THE IRISH TIMES

Nealon's Guide
to the 29th Dáil & Seanad

Edited by
Geraldine Kennedy

Gill & Macmillan

Gill & Macmillan Ltd
Hume Avenue
Park West
Dublin 12
with associated companies throughout the world
www.gillmacmillan.ie

© The Irish Times/Gill & Macmillan 2002
0 7171 3288 9
Original design concept by Elizabeth Fitz-Simon
Print origination by Carole Lynch
Printed by ColourBooks Ltd, Dublin

*The paper used in this book is made from the wood pulp of managed forests.
For every tree felled, at least one tree is planted, thereby renewing natural resources.*

A catalogue record is available for this book
from the British Library.

1 3 5 4 2

Contents

Acknowledgments

This *Nealon's Guide to the Dáil and Seanad* is the tenth in the series which was started by Ted Nealon after the 1973 General Election. With this volume, recording the results of the 2002 general election, we are proud to announce that *The Irish Times* and Gill & Macmillan have secured joint copyright for the future.

It is appropriate, on this occasion, to pay a special tribute to Ted Nealon for the origination and the authorship of the most comprehensive guide to parliamentary elections in Ireland for the last 29 years. It is required reading for political journalists and party strategists, students and academics, and, of course, politicians themselves. We have set out to maintain the qualities that have established *Nealon's Guide to the Dáil and Seanad* as the standard reference book of current Irish politics.

The Irish Times Nealon's Guide to the 29th Dáil and Seanad adopts the same format as previous guides while attempting to broaden the range of information about the results. The biggest change in this edition is that it is produced in full colour for the first time. There are colour photographs of all TDs and colour maps of the 42 constituencies. It also contains profiles of the 15 Irish MEPs, plus analysis of *The Irish Times*/MRBI opinion polls during the campaign and the transfer pattern between parties during the counts.

This Guide could not have been produced without the help and co-operation of many people. I wish to record a special word of thanks to Joe Carroll, former Washington and Parliamentary Correspondent of *The Irish Times*, for the painstaking work which he put into its compilation; Peter Thursfield, Picture Editor, and the Photographic Department of *The Irish Times* for supplying many of the photographs. Thanks also to Donald Menzies, who brought his special mathematical skills to bear on the transfer patterns; and Professor Richard Sinnott who analysed them.

I wish to thank Kieran Coughlan, Clerk of the Dáil; Aisling Hart of the Seanad office in Leinster House; Peter Greene and the Franchise Section of the Department of the Environment and Local Government; Ann Quinlan of the Bills Office in Leinster House; Verona Ní Broinn, Public Relations Officer for the Houses of the Oireachtas; the press officers of Fianna Fáil, Fine Gael, the Labour Party, the Progressive Democrats, the Green Party, Sinn Féin and the Socialist Party; the offices of the European Parliament and the European Commission.

We had the considerable advantage of having Gill & Macmillan as publishers of *The Irish Times Nealon's Guide*. I thank them for their highly professional work and service: Fergal Tobin, Publisher; Mairéad O'Keeffe, Production Director; Deirdre Greenan, Managing Editor, Deirdre Nolan, Editorial Assistant and Carole Lynch.

On this passage of the *Nealon's Guide*, we would like to record that we received maximum co-operation from members of Dáil Éireann and Seanad Éireann. We would welcome suggestions from them, and other students of the *Guide*, as to whether we could provide even more useful information in the next one.

GERALDINE KENNEDY
September 2002

Foreword

by the Taoiseach, Mr Bertie Ahern TD

I congratulate Geraldine Kennedy, Joe Carroll, the publishers Gill & Macmillan and the *Irish Times* team in publishing *Nealon's Guide*. This Hansard of Irish politics breaks new ground in passing from the hands of its founder Ted Nealon. Ted had been pundit, practitioner and insightful analyst. *The Guide* became the essential companion volume for everyone interested in politics. Eagerly awaited and pored over in the wake of every election, it was a standard work of reference thereafter. Until, coming up to the next poll, it was again examined and teased out in great detail as campaigns were planned and the makings of another *Guide* put into the works.

Now new insight has been brought to this *Guide* of the 29th Dáil and Seanad. The last election has given us a more diverse Dáil than I have ever seen in my political lifetime. In an election where the outcome was swung by a handful of votes in a few constituencies, the final national result was a collage of local colour and drama all over the country. With the introduction of electronic voting in three constituencies, the drama was telescoped into the space of a few hours. In other places the tradition of the long count was continued over many days.

This election underpinned the changing nature of Irish politics. Less and less can political support be taken for granted from one election to the next. Bye-elections and referenda similarly give little advance knowledge of what the considered verdict of the sovereign people will be. Our increasingly sophisticated and discerning electorate knows that there are horses for courses and they make their political choices accordingly.

But not only is the substance of politics changing, the regulatory framework is changing as well. This election is the first conducted under the new and exacting legislation governing the conduct of public affairs. Limits on donations and expenditure as well as rigorous disclosure requirements are the appropriate response to the revelations of the Tribunals. These requirements are at least as comprehensive as in any other jurisdiction and mark a major turning point in the conduct of Irish political life. Accountability is now not only a requirement for national parties but for candidates and organisations at local level as well.

Viewed from a distance or exclusively through the national spotlight the general election might appear to have been dominated by the campaigns of the parties. I believe that the reality was much more complex. The judgement of the electorate was arrived at over a longer period and was more likely to be nuanced at local rather than at national level. The people do make judgements based on national issues and on what they believe the future direction of the country should be. But they will seek to voice that view through effective local candidates who will champion the interests of their community. Irish politics always had both feet firmly planted on local ground. In our small country people expect to know their politicians locally and to have access to their Government nationally. While the issues have changed and Ireland is now a much more open society, the fundamental nature of the relationship between politicians and people remains a remarkably personal one.

And the issues have changed radically. Until a decade ago, Irish politics was dominated by mass unemployment and emigration and was permanently overshadowed by the seemingly intractable problems of Northern Ireland. In 2002, our challenge is to sustain the remarkable peace and prosperity we have now achieved. No generation in the history of the state has been given such opportunity. And none bears such heavy responsibility. If

we succeed this generation will be the generation that brought Ireland out of the political turbulence and economic poverty of the twentieth century and into a period where a prosperous island at peace with itself was not only possible but in the making. That is the vision I believe in. Peace, Prosperity and Progress. We cannot, however, take that vision for granted.

Too often in our history we have glimpsed the promise of peace, only to see it wither away again. Too often we have enjoyed the beginning of economic progress only to see it disappear. It is the historic challenge of the 29th Dáil to ensure the Good Friday Agreement is not a false dawn and that our economic development does not prove to be fool's gold.

It is not enough to sustain what we have – much more remains to be done. In Northern Ireland, there are those in both communities who remain to be assured of their place in an inclusive settlement as well as those who have yet to fulfil their commitments to that settlement. Building a lasting and a just peace on this island is the great political goal of this generation. It is the imperative that overrides all others.

We also have the great task of not only extending prosperity in time but expanding it in scope to reach all our people. We must manage the economy prudently not only to meet the needs of today but to safeguard our welfare for many years to come.

The electors have considered the issues put before them and they have given their verdict. This *Guide* details that verdict with insight and style. It makes clear that the final result was an extraordinary mosaic of local colour. It underlines the humility and caution needed by those who would predict the results. For political activists and politicians, this book will be read either with relief at what was, or wistfully at what might have been. Inevitably it will be studied with an eye for next time – the campaign for the 30th Dáil which is already in the mind's eye of many of the readers of this volume.

Bertie Ahern was Taoiseach 1997-2002, leading the first minority Coalition Government with the Progressive Democrats. He leads the first Coalition Government to be re-elected in the history of the State. He has been Leader of Fianna Fáil since 1994. He has served as a Minister in all Fianna Fáil governments since 1987 and as Minister of State and Government Chief Whip since 1982. He was first elected to the Dáil in 1977.

Bertie Ahern

The Election Background

by Geraldine Kennedy

2002 was the strangest election campaign: the longest planned, the best prepared, but the most boring in living memory. The campaign never caught the public imagination. The issues never came alight.

The Taoiseach, Bertie Ahern, went right up to the wire on the calling of the general election. He had led the longest-serving government in the history of the State, with the exception of the Fianna Fáil government which held office during the Second World War and used emergency powers to run for five years and five days. It was the first minority Coalition ever, Fianna Fáil and the Progressive Democrats, supported by four Independent TDs, and it had run its full course.

More relevant to voters, however, the outgoing Coalition had presided, fortuitously, over the period of the Celtic Tiger when unprecedented economic progress was made in the Republic. It had presided also over the introduction of new ethical guidelines for the conduct of politics after the various tribunals of inquiry – particularly Flood and Moriarty – revealed a culture of corruption in the political, business and planning life of this State dating back to the Haughey era in the 1980s.

Mr Ahern managed to surprise his opponents when he took the unusual step of notifying an almost empty Dáil chamber late on the night of Wednesday, 24 April, that he would proceed to Áras an Uachtaráin at 9am the next morning to ask the President to dissolve the 28th Dáil.

He was bidding to go into the history books as leader of the first outgoing government to be returned to office since 1969; the first Coalition ever to be re-elected.

After a marathon lead-in to the election, the Taoiseach asked the President, Mrs McAleese, to dissolve the Dáil shortly after 9am on Thursday, 25 April. He opted for the minimum three-week campaign with polling day set for a Friday, 17 May, for the first time.

There was a clear consensus going into the campaign that Mr Ahern and Fianna Fáil would lead the next government. It was only a matter of picking a partner if, some party strategists dared to believe, a marriage had to be contemplated at all.

That consensus, shared by all of Fianna Fáil, most PDs and even some members of Fine Gael and the Labour Party, ignored the precarious balance of seats held by Government and Opposition parties on the dissolution of the Dáil. Mr Ahern's popularity had not produced electoral results over the previous five years. He had lost six by-elections and two important referenda on the Nice Treaty and abortion.

In his first general election as leader of Fianna Fáil in 1997, Mr Ahern got a 12-seat bonus with 39.33 per cent of the first preference vote. The number of seats won in the 28th Dáil was: Fianna Fáil 77, Fine Gael 54, Labour Party 17, Democratic Left 4, Progressive Democrats 4, Green Party 2, Sinn Féin 1, Socialist Party 1 and Others 6.

After six by-elections, the amalgamation of DL with Labour, and the movement of a couple of TDs from Fianna Fáil to Independent ranks, the state of the parties going into the 2002 election was: Fianna Fáil 76 (including Beverly Cooper-Flynn, ratified as a party candidate although outside the parliamentary party, Denis Foley and Liam Lawlor, both Fianna Fáil TDs, also outside the parliamentary party), Fine Gael 54, Labour 21 (including the Ceann Comhairle, Séamus Pattison, who is automatically re-elected), PDs 4, Green Party 2, Sinn Féin 1, Socialist Party 1, and Others 7.

The battleground for the 2002 election was in 42 constituencies, an increase of one over 1997. The new constituency was the three-seater of Dublin Mid-West.

In a bid to set the agenda for the campaign, the Taoiseach launched Fianna Fáil's election manifesto within two hours of the dissolution of the Dáil. Their campaign slogan, designed to capture the mood of the Celtic Tiger, was 'A lot done. More to do'. It was intended to carry the subliminal message to voters that Fianna Fáil – and its PD partners – were best poised to protect the peace in Northern Ireland, and prosperity and progress in the Republic.

By any standards, the record of the past five years had been impressive:

- The Irish economy had out-performed all others in the OECD with GDP growth averaging 10 per cent per annum;
- Unemployment had fallen from 10 per cent to 4 per cent to what, effectively, economists call full employment;
- The era of mass emigration had ended with the return of thousands of Irish people from abroad;
- The national debt had fallen in relative and absolute terms with the debt/GDP ratio under 35 per cent;
- The standard rate of income tax was reduced from 26 per cent to 20 per cent and the top rate from 48 per cent to 42 per cent.

But, the deterioration in the health services, the length of waiting lists and the state of emergency hospital services had registered in opinion polls for the previous two years as the issue on which the election would be fought.

The commitments in Fianna Fáil's election manifesto were based on conservative economic projections. The 'big idea' was a new National Development Finance Agency designed to take over the job of funding the National Development Plan; to finance roads, public transport, health and schools without raising taxes or borrowing significantly. It promised to cut hospital waiting lists within two years.

There were no hostages to fortune between the Fianna Fáil and the PD manifesto, issued to promote the smaller party's separate identity the previous weekend. The PD's 'big idea' was the establishment of a National Transformation Fund to hold the proceeds of the privatisation of State assets. It promised to sell-off the ESB, Aer Lingus, Bord Gáis and the commercial ports to finance increased spending on infrastructure and health. It aimed to cut the top rate of income tax from 42 per cent to 40 per cent and, significantly, it opposed the building of the Bertie Bowl.

The platform on which the main Opposition parties would challenge for government was revealed over the next few days. It was hampered from the outset, however, by the absence of any perception that there was a real chance of an alternative government being formed.

The new Fine Gael leader, Michael Noonan, had been elected on the 'dream team' with deputy leader, Jim Mitchell, in February, 2001, in a successful challenge to John Bruton. But successive opinion polls had indicated that they were not reviving the party's fortunes. Mr Noonan was not connecting with the public.

Their manifesto 'Vision, with Purpose' sought to introduce a quality of life element onto the economic agenda.

Fine Gael promised the biggest income tax relief in the campaign: 2 billion in concessions mainly to low and middle-income earners. The party offered tax rebates, tax credits and double mortgage relief for first-time house buyers. The most high-profile promise was to compensate Eircom shareholders who had lost money after its flotation.

The Labour Party's manifesto was launched in five parts. The most controversial promise was to reduce contributions to the National Pension Fund from 1 per cent of GNP to 0.25 per cent over the next five years.

In the public relations environment of the election, it encapsulated its separate manifestos into six simple pledges on health, schools, poverty, children, carers and housing.

The main establishment parties had set out their pitch. And after the longest 'unofficial' election campaign in modern history, the first week fell flat. Fianna Fáil tried to hold the agenda on the economy while the Opposition parties engaged in spiceless spats about whose figures stood up to independent scrutiny.

The over-the-top intervention of the Attorney General, Michael McDowell, marked the highpoint of the early part of the campaign. The president of the PDs described the Taoiseach's pet project, Campus and Stadium Ireland, as a 'Ceausescu-era Olympic project' which should be opposed as a matter of basic political morality. Fianna Fáil's enthusiasm for Mr Ahern's £1 billion project underlined 'the dangers of one-party government', he said.

If Mr McDowell's speech brought a sparkle to the campaign, the first *Irish Times*/MRBI opinion poll set it on fire. It showed that Fianna Fáil, on 45 per cent, was on course to lead the next government. It was within shouting distance of that overall majority which had eluded the party since 1977. The PDs were on 2 per cent.

The customary swing to Fine Gael was not materialising. The party was showing 23 per cent; Labour 12 per cent. The smaller parties, Sinn Féin and the Green Party, were holding their base at 6 per cent and 3 per cent respectively. Others were 9 per cent.

For the first time, the *Irish Times*/MRBI poll was conducted on a simulated ballot paper in all 42 constituencies. The introduction of the new methodology meant that there were no legitimate figures with which to compare the parties' ratings.

It would be difficult to exaggerate the impact of the findings: on the parties themselves and on their election strategies. The whole direction of the campaign changed.

Fianna Fáil played down the significance of its high ratings, fearing that the prospect of the party forming a single party government would scare off supporters. Fine Gael hightened its attack on Fianna Fáil publicly while descending into desperation. The

Labour Party still believed that it could make substantial gains at Fine Gael's expense.

One of the most memorable images of the 2002 campaign was created over the second weekend. Michael McDowell, Attorney General and president of the PDs, was pictured erecting a poster 'One-Party Government – No Thanks' on the top of a pole in Ranelagh in Dublin.

The other symbolic image of the election was the photograph of Fine Gael leader, Michael Noonan, being struck in the face with a custard pie in Boyle, Co Roscommon.

The national campaign limped from day to day through the second and third weeks. For days on end, it was off the front pages. Quibbles about economic figures alternated with portraits of the pathetic state of the health service but there was no public engagement with issues.

The Department of Finance published figures for the first four months of the year at an early stage in the campaign. It showed that the Exchequer had recorded a deficit of 112.7 million compared to a surplus of 1.18 billion in the same period in 2001. The shortfall in the public finances was caused by a substantial rise in spending and a major fall-off in income tax receipts.

The former Fine Gael Taoiseach, Dr Garret FitzGerald, had been a lone voice in the columns of *The Irish Times* warning about the poor state of the public finances and the challenge facing the next Government.

Going into the final weekend of the campaign, however, the Fine Gael leader, Mr Noonan, launched a major change in electoral strategy warning about the dangers of a Fianna Fáil majority and tougher financial times ahead. The Labour Party also questioned the veracity of many of Fianna Fáil's election promises.

Public spending would have to be brought under control, Mr Noonan said. And in a statement which undermined its own 2 billion in concessions, he added that, otherwise, the commitments of all the parties would be null and void.

The Election Background

By the time the presidential head-to-head TV debate was held by the two alternative Taoisigh, Mr Ahern and Mr Noonan, the die had been cast. Mr Noonan performed well but it was too late to over-turn the trends of the past five years.

The last *Irish Times*/MRBI opinion poll of the campaign confirmed that Mr Ahern was set to be re-elected Taoiseach with the real prospect of leading a single party government. The state of the parties was: Fianna Fáil 45 per cent (unchanged); Fine Gael 21 per cent (down 2 percentage points); Labour 12 per cent (unchanged); Sinn Féin 7 per cent (up 1 point); Green Party 3 per cent (unchanged); Progressive Democrats 2 per cent (unchanged); and Others 10 per cent (up 2 points).

With the arrival of polling day, 17 May, it was clear that the only question to be answered by voters was what kind of Fianna Fáil Government would be returned.

The introduction of electronic voting in three constituencies – Dublin North, Dublin West and Meath – produced the first results overnight. There were omens for things to come for Fine Gael when its high-profile deputy leader, Nora Owen, lost her seat to Fianna Fáil. Sinn Féin was polling well.

The traditional counts on Saturday, 18 May, produced the greatest turbulence in Irish politics for generations. The final result was Fianna Fáil 81 seats, Fine Gael 31, Labour 21, PDs 8, Green Party 6, Sinn Féin 5, Others, including Mr Joe Higgins of the Socialist Party, 14.

The outgoing Taoiseach, Mr Ahern, held all of the options. The Progressive Democrats, by virtue of Mr McDowell's high-profile interventions, won eight seats with a decrease in its vote to 3.96 per cent.

The story of the 2002 election, however, was the meltdown of the Fine Gael party. The party paid a huge penalty for rendering itself irrelevent in the election. With a drop of 5 percentage points in its first preference vote to 22.5 per cent, Fine Gael paid the unprecedented price of losing 23 Dáil seats.

It entered the 29th Dáil with 31 seats – a level last seen by John A Costello's inter-party government in 1948.

The whole leadership structure of the party was removed. Mr Noonan resigned on Saturday night. The party lost its deputy leader, Jim Mitchell, its former leader, Alan Dukes and its former deputy leader, Nora Owen. The outgoing front bench was decimated. The party was reduced from 12 to 3 seats in Dublin.

The scale of the Fine Gael losses took the focus off the Labour Party. It had performed poorly also. Against its own expectations, it made no gains. It returned with 21 seats.

The outstanding successes of the 2002 election were recorded by the Green Party and Sinn Féin. They have broken the stranglehold of the main parties in the Dáil.

The new Coalition Government of Fianna Fáil and the PDs was formed on 6 June. Mr Ahern won the prize of being leader of the first outgoing government to be re-elected since 1969, but, within weeks, it was obvious that it was based on questionable financial foundations. The cutbacks started. For the first time in electoral history, the electorate voted out the opposition, not the government. The composition of the 29th Dáil has irrevocably changed. It remains to be seen whether the traditional balance of Opposition parties will ever be the same again.

Geraldine Kennedy is Editor of
The Irish Times

HOUSES OF THE OIREACHTAS
Address
Leinster House, Kildare Street, Dublin 2

Switchboard
Dáil Éireann (01) 618 3333; From outside Dublin 1890 337 889
Seanad Éireann (01) 618 3111. From outside Dublin 1890 732 623

E-mail: The e-mail address for deputies and senators follows the convention: firstname.surname@oireachtas.ie. Ministers and Ministers of State have individual e-mail addresses, but some deputies and senators use their own e-mail address and some may opt not to use the address provided for them by the Houses of the Oireachtas.

KEY TO ABBREVIATIONS

FF	Fianna Fáil
FG	Fine Gael
Lab	Labour
PD	Progressive Democrats
GP	Green Party
SF	Sinn Féin
SWP	Socialist Workers' Party
CSP	Christian Solidarity Party
WP	Workers' Party
Ind	Independent
*	Outgoing

Subscribe Now
to ireland.com premium content
Ireland's leading news and information website

The 29th Dáil has 166 deputies returned by 42 constituencies. Position of parties as returned in the General Election:

Fianna Fáil	**81**
Fine Gael	**31**
Labour	**21**
Progressive Democrats	**8**
Green Party	**6**
Sinn Féin	**5**
Socialist Party	**1**
Others	**13**

Deputy	Party	Constituency
* Ahern, Bertie	FF	Dublin Central
* Ahern, Dermot	FF	Louth
* Ahern, Michael	FF	Cork East
* Ahern, Noel	FF	Dublin North-West
* Allen, Bernard	FG	Cork North-Central
Andrews, Barry	FF	Dún Laoghaire
* Ardagh, Seán	FF	Dublin South-Central
* Aylward, Liam	FF	Carlow-Kilkenny
Blaney, Niall	Ind	Donegal North-East
Boyle, Dan	GP	Cork South-Central
* Brady, Johnny	FF	Meath
* Brady, Martin	FF	Dublin North-East
Breen, James	Ind	Clare
Breen, Pat	FG	Clare
* Brennan, Séamus	FF	Dublin South
* Broughan, Tommy	Lab	Dublin North-East
* Browne, John	FF	Wexford
* Bruton, John	FG	Meath
* Bruton, Richard	FG	Dublin North-Central
† Burton, Joan	Lab	Dublin West
Callanan, Joe	FF	Galway East
* Callely, Ivor	FF	Dublin North-Central
* Carey, Pat	FF	Dublin North-West
Carty, John	FF	Mayo
Cassidy, Donie	FF	Westmeath
* Collins, Michael	FF	Limerick West
* Connaughton, Paul	FG	Galway East
Connolly, Paudge	Ind	Cavan-Monaghan
* Cooper-Flynn, Beverly	FF	Mayo
† Costello, Joe	Lab	Dublin Central
* Coughlan, Mary	FF	Donegal South-West
* Coveney, Simon	FG	Cork South-Central
* Cowen, Brian	FF	Laois-Offaly
Cowley, Jerry	Ind	Mayo

Deputy	Party	Constituency
* Crawford, Seymour	FG	Cavan-Monaghan
Cregan, John	FF	Limerick West
Crowe, Seán	SF	Dublin South-West
Cuffe, Ciaran	GP	Dún Laoghaire
* Cullen, Martin	FF	Waterford
Curran, John	FF	Dublin Mid-West
* Davern, Noel	FF	Tipperary South
Deasy, John	FG	Waterford
* Deenihan, Jimmy	FG	Kerry North
* Dempsey, Noel	FF	Meath
Dempsey, Tony	FF	Wexford
* Dennehy, John	FF	Cork South-Central
* de Valera, Síle	FF	Clare
Devins, Jimmy	FF	Sligo-Leitrim
* Durkan, Bernard	FG	Kildare North
* Ellis, John	FF	Sligo-Leitrim
English, Damien	FG	Meath
Enright, Olwyn	FG	Laois-Offaly
* Fahey, Frank	FF	Galway West
Ferris, Martin	SF	Kerry North
Finneran, Michael	FF	Longford-Roscommon
† Fitzpatrick, Dermot	FF	Dublin Central
* Fleming, Seán	FF	Laois-Offaly
* Fox, Mildred	Ind	Wicklow
† Gallagher, Pat the Cope	FF	Donegal South-West
* Gilmore, Éamon	Lab	Dún Laoghaire
Glennon, Jim	FF	Dublin North
Gogarty, Paul	GP	Dublin Mid-West
* Gormley, John	GP	Dublin South-East
Grealish, Noel	PD	Galway West
* Gregory, Tony	Ind	Dublin Central
* Hanafin, Mary	FF	Dún Laoghaire
Harkin, Marian	Ind	Sligo-Leitrim
* Harney, Mary	PD	Dublin Mid-West
* Haughey, Seán	FF	Dublin North-Central
* Hayes, Tom	FG	Tipperary South
* Healy, Seamus	Ind	Tipperary South
* Healy-Rae, Jackie	Ind	Kerry South
* Higgins, Joe	SP	Dublin West
* Higgins, Michael D.	Lab	Galway West
Hoctor, Máire	FF	Tipperary North
* Hogan, Philip	FG	Carlow-Kilkenny
* Howlin, Brendan	Lab	Wexford
* Jacob, Joe	FF	Wicklow
* Keaveney, Cecilia	FF	Donegal North-East
Kehoe, Paul	FG	Wexford

* Kelleher, Billy	FF	Cork North-Central
Kelly, Peter	FF	Longford-Roscommon
* Kenny, Enda	FG	Mayo
* Killeen, Tony	FF	Clare
* Kirk, Séamus	FF	Louth
* Kitt, Tom	FF	Dublin South
* Lenihan, Brian	FF	Dublin West
* Lenihan, Conor	FF	Dublin South-West
* Lowry, Michael	Ind	Tipperary North
† Lynch, Kathleen	Lab	Cork North-Central
* Martin, Mícheál	FF	Cork South-Central
* McCormack, Pádraic	FG	Galway West
* McCreevy, Charlie	FF	Kildare North
* McDaid, James	FF	Donegal North-East
† McDowell, Michael	PD	Dublin South-East
McEllistrim, Tom	FF	Kerry North
* McGinley, Dinny	FG	Donegal South-West
McGrath, Finian	Ind	Dublin North-Central
* McGrath, Paul	FG	Westmeath
* McGuinness, John	FF	Carlow-Kilkenny
McHugh, Paddy	Ind	Galway East
* McManus, Liz	Lab	Wicklow
* Mitchell, Gay	FG	Dublin South-Central
* Mitchell, Olivia	FG	Dublin South
* Moloney, John	FF	Laois-Offaly
Morgan, Arthur	SF	Louth
* Moynihan, Donal	FF	Cork North-West
* Moynihan, Michael	FF	Cork North-West
* Moynihan-Cronin, Breeda	Lab	Kerry South
Mulcahy, Michael	FF	Dublin South-Central
Murphy, Gerard	FG	Cork North-West
* Naughten, Denis	FG	Longford-Roscommon
* Neville, Dan	FG	Limerick West
† Nolan, M.J.	FF	Carlow-Kilkenny
* Noonan, Michael	FG	Limerick East
* Ó Caoláin, Caoimhghín	SF	Cavan-Monaghan
O'Connor, Charlie	FF	Dublin South-West
* Ó Cuív, Éamon	FF	Galway West
* O'Dea, Willie	FF	Limerick East
* O'Donnell, Liz	PD	Dublin South
* O'Donoghue, John	FF	Kerry South
O'Donovan, Denis	FF	Cork South-West
O'Dowd, Fergus	FG	Louth
O'Fearghail, Seán	FF	Kildare South
* O'Flynn, Noel	FF	Cork North-Central
* O'Hanlon, Rory	FF	Cavan-Monaghan
* O'Keeffe, Batt	FF	Cork South-Central
* O'Keeffe, Jim	FG	Cork South-West
* O'Keeffe, Ned	FF	Cork East

O'Malley, Fiona	PD	Dún Laoghaire
O'Malley, Tim	PD	Limerick East
* O'Shea, Brian	Lab	Waterford
Ó Snodaigh, Aengus	SF	Dublin South-Central
* O'Sullivan, Jan	Lab	Limerick East
Parlon, Tom	PD	Laois-Offaly
* Pattison, Séamus	Lab	Carlow-Kilkenny
* Penrose, Willie	Lab	Westmeath
* Perry, John	FG	Sligo-Leitrim
Power, Peter	FF	Limerick East
* Power, Seán	FF	Kildare South
* Quinn, Ruairí	Lab	Dublin South-East
* Rabbitte, Pat	Lab	Dublin South-West
* Ring, Michael	FG	Mayo
* Roche, Dick	FF	Wicklow
Ryan, Eamonn	GP	Dublin South
* Ryan, Eoin	FF	Dublin South-East
† Ryan, Seán	Lab	Dublin North
* Sargent, Trevor	GP	Dublin North
Sexton, Mae	PD	Longford-Roscommon
† Sherlock, Joe	Lab	Cork East
* Shortall, Róisín	Lab	Dublin North-West
* Smith, Brendan	FF	Cavan-Monaghan
* Smith, Michael	FF	Tipperary North
* Stagg, Emmet	Lab	Kildare North
* Stanton, David	FG	Cork East
* Timmins, Billy	FG	Wicklow
* Treacy, Noel	FF	Galway East
Twomey, Liam	Ind	Wexford
* Upton, Mary	Lab	Dublin South-Central
* Wall, Jack	Lab	Kildare South
* Wallace, Dan	FF	Cork North-Central
* Wallace, Mary	FF	Meath
* Walsh, Joe	FF	Cork South-West
Wilkinson, Ollie	FF	Waterford
* Woods, Michael J.	FF	Dublin North-East
* Wright, G.V.	FF	Dublin North

The 29th Dáil has 166 deputies, the same as the previous Dáil. Of these, 111 (66.87%) were outgoing members of the 28th Dail, denoted here by an asterisk (*); 8 (4.82%) denoted here by † were previous members of the House but not of the 28th Dáil, and 47 (28.31%) are new deputies.

Seated: Charlie McCreevy, TD (Minister for Finance), Michael Smith, TD (Minister for Defence), Bertie Ahern, TD (Taoiseach), (President Mary McAleese), Mary Harney, TD (Tánaiste and Minister for Enterprise, Trade and Employment), Joe Walsh, TD (Minister for Agriculture and Food), Brian Cowen, TD (Minister for Foreign Affairs)

Standing: Mary Hanafin, TD (Minister of State at the Department of the Taoiseach and Government Chief Whip), Éamon Ó Cuív, TD (Minister for the Community, Rural and Gaeltacht Affairs), Michael McDowell, TD (Minister for Justice, Equality and Law Reform), Martin Cullen, TD (Minister for the Environment and Local Government), Séamus Brennan, TD (Minister for Transport), Noel Dempsey, TD (Minister for Education and Science), Dermot Ahern, TD (Minister for Communications, Marine and Natural Resources), John O'Donoghue, TD (Minister for Arts, Sport and Tourism), Micheál Martin, TD (Minister for Health and Children), Mary Coughlan, TD (Minister for Social and Family Affairs) and Rory Brady, SC, (Attorney General)

Taoiseach	Bertie Ahern
Tánaiste and Minister for Enterprise, Trade and Employment	Mary Harney
Minister for Defence	Michael Smith
Minister for Agriculture and Food	Joe Walsh
Minister for Finance	Charlie McCreevy
Minister for Foreign Affairs	Brian Cowen
Minister for Education and Science	Noel Dempsey
Minister for Communications, Marine and Natural Resources	Dermot Ahern
Minister for Arts, Sport and Tourism	John O'Donoghue
Minister for Health and Children	Micheál Martin
Minister for Transport	Seamus Brennan
Minister for Justice, Equality and Law Reform	Michael McDowell
Minister for the Environment and Local Government	Martin Cullen
Minister for Community, Rural and Gaeltacht Affairs	Éamon Ó Cuív
Minister for Social and Family Affairs	Mary Coughlan
Attorney General	Rory Brady

Ministers of State (appointed 6 June and 18 June 2002)

Department	Special Responsibilities	Name
Taoiseach, Defence	Government Chief Whip, Information Society	Mary Hanafin
Taoiseach, Foreign Affairs	European Affairs	Dick Roche
Education and Science	Adult Education, Youth Affairs and Educational Disadvantage	Síle de Valera
Transport	Road Traffic, including Road Haulage	Jim McDaid
Enterprise, Trade and Employment	Labour Affairs, including Training	Frank Fahey
Agriculture and Food	Food and Horticulture	Noel Treacy
Justice, Equality and Law Reform	Equality Issues, including Disability	Willie O'Dea
Foreign Affairs	Overseas Development and Human Rights	Tom Kitt
Environment and Local Government		Pat the Cope Gallagher
Agriculture and Food	Animal Health and Welfare and Customer Services	Liam Aylward
Communications, Marine and Natural Resources		John Browne
Enterprise, Trade and Employment	Trade and Commerce	Michael Ahern
Health and Children	Services for Older People	Ivor Callely
Environment and Local Government; Community, Rural and Gaeltacht Affairs	Housing and Urban Renewal, Drugs Strategy and Community Affairs	Noel Ahern
Health and Children; Justice, Equality and Law Reform; Education and Science	Children	Brian Lenihan
Health and Children	Disability and Mental Health Services and Food Safety	Tim O'Malley
Finance	Office of Public Works	Tom Parlon

Note that two of the above have no 'special responsibilities' allocated to them. They come under the general name of the Department.

The general election of 17 May 2002 brought a Government of Fianna Fáil and the Progressive Democrats to power. This became the first Coalition Government to be returned to office in the history of the State. When the 29th Dáil assembled on 6 June 2002, Bertie Ahern, leader of Fianna Fáil since 1994, was nominated for appointment by the President as Taoiseach by 93 votes to 68.

In addition to the 80 votes of his own party – after the election of Dr Rory O'Hanlon as Ceann Comhairle – and the 8 votes of the Progressive Democrats, Mr Ahern was supported by five Independent TDs.

Mildred Fox (Wicklow) and Jackie Healy-Rae (Kerry South) were two of the four Independents who had supported the outgoing Fianna Fáil/Progressive Democrats minority Coalition Government. Niall Blaney (Donegal North-East), Paudge Connolly (Cavan-Monaghan) and Paddy McHugh (Galway East) also voted for Mr Ahern.

A further four newly-elected Independent TDs abstained on the nomination: Dr Jerry Cowley (Mayo), Dr Liam Twomey (Wexford), James Breen (Clare) and Marian Harkin (Sligo-Leitrim).

The motion for approval of the nomination by the Taoiseach of other members of the Government was carried by 91 votes to 65.

Michael McDowell of the Progressive Democrats erecting a poster in Ranelagh, Dublin, against the possibility of a single-party government.

The May 2002 General Election was declared on 25 April 2002. Voting took place on 17 May 2002. A total of 463 candidates were nominated for the 166 seats to be contested. The outgoing Ceann Comhairle, Séamus Pattison (Lab) was automatically returned for his constituency of Carlow-Kilkenny. Ten registered political parties nominated candidates: Fianna Fáil, Fine Gael, the Labour Party, Progressive Democrats, the Green Party—Comhaontas Glas, Sinn Féin, the Socialist Party, the Workers' Party, the Socialist Workers' Party, and the Christian Solidarity Party. Those who were nominated as Independents totalled 95. Eight of these informally called themselves representatives of the Independent Health Alliance. For the first time electronic voting and counting was used in three constituencies on a trial basis.

*Democratic Left formally merged with the Labour Party on 1 February 1999.

State of the Parties

Election	FF	FG	Lab	PD	DL	GP	SF	SP	Others
2002	81	31	21	8	—	6	5	1	13
1997	77	54	17	4	4	1	1	1	7
1992	68	45	33	10	4	—	—	—	6
1989	77	55	15	6	—	—	—	—	13
1987	81	51	12	14	—	—	—	—	8
Nov. 1982	75	70	16	—	—	—	—	—	5
Feb. 1982	81	63	15	—	—	—	—	—	7

Line-up

Election	Electorate	Candidates	Seats
2002	2,994,642	463	166
1997	2,741,262	484	166
1992	2,557,036	481	166
1989	2,448,813	370	166
1987	2,445,515	466	166
Nov. 1982	2,335,153	364	166
Feb. 1982	2,275,450	365	166

First-Preference Votes

Election	FF		FG		Lab		PD		GP		SF		DL		Others	
2002	770,846	41.49%	417,653	22.48%	200,138	10.77%	73,628	3.96%	71,480	3.85%	121,039	6.51%			203,329	10.94%
1997	703,682	39.33%	499,936	27.95%	186,044	10.40%	83,765	4.68%	—		—		44,901	2.51%	270,657	15.13%
1992	674,650	39.11%	422,106	24.47%	333,013	19.31%	80,787	4.68%	—		—		47,945	2.78%	166,352	9.64%
1989	731,472	44.15%	485,307	29.29%	156,989	9.48%	91,013	5.49%	—		—		—		192,032	11.59%
1987	784,547	44.15%	481,127	27.07%	114,551	6.44%	210,583	11.85%	—		—		—		186,357	10.49%
Nov. 1982	763,313	45.20%	662,284	39.22%	158,115	9.36%	—		—		—		—		105,008	6.22%
Feb. 1982	786,951	47.26%	621,088	37.30%	151,875	8.12%	—		—		—		—		105,219	6.32%

Turnout

Election	Total Poll		Spoiled Votes		Valid Poll	
2002	1,878,393	62.73%	20,280	1.08%	1,858,113	62.05%
1997	1,807,016	65.92%	18,031	1.00%	1,789,985	65.26%
1992	1,751,351	68.49%	26,498	1.51%	1,724,853	67.46%
1989	1,677,592	68.51%	20,779	1.24%	1,656,813	67.66%
1987	1,793,406	73.33%	16,241	0.91%	1,777,165	72.69%
Nov. 1982	1,701,393	72.86%	12,673	0.74%	1,688,720	72.32%
Feb. 1982	1,679,500	73.81%	14,367	0.86%	1,665,133	73.18%

Regional First-Preference Percentages by Euro Constituencies

Constituency	FF	FG	Lab	PD	GP	SF	Others
Connacht-Ulster	41.24%	27.45%	2.77%	3.27%	1.37%	8.01%	15.89%
Dublin	37.13%	14.45%	14.89%	7.09%	8.04%	8.91%	9.48%
Rest of Leinster	43.82%	22.22%	13.69%	3.75%	3.59%	5.66%	7.27%
Munster	43.31%	25.70%	10.72%	2.08%	2.40%	4.20%	11.60

Carlow-Kilkenny

Elected

Liam Aylward (FF)*	1st Count
Philip Hogan (FG)*	6th Count
John McGuiness ((FF)*	8th Count
M.J. Nolan (FF)	8th Count

Voting by Party

1st Preference	Number	%	% 1997
Fianna Fáil	30,543	50.20	42.19
Fine Gael	13,309	21.87	29.19
Labour	8,004	13.15	15.19
Green Party	4,961	8.15	5.52
Sinn Féin	2,078	3.42	–
Others	1,949	3.20	4.66

Statistics

Population	113,543	
Electorate	97,071	
Total Poll	61,688	63.55
Spoiled Votes	844	1.37
Valid Poll	60,844	62.68
Seats	5	
Quota	12,169	
Candidates	11	

Seats

FF	3
FG	1
Lab	1

**(The fifth seat was taken by outgoing Ceann Comhairle, Séamus Pattison (Lab), who was returned automatically)
FF gain from FG**

The constituency of Carlow-Kilkenny is unchanged since the 1997 General Election.

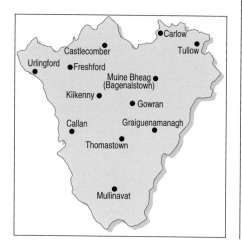

Liam Aylward (FF)

Home Address
Aghaviller, Hugginstown, Co Kilkenny
Office
Department of Agriculture and Food;
Agriculture House, Kildare Street, Dublin 2
Telephone
Home (056) 68703; *Office* (01) 6072000
Birth Place/Date
Knockmoylon, Mullinavat, Co Kilkenny.
September 1952
Married
Kathleen Noonan. 2 sons, 2 daughters
Education
St Kieran's College, Kilkenny (Diploma in Building and Construction)
Occupation
Minister of State. Formerly laboratory technician

Liam Aylward was appointed in June 2002 as Minister of State at the Department of Agriculture and Food with responsibility for animal health, welfare and customer service. His promotion from the back benches was seen as partly due to the excellent performance of Fianna Fáil in Carlow-Kilkenny where the party won three out of four seats with 50 per cent of the first preferences.

He was first elected to the Dáil for Carlow-Kilkenny in 1977. He was Minister of State at the Department of Education February 1992–94, with special responsibility for Youth and Sport. He was Minister of State at the Department of Forestry, November 1988–July 1989. Party spokesperson on Sport, Leisure and Tourism 1995–97.

He served on Kilkenny County Council 1974–92 and 1999–2002.

Member, Gaelic Athletic Association.

He is a son of Bob Aylward, Senator, Agricultural Panel, 1973 until his death in July 1974, and a Dáil candidate in Carlow-Kilkenny constituency in the general elections of 1965, 1969 and 1973.

Philip Hogan (FG)

Home Address
39 The Fairways, Kilkenny
Business Adress
1 High Street, Kilkenny
Telephone
Constituency Office (056) 71490; *Fax* (056) 71491
Birth Place/Date
Kilkenny. 4 July 1960
Married
Kathleen Murphy. 1 son
Education
St Joseph's College, Freshford; St Kieran's College, Kilkenny; University College, Cork (BA, HDipEd)
Occupation
Public representative. Auctioneer

Phil Hogan was appointed party spokesperson on Enterprise, Trade and Employment in June 2002. He had been an unsuccessful candidate in the leadership contest following the resignation of Michael Noonan.

He was first elected to the Dáil in 1989. He was appointed Minister of State at the Department of Finance with special responsibility for Public Expenditure and the Office of Public Works in December 1994. He resigned in February 1995. Since 1997 has been Political Director of the Fine Gael Organisation and a member of the Fine Gael Front Bench. Chairman of the Parliamentary Party 1995–2001. Member in last Dáil of Oireachtas Committee on European Affairs and of the Inter-Parliamentary Union. Front Bench Spokesperson on Regional Affairs and European Development 1993–94; on Consumer Affairs 1991–93; on the Food Industry 1989–91.

He was a Senator, Industrial and Commercial panel, 1987–89.

Member of Kilkenny County Council since 1982 (Chairman 1985–86 and 1998–99); South-Eastern Health Board 1991–99.

Member, Gaelic Athletic Association; Kilkenny Archaeological Society; Castlecomer Golf Club.

John McGuinness (FF)

Home Address
Windsmoor, Brooklawn, Ballyfoyle Road, Kilkenny
Constituency Office
11 O'Loughlin Road, Kilkenny
Telephone
Mobile 087 2855834; *Fax* (056) 70674; *Office* (056) 70672/73; *Fax* (056) 62706.
Website: www.johnmcguinness.com
Birth Place/Date
Kilkenny. 15 March 1955
Married
Margaret Redmond, Graigecullen, Co Carlow. 3 sons, 1 daughter
Education
Kilkenny CBS. Diploma in Business Management
Occupation
Full-time public representative

John McGuinness was elected in 1997 in his first general election.

Was member in last Dáil of Joint Oireachtas Committees for European Affairs, Enterprise and Small Business (Government Whip), Justice, Equality and Women's Rights.

Member Kilkenny Corporation since 1979. Mayor of Kilkenny 1996–97 (third generation of family to serve as Mayor of the Borough); member, Kilkenny County Council since 1991; Kilkenny Enterprise Board; Kilkenny Chamber of Commerce and Industry; Kilkenny Third Level Education Committee; Board member Young Irish Film Makers.

M.J. Nolan (FF)

Home Address
Shandon House, Strawhall, Carlow
Telephone
Home (0503) 30800; *Mobile* 087 224 1967
Birth Place/Date
Bagenalstown, Co Carlow. 25 January 1951
Married
Mary Forde. 2 daughters, 2 sons
Education
De La Salle, Bagenalstown; Mount St Joseph's, Roscrea
Occupation
Public representative

M.J. Nolan returns to the Dáil after an absence of five years. He was first elected for the Carlow-Kilkenny constituency at his first attempt in November 1982 and re-elected at subsequent general elections until he lost his seat in 1997 and also failed to get elected to the Seanad in that year. He began his national political career when the then Taoiseach, Mr Charles Haughey, nominated him as a Senator in 1981. M.J. Nolan was 10 years' later to criticise Mr Haughey as one of the 'Gang of Four' in the Autumn of 1991.

Member, Carlow County Council since 1979.

He is a son of former Fianna Fáil minister, Tom Nolan, who was a TD for Carlow-Kilkenny 1965–82. He was Minister for Labour December 1980–81 and Minister of State at the Department of Health and Social Welfare in 1980.

Séamus Pattison (Lab)

Home Address
6 Upper New Street, Kilkenny
Telephone
Home (056) 21295; *Fax* (056) 52533
Birth Place/Date
Kilkenny. 19 April 1936
Education
St Kieran's College, Kilkenny; University College, Dublin, extra-mural (Diploma in Social and Economic Science)
Occupation
Full-time public representative. Formerly trade union official

Séamus Pattison, who is now the Father of the House as longest serving member, was elected Leas-Cheann Comhairle of the 29th Dáil on 6 June 2002. He had been Ceann Comhairle 1997–2002 and Minister of State at the Department of Social Welfare 1983–87.

He was first elected to the Dáil in 1961. Member of the European Parliament 1981–83. Member of the Parliamentary Assembly of the Council of Europe and its Committees on Social and Legal Affairs 1989–90 and 1996–97.

Member of the British-Irish Inter-Parliamentary Body 1993–97. Chairman of the Select Committee on Social Affairs 1993–97. Party spokesman on Education 1963–67; Justice 1967–72; Lands 1972–73; Defence and Marine Affairs 1987; Energy and Forestry 1989–91.

Member of Kilkenny County Council 1964–97. Chairman 1975–76, 1980–81. Member of Kilkenny Corporation 1964–97 and Alderman 1967–97. Mayor of Kilkenny 1967–68, 1976–77 and 1992–93. Member of Kilkenny Vocational Education Committee 1964–97 and Vice-Chairman 1990–97. Member of South-Eastern Health Board 1971–84.

He is son of James P. Pattison, Dáil deputy 1932–51 and 1954–57.

Carlow-Kilkenny

Seats 5 Quota 12,169	1st Count	2nd Count Transfer of **Nolan, B** Votes	3rd Count Transfer of **Collins-Hughes** Votes
AYLWARD, Liam* (FF)	12,489		
BROWNE, Fergal (FG)	5,468	*(+62)* 5,530	*(+140)* 5,670
COLLINS-HUGHES, Eddie (Ind)	1,614	*(+30)* 1,644	
HOGAN, Phil* (FG)	7,841	*(+11)* 7,852	*(+222)* 8,074
KIERNAN, Tom (SF)	2,078	*(+20)* 2,098	*(+118)* 2,216
MCGUINNESS, John* (FF)	9,343	*(+28)* 9,371	*(+286)* 9,657
NOLAN, Billy (Ind)	335		
NOLAN, MJ (FF)	8,711	*(+61)* 8,772	*(+115)* 8,887
O'BRIEN, Michael (Lab)	3,732	*(+7)* 3,739	*(+207)* 3,946
TOWNSEND, Jim (Lab)	4,272	*(+58)* 4,330	*(+85)* 4,415
WHITE, Mary (GP)	4,961	*(+42)* 5,003	*(+398)* 5,401
NON-TRANSFERABLE		16	73

4th Count Transfer of **Kiernan** Votes	5th Count Transfer of **O'Brien** Votes	6th Count Transfer of **Browne** Votes	7th Count Transfer of **Aylward** Surplus	8th Count Transfer of **White** Votes
(+92) 5,762	(+132) 5,894			
(+165) 8,239	(+664) 8,903	(+3,335) 12,238		
(+428) 10,085	(+442) 10,527	(+127) 10,654	(+224) 10,878	(+1,233) 12,111
(+253) 9,140	(+64) 9,204	(+628) 9,832	(+63) 9,895	(+1,114) 11,009
(+274) 4,220				
(+153) 4,568	(+2,057) 6,625	(+1,021) 7,646	(+7) 7,653	(+2,962) 10,615
(+654) 6,055	(+641) 6,696	(+633) 7,329	(+26) 7,355	
197	220	150		2,046

Cavan-Monaghan

Elected

Caoimhghín Ó Caoláin (SF)*	1st Count
Brendan Smith (FF)*	1st Count
Paudge Connolly (Ind)	9th Count
Rory O'Hanlon (FF)*	9th Count
Seymour Crawford (FG)*	12th Count

Voting by Party

1st Preference	Number	%	% 1997
Fianna Fáil	21,614	34.95	38.44
Fine Gael	15,571	25.18	34.67
Labour	550	0.89	3.96
Prog Democrats	1,131	1.83	—
Green Party	1,100	1.78	—
Sinn Féin	10,832	17.51	19.37
CSP	358	0.58	3.40
Others	10,691	17.29	0.17

Statistics

Population	104,257	
Electorate	87,087	
Total Poll	62,710	72.01
Spoiled Votes	863	1.34
Valid Poll	61,847	71.02
Seats	5	
Quota	10,308	
Candidates	14	

Seats

FF	2
FG	1
Sinn Féin	1
Ind	1
Ind gain from FG	

The constituency of Cavan-Monaghan is unchanged since the 1997 General Election.

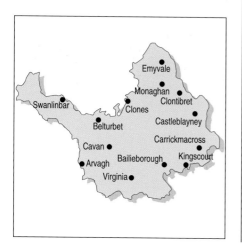

Caoimhghín Ó Caoláin (SF)

Home Address
Mullaghdun, Monaghan
Constituency Office
21 Dublin Street, Monaghan
Telephone
Constituency Office (047) 82917;
Fax (047) 71849
Birth Place/Date
Monaghan. 18 September 1953
Married
Briege McGinn. 4 daughters, 1 son
Education
St Mary's CBS, Monaghan
Occupation
Full-time public representative. Formerly bank official

Caoimhghín Ó Caoláin was appointed parliamentary leader of the five Sinn Féin deputies in the 29th Dáil in June 2002.

He was first elected a Dáil deputy in 1997. He was the first Sinn Féin representative to be elected since the party abandoned the policy of abstentionism. He was a candidate in the general elections of 1987, 1989 and 1992.

Was member of Oireachtas Committee on Environment and Local Government. Member of British-Irish Inter-Parliamentary Body.

Member of Monaghan County Council since 1985. Member Sinn Féin Ardchomairle since 1983; Sinn Féin delegation to the Forum for Peace and Reconciliation. Member of Sinn Féin delegation in direct talks with British Government representatives.

Brendan Smith (FF)

Home Address
3 Carrickfern, Cavan
Telephone
Home (049) 4362366; *Fax* (049) 4362367
Birth Place/Date
Cavan. June 1956
Married
Anne McGarry
Education
St Camillus's College, Killucan, Co Westmeath; University College, Dublin (BA)
Occupation
Full-time public representative. Former adviser to Government minister

Brendan Smith was elected on the first count, his best performance since he was first elected in 1992. In that year he replaced the senior Fianna Fáil minister John Wilson who retired from active politics. Brendan Smith was political advisor to the former Tánaiste John Wilson for 15 years. Government Whip on Oireachtas Joint Committee on Foreign Affairs in last Dáil. Member of British-Irish Inter-Parliamentary Body.

Member, Co Cavan Vocational Educational Committee; Templeport Gaelic Football Club; Cavan GAA Supporters' Club; Cavan Drama Festival; Cumann Seanchais Bhreifne.

Paudge Connolly (Ind)

Home Address
Tullylush, Silver Stream, Monaghan
Telephone
Home (047) 82386
Birth Place/Date
Monaghan. 23 September 1953
Married
Winnie McGuinness. 4 sons
Education
St Macartan's College, Monaghan
Occupation
Full-time public representative. Formerly psychiatric nurse and part-time secretary health services branch of SIPTU

Paudge Connolly is a new Dáil deputy. He topped the poll in the Monaghan part of the constituency as an Independent campaigning as a 'Hospital Action' candidate. His win deprived Fine Gael of their second seat in the constituency.

Member, North-Eastern Health Board since 1997 and of its Partnership Committee; County Enterprise Board; Monaghan County Partnership. Member, Gaelic Athletic Association. Played gaelic football at county level for minor and under-21 teams. Chairman and founder, Tyholland Boxing Club. Member, Ulster Boxing Council.

Rory O'Hanlon (FF)

Home Address
Mullinarry, Carrickmacross, Co Monaghan
Constituency Office
Carrickmacross
Telephone
Home (042) 966 1530; *Fax* (042) 966 3220;
Office (042) 966 1530; *Fax* (042) 966 1530;
Website www.roryohanlon.ie
Birth Place/Date
Dublin. 7 February 1934
Married
Teresa Ward. 4 sons, 2 daughters
Education
St Mary's College, Dundalk; Blackrock College; University College, Dublin (MB, BCh, BAO, DCh, LM)
Occupation
Public representative. Doctor

Rory O'Hanlon was elected Ceann Comhairle of the 29th Dáil on 6 June 2002.

He was first elected a Dáil deputy in 1977. Leas-Cheann Comhairle 1997–2002. Chairman of the Fianna Fáil Parliamentary Party 1995–2002. Was Minister for the Environment November 1991 to February 1992; Minister for Health 1987–91; Minister of State, Department of Health and Social Welfare October-December 1982. Party spokesperson on Health 1983–87.

Member and vice-chairperson British-Irish Inter-Parliamentary Body. Member of National Forum on Europe. Member New Ireland Forum. Former chairman of Cross-Border Development Committee, Eastern Region.

Member of Monaghan County Council 1979–87. Medical representative on North-Eastern Health Board 1970–87.

Seymour Crawford (FG)

Home Address
Drumkeen, Aghabog, Co Monaghan
Constituency Office
18 The Diamond, Monaghan
Telephone
Office (047) 71911; *Fax* (047) 71912; *Mobile* 087 2544886
Birth Place/Date
Monaghan. June 1944
Education
Mullagreenan National School; High School, Clones
Occupation
Public representative. Farmer

Seymour Crawford was appointed deputy spokesperson for Community, Rural and Gaeltacht Affairs in June 2002.

He was first elected to the Dáil in 1992. Junior spokesperson on Agriculture in last Dáil. Member of British-Irish Inter-Parliamentary Body 1993–2002.

Member of Monaghan County Council since 1991.

Member of the Irish Farmers' Association since 1965 (Vice-President 1984–88). Chairperson of the National Livestock Committee 1979–84. Chairperson of the EU Beef and Veal Committee (1981–86) and a member of the CBF (Irish Livestock and Meat Board) 1979–86. Received Bastow Award for service in meat and livestock in 1986.

Cavan-Monaghan

Seats 5 Quota 10,308	1st Count	2nd Count Transfer of **Ó Caoláin** Surplus	3rd Count Transfer of **Smith, B** Surplus	4th Count Transfer of **Cullen, Smith, T** Votes	5th Count Transfer of **Brennan** Votes
BRENNAN, Joe (Ind)	1,026	*(+20)* 1,046	*(+1)* 1,047	*(+67)* 1,114	
BOYLAN, Andrew* (FG)	4,819	*(+36)* 4,855	*(+34)* 4,889	*(+172)* 5,061	*(+23)* 5,084
CONNOLLY, Paudge (Ind)	7,722	*(+145)* 7,867	*(+4)* 7,871	*(+75)* 7,946	*(+429)* 8,375
CRAWFORD, Seymour* (FG)	6,113	*(+23)* 6,136	*(+3)* 6,139	*(+39)* 6,178	*(+108)* 6,286
CULLEN, Des (Lab)	550	*(+16)* 566	*(+6)* 572		
GALLAGHER, Robbie (FF)	3,731	*(+58)* 3,789	*(+85)* 3,874	*(+47)* 3,921	*(+83)* 4,004
MARTIN, Vincent P (Ind)	1,943	*(+49)* 1,992	*(+5)* 1,997	*(+90)* 2,087	*(+178)* 2,265
MCCABE, Marcus (GP)	1,100	*(+38)* 1,138	*(+5)* 1,143	*(+158)* 1,301	*(+84)* 1,385
MCCAUGHEY, Gerard (PD)	1,131	*(+13)* 1,144	*(+10)* 1,154	*(+65)* 1,219	*(+42)* 1,261
Ó CAOLÁIN, Caoimhghín* (SF)	10,832				
O'HANLON, Rory* (FF)	7,204	*(+91)* 7,295	*(+184)* 7,479	*(+62)* 7,541	*(+107)* 7,648
O'REILLY, Paddy (FG)	4,639	*(+28)* 4,667	*(+31)* 4,698	*(+119)* 4,817	*(+19)* 4,836
SMITH, Brendan* (FF)	10,679				
SMITH, Tony (CSP)	358	*(+7)* 365	*(+3)* 368		
NON-TRANSFERABLE				46	41

6th Count	7th Count	8th Count	9th Count	10th Count	11th Count	12th Count
Transfer of **McCaughey** Votes	Transfer of **McCabe** Votes	Transfer of **Martin** Votes	Transfer of **Gallagher** Votes	Transfer of **O'Hanlon** Surplus	Transfer of **Connolly** Surplus	Transfer of **O'Reilly** Votes
(+127) 5,211	(+163) 5,374	(+142) 5,516	(+117) 5,633	(+211) 5,844	(+61) 5,905	(+3,139) 9,044
(+239) 8,614	(+359) 8,973	(+705) 9,678	(+1,192) 10,870			
(+111) 6,397	(+112) 6,509	(+294) 6,803	(+275) 7,078	(+314) 7,392	(+310) 7,702	(+1,463) 9,165
(+193) 4,197	(+122) 4,319	(+216) 4,535				
(+106) 2,371	(+275) 2,646					
(+128) 1,513						
(+159) 7,807	(+136) 7,943	(+719) 8,662	(+2,370) 11,032			
(+119) 4,955	(+153) 5,108	(+212) 5,320	(+109) 5,429	(+199) 5,628	(+82) 5,710	
79	193	358	472		109	1,108

Clare

Elected

Voting by Party

1st Preference	Number	%	% 1997
Fianna Fáil	22,602	45.38	50.36
Fine Gael	12,680	25.46	30.08
Labour	1,720	3.45	3.59
Green Party	2,903	5.83	3.59
Christian Solidarity	176	0.35	1.06
Others	9,721	19.52	2.51

Statistics

Population	90,530	
Electorate	80,412	
Total Poll	50,341	62.60
Spoiled Votes	539	1.07
Valid Poll	49,802	61.93
Seats	4	
Quota	9,961	
Candidates	10	

Seats

FF   2
FG   1
Ind   1
Ind gain from FG

The constituency of Clare is unchanged since the 1997 General Election.

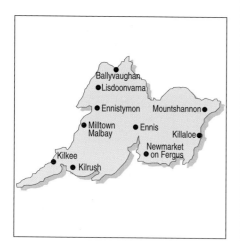

James Breen (Ind)

Home Address
Ballyknock, Kilnamona, Co Clare
Telephone
Home (065) 6828180
Birth Place/Date
Ballyknock. 23 May 1945
Married
Eileen Galvin. 3 sons, 1 daughter
Education
Kilnamona National School
Occupation
Public representative. Farmer

James Breen is a new Dáil deputy. He topped the poll in Clare running as an Independent on local issues. He had been 36 years a member of Fianna Fáil.

Member, Clare County Council.

Tony Killeen (FF)

Home Address
Kilnaboy, Corofin, Co Clare
Constituency Office
Upper Market Street, Ennis, Co Clare
Telephone
Office (065) 6841500; *Fax* (065) 6841514;
Mobile 087 2525304
Birth Place/Date
Clare. 9 June 1952
Married
Lily O'Keeffe. 5 sons
Education
St Flannan's College, Ennis; Mary Immaculate College of Education, Limerick
Occupation
Full-time public representative. Formerly national school teacher

Tony Killeen was first elected to the Dáil in 1992. In the last Dáil he has been a member of the following committees: Dáil Committee on Privileges and Procedures; Joint Committee on Environment and Local Government; Committee on Sustainable Development.

Chairman, Committee on Members' Interests. Member, Working Group of Committee Chairmen. Member, British-Irish Inter-Parliamentary Body.

Member, Clare County Council 1985–97 (vice-chairman 1987–89 and chairman 1989–91). Member, County Clare Vocational Education Committee 1979–94 (chairman 1991–94).

Former member, Management Boards of Killaloe and Shannon Community Schools and Limerick Regional Technical College.

Founder member, Shannon Status Committee and Chairman 1989–91.

Member, Gaelic Athletic Association; Irish Farmers' Association; Irish National Teachers' Organisation; Conradh na Gaeilge and other community and cultural organisations.

Former national chairman of Fianna Fáil Councillors' Association.

Síle de Valera (FF)

Home Address
6 Riverdale, Tulla Road, Ennis, Co Clare
Constituency Office
9 Chapel Lane, Ennis
Office
Department of Education and Science,
Marlborough Street, Dublin 1.
Telephone
Constituency Office (065) 6821100/6840208;
Fax (065) 6840695; *Office* (01) 889 2028
Birth Place/Date
Dublin. December 1954
Education
Loreto Convent, Foxrock, Co Dublin;
University College, Dublin (BA, HDipEd, Dip
Career Guidance, D Psych Sc)
Occupation
Minister of State. Formerly teacher

Síle de Valera was appointed Minister of State
at the Department of Education and Science in
June 2002, responsible for Adult Education,
Youth Affairs and Educational Disadvantage.
The de Valera family continues to be
represented at Cabinet in the person of her
cousin, Éamon Ó Cuív. Síle de Valera was
Minister for Arts, Heritage, Gaeltacht and the
Islands 1997–2002. She was first elected to the
Dáil as the youngest deputy in 1977 for the
constituency of Dublin Mid-County. She
unsuccessfully contested the constituency of
Dublin South in 1981 and February 1982 and
the constituency of Clare in November 1982.
She was elected for Clare in 1987 and has been
re-elected in subsequent general elections.

Member, European Parliament 1979–84.
Served on the Parliament's committees for
Social Affairs and Employment, Youth
Education and Sport, and the Ad Hoc
Women's Committee.

She is a grand-daughter of Éamon de Valera,
President of Ireland 1959–73; Taoiseach
1937–48, 1951–54, 1957–59; President of the
Executive Council of the Irish Free State
1932–37; President, First Dáil 1919–21;
President, Second Dáil, 1921–January 1922.

Pat Breen (FG)

Home Address
Lisduff, Ballynacally, Co Clare
Constituency Office
Parkview House, Lower Market Street Car
Park, Ennis, Co Clare
Telephone
Home (065) 6838229; *Office* (065) 6868466;
Fax (065) 6868486
Birth Place/Date
Ennis. 21 March 1957
Married
Anne McInerney. 2 sons
Education
Lisheen National School; St Flannan's College,
Ennis; Limerick Technical College
Occupation
Public representative. Farmer. Former
architectural technician

Pat Breen is a new Dáil deputy. He won the
only Fine Gael seat in Clare, defeating his
running mate and incumbent, Donal Carey. He
has been appointed deputy spokesperson for
Transport and Infrastructure.

Member, Clare County Council since 1999.

Clare

Seats 4 Quota 9,961	1st Count	2nd Count Transfer of **Corley, Whelan** Votes	3rd Count Transfer of **Meaney** Votes	4th Count Transfer of **Carey** Votes	5th Count Transfer of **Taylor-Quinn** Votes
BREEN, James (Ind)	9,721	*(+333)* 10,054			
BREEN, Pat (FG)	4,541	*(+160)* 4,701	*(+564)* 5,265	*(+1,669)* 6,934	*(+4,462)* 11,396
CAREY, Donal* (FG)	4,015	*(+212)* 4,227	*(+364)* 4,591		
CORLEY, Michael (Lab)	1,720				
DALY, Brendan* (FF)	6,717	*(+69)* 6,786	*(+128)* 6,914	*(+172)* 7,086	*(+597)* 7,683
DE VALERA, Síle* (FF)	7,755	*(+111)* 7,866	*(+598)* 8,464	*(+355)* 8,819	*(+551)* 9,370
KILLEEN, Tony* (FF)	8,130	*(+122)* 8,252	*(+388)* 8,640	*(+424)* 9,064	*(+418)* 9,482
MEANEY, Brian (GP)	2,903	*(+605)* 3,508			
TAYLOR-QUINN, Madeleine (FG)	4,124	*(+225)* 4,349	*(+685)* 5,034	*(+1,692)* 6,726	
WHELAN, Derek J (CSP)	176				
NON-TRANSFERABLE		59	840	1,119	1,817

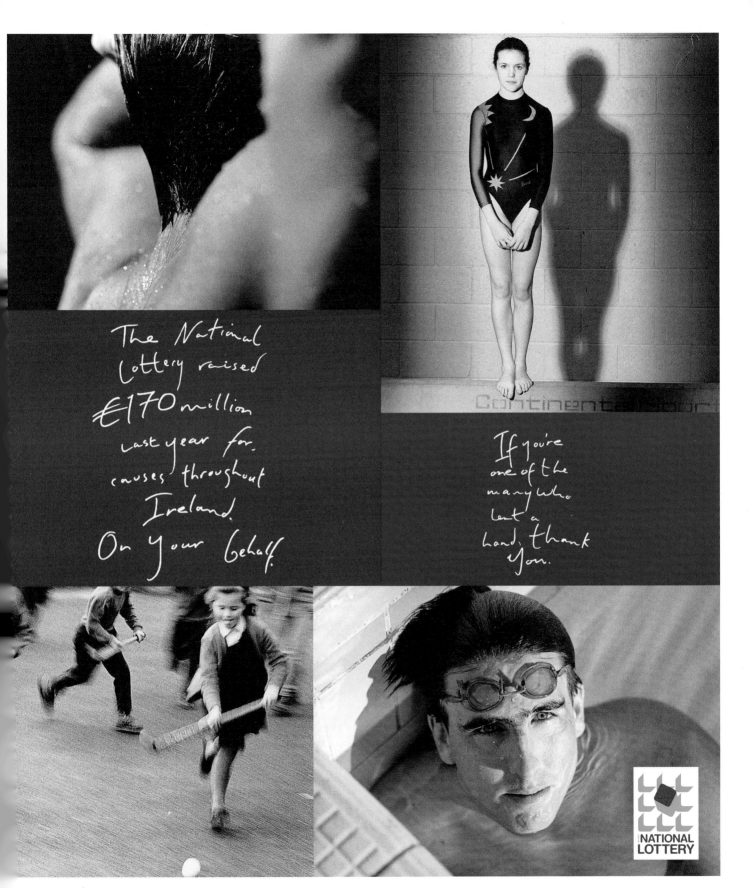

The National
Lottery raised
€170 million
last year for
causes throughout
Ireland.
On Your behalf

If you're
one of the
many who
lent a
hand, thank
you.

NATIONAL
LOTTERY

Cork East

Elected

Ned O'Keeffe (FF)*	1st Count
Michael Ahern (FF)*	2nd Count
David Stanton (FG)*	4th Count
Joe Sherlock (Lab)	4th Count

Voting by Party

1st Preference	Number	%	% 1997
Fianna Fáil	18,914	41.31	36.44
Fine Gael	13,322	29.09	30.12
Labour	9,605	20.98	8.13
Green Party	1,136	2.48	—
Sinn Féin	2,624	5.73	3.56
Christian Solidarity	187	0.40	—

Statistics

Population	83,001	
Electorate	72,702	
Total Poll	46,334	63.73
Spoiled Votes	546	1.18
Valid Poll	45,788	62.98
Seats	4	
Quota	9,158	
Candidates	9	

Seat

FF	2
FG	1
Lab	1
Lab gain from FG	

The constituency of Cork East gained 1,171 population from Cork North-Central in the 1998 revision.

Ned O'Keeffe (FF)

Home Address
Ballylough, Mitchelstown, Co Cork
Telephone
Home (022) 25285; *Fax* (022) 25495
Birth Place/Date
Ballylough. Mitchelstown, August 1942
Married
Ann Buckley. 3 sons, 2 daughters
Education
Darra College, Clonakilty, Co Cork; University College, Cork (Diploma in Social and Rural Science)
Occupation
Formerly company director, farmer

Ned O'Keeffe was first elected to the Dáil in November 1982. He was appointed Minister of State at the Department of Agriculture and Food with special responsibility for Food in July 1997. He resigned in 2001 following an inquiry into his declaration of personal interests. Senator, Taoiseach's nominee, May-November 1982. Party spokesman on Industry 1982–87. Deputy spokesperson on Enterprise and Employment with responsibility for Commerce, Science and Technology and Small Businesses 1994–97.

Member Cork County Council 1985–97. Chairman Northern Committee 1985–86; member Library Committee.

He has served as member, Regional Council and Council of Dairygold Co-operative Society.

Director Mitchelstown Co-operative Society 1974–82; director Agricultural Credit Corporation 1980–82; member Irish Co-operative Organisation Society (ICOS) 1978–81.

Member, Macra na Feirme 1958–71; Irish Farmers' Association 1969–82; chairman, Cork County Executive1979–82. Member, Gaelic Athletic Association.

Michael Ahern (FF)

Home Address
Libermann, Barryscourt, Carrigtwohill, Co Cork
Business Address
Department of Enterprise, Trade and Employment; Kildare Street, Dublin 2
Telephone
Home (021) 4883592; *Fax* (021) 4883436; *Office* (01) 631 2242/3; *Fax* (01)6312808
Birth Place/Date
Dungourney, Co Cork. January 1949
Married
Margaret Monahan. 3 daughters
Education
Rockwell College, Cashel, Co Tipperary; University College, Dublin (BA)
Occupation
Minister of State. Registered auditor and accountant

Michael Ahern was appointed in June 2002 as Minister of State at the Department of Enterprise, Trade and Employment with special responsibility for Trade and Commerce. He was first elected to the Dáil in February 1982. He was Minister of State at the Department of Industry and Commerce, with special responsibility for Science and Technology 1992–93. Chairperson of the Oireachtas Joint Committee on Finance and the Public Service and of the Committee on Consolidation of Bills 1997–2002. Party deputy spokesperson on Transport 1984–87. Spokesperson on the Office of Public Works and Taxation Policy 1995–97.

Member, Carrigtwohill Community Council; Dungourney Hurling Club; Midleton Gaelic Football Club; Midleton Rugby Club; Muintir na Tíre.

Michael Ahern is a son of the late Liam Ahern, Senator 1957–73 and Dáil deputy for Cork North-East 1973–74.

His grand-uncle, John Dineen, was Farmers' Party Dáil deputy 1922–27.

David Stanton (FG)

Home Address
Coppingerstown, Midleton, Co Cork
Telephone
Constituency Office (021) 4632867;
Fax (021) 4621133 *Website* www.stanton.ie
Birth Place/Date
Cork. 15 February 1957
Married
Mary Lehane. 4 sons
Education
St Colman's Vocational School, Midleton;
Sharman Crawford Technical Institute, Cork;
University College, Cork (BA, MEd, Diploma in
Career Guidance, Diploma in Educational
Administration)
Occupation
Full-time public representative. Formerly
teacher, career guidance counsellor

David Stanton was appointed Deputy
Spokesperson on Education and Science in
June 2002.

He was first elected to the Dáil in 1997 at his
first attempt. He won a seat formerly held by
Labour and the Workers' Party. Front Bench
spokesperson on Labour Affairs, Consumer
Rights and Trade 1997–2002.

Served as a commissioned officer in An Fórsa
Cosanta Áitiúil. Was Public Relations Officer
for Midleton and District Day Care Centre.

Joe Sherlock (Lab)

Home Address
20 Blackwater Drive, Mallow, Co Cork
Telephone
Home (022) 21053; *Fax* (022) 21053;
Mobile 086 813 5828
Birth Place/Date
Kildorrery, Co Cork. 26 September 1935
Married
Ellen Spillane. 2 sons, 1 daughter
Education
Graigue National School
Occupation
Full-time public representative. Former Sugar
Company employee

Joe Sherlock returns to the Dáil after a most
varied political career involving changing
parties and electoral successes and defeats.
He was the first Sinn Féin–The Workers' Party
candidate to be elected to the Dáil in 1981. He
had unsuccessfully contested the general
elections of 1973 and 1977 and by-elections in
1974 and 1979. He was re-elected in February
1982, but lost his seat in November 1982. He
was re-elected in 1987 as a Workers' Party
deputy and elected again in 1989. He lost his
seat in 1992 when running as a Democratic
Left candidate after the split within the
Workers' Party. Member of the Seanad
(Labour Panel) 1993–97. He stood
unsuccessfully for the Dáil again in 1997 but
was elected in 2002 as a Labour Party
candidate.

He has been a member of Mallow Urban
District Council since 1967 and a member of
Cork County Council since 1974.

Member, Southern Health Board. Former
member, Cork County Vocational Education
Committee. Chairperson of Mallow Hospital
Co-ordinating Committee. Member, Mallow
GAA club.

Cork East

Seats 4 Quota 9,158	1st Count	2nd Count Transfer of **O'Keeffe, N** Surplus	3rd Count Transfer of **Murphy, Manning, and O'Keeffe, M** Votes	4th Count Transfer of **Mulvihill** Votes
AHERN, Michael* (FF)	8,340	*(+864)* 9,204		
BRADFORD, Paul* (FG)	7,053	*(+171)* 7,224	*(+494)* 7,718	*(+513)* 8,231
MANNING, Pat (CSP)	187	*(+2)* 189		
MULVIHILL, John (Lab)	4,813	*(+25)* 4,838	*(+721)* 5,559	
MURPHY, June (SF)	2,624	*(+61)* 2,685		
O'KEEFFE, Martin (GP)	1,136	*(+15)* 1,151		
O'KEEFFE, Ned* (FF)	10,574			
SHERLOCK, Joe (Lab)	4,792	*(+223)* 5,015	*(+1,177)* 6,192	*(+2,468)* 8,660
STANTON, David* (FG)	6,269	*(+55)* 6,324	*(+654)* 6,978	*(+1,460)* 8,438
NON-TRANSFERABLE			979	2,097

Labour Leader Ruairí Quinn speaking with lollipop lady Dolores Kinsella while on the campaign trail in Sandyford, Dublin.

Cork North-Central

Elected

Voting by Party

1st Preference	Number	%	% 1997
Fianna Fáil	18,725	41.48	35.53
Fine Gael	9,202	20.38	30.16
Labour	5,313	11.77	5.27
Prog Democrats	3,126	6.92	7.51
Green Party	1,155	2.56	3.04
Sinn Féin	2,860	6.34	3.76
Others	4,763	10.55	2.04

Statistics

Population	104,787	
Electorate	79,063	
Total Poll	45,692	57.79
Spoiled Votes	548	1.20
Valid Poll	45,144	57.01
Seats	5	
Quota	7,525	
Candidates	13	

Seats

FF	3
FG	1
Lab	1
Lab gain from FG	

The constituency of Cork North-Central in the 1998 revision gained 4,643 population from Cork South-Central. It lost 1,171 to Cork East and 1,666 to Cork North-West.

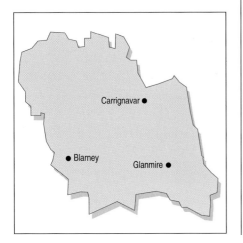

Noel O'Flynn (FF)

Home Address
Melvindale House, Coolowen, Blarney, Co Cork
Constituency Office
Unit 3A, N.O.F. Commercial Centre, Kilnap, Mallow Road, Cork
Telephone
Home (021) 4382500; *Constituency Office* (021) 4211200; *Fax* (021) 4211110
Website www.noeloflynn.ie
Birth Place/Date
Cork. December 1951
Married
Frances O'Keeffe. 3 sons
Education
Regional Technical College, Cork
Occupation
Full-time public representative. Company director

Noel O'Flynn was first elected a Dáil deputy in 1997. Served in last Dáil on Oireachtas Committees on Justice, Equality and Women's Rights; Public Enterprise, Enterprise and Small Business and was Government Whip on Finance and Public Services Committee. Was member of Mini CTC Sub-Committee which inquired into CIÉ/Iarnrod Éireann.

Member, Cork City Council since 1991. Alderman since 1999. Member, Southern Health Board; Institute of Motor Industry; Society of Operations Engineers; Society of Irish Motor Industry.

Kathleen Lynch (Lab)

Home Address
Farrancleary House, 5 Assumption Road, Blackpool, Cork
Telephone
Home/Office (021) 439 9930;
Fax (021) 430 4293
Birth Place/Date
Cork. 7 June 1953
Married
Bernard Lynch. 3 daughters, 1 son
Education
Blackpool School, Cork
Occupation
Full-time public representative

Kathleen Lynch was appointed party spokesperson for Arts, Sports and Tourism in June 2002. She was first elected to the Dáil in 1994 as a Democratic Left candidate in the Cork North Central by-election caused by the death of the Labour TD Gerry O'Sullivan. She lost her seat in the 1997 general election. She had previously contested the Cork South Central constituency in the 1992 general election. Served as a member of the Constitutional Review Committee.

Member of Cork Corporation since 1985. Member, Southern Health Board. Chairperson of the Housing and Strategic Policy Committee, Cork Corporation. Member, Cork City Development Board. Member, Cork Opera House Board.

Cork North-Central

Bernard Allen (FG)

Home Address
Mount Prospect, Shanakiel, Cork
Telephone
Home (021) 4303068; *Fax* (021) 4304200
Birth Place/Date
Cork. 9 September 1944
Married
Marie Dorney. 3 daughters
Education
North Monastery CBS, Cork; Regional Technical College; University College, Cork (Diploma in Chemical Technology)
Occupation
Full-time public representative. Formerly laboratory technologist

Bernard Allen was appointed party spokesperson for the Environment and Local Government in June 2002.

He was first elected to the Dáil in 1981. He was Minister of State at the Department of Education, with special responsibility for Youth and Sport, 1994–97; Minister of State at the Department of the Environment, with special responsibility for Local Government Reform and Urban Traffic Management, 1994–97. Front Bench spokesperson on Tourism, Sport and Recreation 1997–2002; on Social Welfare 1993–94; on Health 1987–88; on Environmental Protection 1982. Was member of Oireachtas Committee on Health and Children.

Alderman, Cork City Council 1979–95 (Lord Mayor, 1988–89); Southern Health Board 1982–95. Former chairman, Southern Health Advisory Board. Served on Board of Management, North Infirmary, Cork.

Member, Pitch and Putt Union of Ireland; Bol-Chumann na hÉireann; Golfing Union of Ireland.

Billy Kelleher (FF)

Home Address
Ballyphilip, White's Cross, Glanmire, Co Cork
Constituency Office
28A Ballyhooley Road, Dillon's Cross, Cork
Telephone
Home (021) 4821045; *Constituency office* (021)4502289; *Mobile* 087 258 0521; *Fax* (021) 502356
Birth Place/Date
Cork. 20 January 1968
Education
Sacred Heart College, Carignavar, Co Cork; Agricultural College, Limerick
Occupation
Full-time public representative. Farmer

Billy Kelleher was first elected to the Dáil in 1997. He was Government Whip on the Committee on the Environment and Local Government and a member of the Committes on Agriculture, Food and the Marine, and on Tourism and Sport. He was a Senator, Taoiseach's nominee, 1992–97. He was a candidate in the 1992 general election in Cork North Central, losing out on the last seat by 25 votes. He was also a candidate in the by-election in the same constituency in 1994 caused by the death of Gerry O'Sullivan (Lab).

Dan Wallace (FF)

Home Address
13 Killeens Place, Farranree, Cork
Constituency Office
60 Thomas Davis Street, Blackpool, Cork
Telephone
Home (021) 4307465; *Fax* (021) 4393098; *Constituency office* (021) 4393111; *Fax* (021) 4308969
Birth Place/Date
Cork. 14 June 1942
Married
Ethel Sutton. 2 sons, 3 daughters
Education
North Presentation Convent, Cork; North Monastery CBS, Cork; College of Commerce, Cork
Occupation
Public representative. Formerly customs clerk with Henry Ford Ltd

Dan Wallace was first elected to the Dáil in November 1982. He was Minister of State at the Department of the Environment and Local Government with special responsibility for Environment Information and Awareness and the Environmental Protection Agency 1997–2002. He was Minister of State at the Department of the Environment with special responsibility for Urban Renewal, February 1992–January 1993.

Chairman, Select Committee on Legislation and Security 1993–95. He has served on the Women's Rights Committee; Oireachtas Joint Committee on the Secondary Legislation of the European Communities; Committee on Crime, Lawlessness and Vandalism; Select Committee on Finance and General Affairs.

Member, Cork City Council 1979–92 (Alderman 1985–92 and Lord Mayor 1985/86).

Cork North-Central

Seats 5 Quota 7,525	1st Count	2nd Count Transfer of **Duffy and Tynan** Votes	3rd Count Transfer of **Barry** Votes
ALLEN, Bernard* (FG)	5,458	(+45) 5,503	(+94) 5,597
BARRY, Mick (SP) (Ind)	936	(+90) 1,026	
DUFFY, Gerry (CSP) (Ind)	215		
KELLEHER, Billy* (FF)	5,801	(+48) 5,849	(+36) 5,885
KELLY, Gerry (FG)	3,744	(+23) 3,767	(+51) 3,818
LYNCH, Kathleen (Lab)	5,313	(+89) 5,402	(+226) 5,628
MCMURRAY, Nicholas (GP)	1,155	(+41) 1,196	(+133) 1,329
MINIHAN, John (PD)	3,126	(+26) 3,152	(+21) 3,173
O'BRIEN, Jonathan (SF)	2,860	(+105) 2,965	(+258) 3,223
O'CALLAGHAN, Joe (Ind)	3,154	(+68) 3,222	(+97) 3,319
O'FLYNN, Noel* (FF)	7,387	(+54) 7,441	(+54) 7,495
TYNAN, Ted (WP) (Ind)	458		
WALLACE, Dan* (FF)	5,537	(+71) 5,608	(+24) 5,632
NON-TRANSFERABLE		13	45

4th Count	5th Count	6th Count	7th Count
Transfer of **McMurray** Votes	Transfer of **Minihan** Votes	Transfer of **O'Brien** Votes	Transfer of **O'Callaghan** Votes
(+75) 5,672	*(+512)* 6,184	*(+417)* 6,601	*(+1,049)* 7,650
(+55) 5,940	*(+690)* 6,630	*(+339)* 6,969	*(+487)* 7,456
(+93) 3,911	*(+493)* 4,404	*(+164)* 4,568	*(+369)* 4,937
(+514) 6,142	*(+541)* 6,683	*(+813)* 7,496	*(+922)* 8,418
(+113) 3,286			
(+182) 3,405	*(+78)* 3,483		
(+138) 3,457	*(+248)* 3,705	*(+760)* 4,465	
(+30) 7,525			
(+43) 5,675	*(+560)* 6,235	*(+342)* 6,577	*(+610)* 7,187
131	295	943	1,971

Cork North-West

Elected

Voting by Party

1st Preference	Number	%	% 1997
Fianna Fáil	19,433	50.06	46.50
Fine Gael	16,335	42.08	41.12
Labour	2,668	6.87	7.40
Christian Solidarity	383	0.99	—

Statistics

Population	62,453	
Electorate	53,699	
Total Poll	39,393	73.36
Spoiled Votes	574	1.46
Valid Poll	38,819	72.29
Seats	3	
Quota	9,705	
Candidates	6	

Seats

FF	2
FG	1
No change	

The Cork North-West constituency in the 1998 revision gained 1,666 population from Cork North-Central and 993 from South-Central.

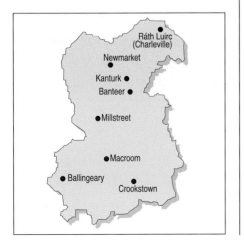

Michael Moynihan (FF)

Home Address
Meens, Kiskeam, Mallow, Co Cork
Constituency Office
Kanturk, Co Cork
Telephone
Home (029) 76200; *Constituency office* (029) 51299; *Fax* (029) 51300; *Mobile* 087 274 5810
Birth Place/Date
Cork. 12 January 1968
Education
Boherbue Comprehensive School, Mallow
Occupation
Full-time public representative. Farmer

Michael Moynihan was first elected to the Dáil in 1997 in his first general election. He was a member of the Committees on Heritage and the Irish Language and Agriculture, Food and the Marine during the 28th Dáil.

Donal Moynihan (FF)

Home Address
Gortnascorty, Ballymakeera, Macroom, Co Cork
Constituency Office
Railway View, Macroom
Telephone
Home (026) 45019; *Office* (026) 43937; *Fax* (026) 43938
Birth Place/Date
Ballymakeera. 2 October 1941
Married
Catherine Twomey. 4 sons, 5 daughters
Education
Ballyvourney Vocational School, Co Cork
Occupation
Full-time public representative. Farmer

Donal Moynihan has been a Dáil deputy since 1992 when he regained a seat he had previously held in Cork North-West, November 1982–89.

Member, Oireachtas All-Party Committees on Tourism, Sport and Recreation and on Heritage and the Irish Language in last Dáil.

Gerard Murphy (FG)

Home Address
New Street, Newmarket, Co Cork
Constituency Office
Percival Street, Kanturk, Co Cork; Main Street,
Charleville, Co Cork
Telephone
Home (029) 60780; *Fax* (029) 20928;
Constituency office (029) 51922;
Fax (029) 20928
Birth Place/Date
Newmarket. 25 March 1951
Married
Marian Kelly. 1 son, 1 daughter
Education
Cistercian College, Mount St Joseph,
Roscrea, Co. Tipperary
Occupation
Full-time public representative

Gerard Murphy is a new Dáil deputy. He has been appointed deputy party spokesperson for Enterprise, Trade and Employment.

He has been a member of Cork County Council since 1991. He is the leader of the Fine Gael group on the council. He is chairman of the Policy Committee on Planning and chairman of the County Development Board. He is also chairman of the Newmarket Community Development Association and of the FÁS Community Employment Scheme.

Seats 3 Quota 9,705	1st Count	2nd Count Transfer of **Moynihan, M** Surplus	3rd Count Transfer of **Coughlan, Duffy** Votes	4th Count Transfer of **Moynihan, D** Surplus
CREED, Michael* (FG)	7,787	*(+30)* 7,817	*(+1,340)* 9,157	*(+303)* 9,460
COUGHLAN, Martin (Lab)	2,668	*(+26)* 2,694		
DUFFY, Gerry (CSP)	383	*(+6)* 389		
MOYNIHAN, Donal* (FF)	8,893	*(+592)* 9,485	*(+669)* 10,154	
MOYNIHAN, Michael* (FF)	10,540			
MURPHY, Gerard (FG)	8,548	*(+181)* 8,729	*(+688)* 9,417	*(+90)* 9,507
NON-TRANSFERABLE			386	442

Cork South-Central

Elected

Voting by Party

1st Preference	Number	%	% 1997
Fianna Fáil	26,879	48.57	42.62
Fine Gael	10,735	19.40	30.57
Labour	3,286	5.94	8.92
Green Party	4,956	8.96	6.58
Sinn Féin	2,073	3.75	—
Socialist Workers' Party	218	0.39	—
Others	7,191	12.99	6.80

Statistics

Population	107,591	
Electorate	90,237	
Total Poll	55,785	61.82
Spoiled Votes	545	0.80
Valid Poll	55,240	61.22
Seats	5	
Quota	9,207	
Candidates	12	

Seats

FF	3
FG	1
GP	1
GP gain from FG	

The constituency of Cork South-Central in the 1998 revision lost 4,643 population to Cork North-Central and 993 to Cork North-West.

Micheál Martin (FF)

Home Address
Lios Laoi, 16 Silver Manor, Ballinlough, Cork
Business Address
Department of Health and Children, Hawkins House, Poolbeg Street, Dublin 1
Telephone
Home (021) 4320088; *Office* (01) 6354000; *Fax* (01) 6354108
Birth Place/Date
Cork. August 1960
Married
Mary O'Shea. 2 sons, 1 daughter
Education
Coláiste Chríost Rí, Cork; University College, Cork (BA, HDipEd, MA)
Occupation
Government Minister. Formerly secondary school teacher

Micheál Martin was re-appointed Minister for Health and Children in June 2002. He had been appointed Minister for Education in June 1997 and moved to Health in January 2000 as part of a Cabinet re-shuffle. He was first elected to the Dáil in 1989. He had been a candidate in the 1987 general election.

Party spokesperson on Education and the Gaeltacht 1995–97.

Member, Cork City Council 1985–97 (Lord Mayor, 1992/93, Alderman from 1991). Chairman of Arts Committee 1987/88. Former chairman, City of Cork Vocational Education Committee. He has served on the Governing Body of University College, Cork and of Cork Regional Technical College.

He has served as a member, Association of Secondary Teachers of Ireland (shop steward); Nemo Rangers Hurling and Football clubs.

Former national chairman, Ógra Fianna Fáil.

Simon Coveney (FG)

Home Address
1 Abbotswood, Monastery Road, Cork
Constituency Office
6a Anglesea Street, Cork
Telephone
Mobile 087 8321755; *Constituency office* (021) 4313100; *Fax* (021) 4316696
Website: www.simoncoveney.ie
Birth Place/Date
Cork. 16 June 1972
Education
Clongowes Wood College, Co Kildare; University College, Cork; Gurteen Agricultural College; Royal Agricultural College, Gloucestershire, England (BSc Agriculture and Land Management)
Occupation
Full-time public representative. Formerly farmer

Simon Coveney is front bench spokesperson for Communications, Marine and Natural Resources. He was first elected to the Dáil in a by-election for Cork South Central in October 1998 following the death of his father, Hugh Coveney TD. In the last Dáil he was Assistant Chief Whip and Secretary of the Fine Gael Parliamentary Party. He was spokesperson on Drugs and Youth Issues. In the last Dáil he was a member of Oireachtas Committees on Family, Social and Community Affairs and on Education and Science; Strategic Management Initiative Committee.

Member, Cork County Council since 1999. Member, Southern Health Board. Former Chairperson of Joint City and County Committee.

Led the Sail Chernobyl Project which involved sailing a boat 30,000 miles around the world and raising £500,000 for the charity. Is a qualified sailing instructor and lifeguard. Played rugby with Garryowen, Cork Constitution and Crosshaven.

Batt O'Keeffe (FF)

Home Address
8 Westcliffe, Ballincollig, Co Cork
Constituency Office
Commercial Park, Ballincollig, Co Cork
Telephone
Home/Office (021) 4871393;
Fax (021) 4871393
Birth Place/Date
Cullen, Mallow, Co Cork. April 1945
Married
Mary Murphy. 1 son, 3 daughters
Education
St Brendan's College, Killarney, Co Kerry;
University College, Cork (BA, HDipEd)
Occupation
Public representative. Lecturer in Cork
Institute of Technology

Batt O'Keeffe has been a Dáil deputy since
1992 and previously 1987–89. Senator, Labour
panel, 1989–92. He was a candidate in the
1989 general election. Chairman Oireachtas
Committee on Health and Children
1997–2002.

Member, Cork County Council since 1985;
Cork Vocational Education Sports Advisory
Committee; Higher Education Committee;
Chairman, Southern Health Board.

Member, Gaelic Athletic Association and Cork
Handball Board. Vice-Chairman Ballincollig
Community Centre Management Committee.

Cork footballer and holder of Munster medals
at under-21, junior and senior levels. Cork
intermediate Handball Champion 1980.

Dan Boyle (GP)

Home Address
45 Capwell Avenue, Turner's Cross, Cork
Constituency Office
99 Douglas Street, Cork
Telephone
Home (021) 496 5663; *Mobile* 087 277 2701;
Constituency office (021) 4704238
Birth Place/Date
Chicago, USA. 14 August 1962
Married
Bláithín Hurley. 1 daughter
Education
Coláiste Chríost Rí; Cork Institute of
Technology (Diploma in Child/Community
Care)
Occupation
Full-time public representative. Former
community youth worker

Dan Boyle is a new Dáil deputy. His election
follows several attempts to win a seat in Cork
South Central. He is party spokesperson on
Finance, Social and Family Affairs, Rural
Development, the Gaeltacht and the Islands.

Member of Cork City Council 1991–2002.
Former Vice-President of the National Youth
Council of Ireland; member, the National
Economic and Social Council 1998–2002 and
the Public Transport Partnership Forum
1999–2002.

Member, National Council of Friends of the
Earth and former Director.

John Dennehy (FF)

Home Address
Avondale, 13 Westside Estate, Togher, Cork
Telephone
Home (021) 4962908; *Fax* (021) 4320799;
Mobile 087 239 2517
Birth Place/Date
Togher, Cork. 22 March 1940
Married
Philomena Martin. 5 sons, 2 daughters
Education
Sharman Crawford Technical College, Cork;
Cork School of Commerce (Diploma in
Supervisory Studies)
Occupation
Full-time public representative. Formerly
engineering supervisor

John Dennehy was a Dáil deputy 1987–92 and
1997–2002. He was a candidate in Cork-Mid
constituency in 1977, in a by-election in Cork
City in 1979 and in the 1992 general election
in 1992 in Cork South-Central.

He was Assistant Government Chief Whip
1989–92. Member of the British-Irish Inter-
Parliamentary Body and Co-Chairman of its
Committee on Environment, Culture and
Education. Government Whip on Finance and
Public Service Committee 1997–2001. Vice-
Chairman Public Accounts Committee
2001–02. Member, Health and Children's
Committee.

Member, Cork City Council since 1974.
Alderman since 1985. Lord Mayor 1983–84.
Chairman of Southern Health Board 1984–86
and 1995–97 and Chairman of its Committee
on Drugs and Alcohol Prevention since 1995.

Cork South-Central

Seats 5 Quota 9,207	1st Count	2nd Count Transfer of **Martin** Surplus	3rd Count Transfer of **Neville, O'Sullivan** Votes	4th Count Transfer of **O'Connell** Votes
BOYLE, Dan (GP)	4,952	*(+442)* 5,394	*(+112)* 5,506	*(+260)* 5,766
CLUNE, Deirdre* (FG)	5,535	*(+313)* 5,848	*(+38)* 5,886	*(+96)* 5,982
COVENEY, Simon* (FG)	5,183	*(+574)* 5,757	*(+36)* 5,793	*(+113)* 5,906
DENNEHY, John* (FF)	5,533	*(+1,723)* 7,256	*(+39)* 7,295	*(+402)* 7,697
HANLON, Tom (SF)	2,063	*(+113)* 2,176	*(+78)* 2,254	*(+226)* 2,480
MARTIN, Micheál* (FF)	14,742			
NEVILLE, Ted (Ind)	372	*(+11)* 383		
O'CONNELL, Con (Ind)	1,821	*(+93)* 1,914	*(+90)* 2,004	
O'KEEFFE, Batt* (FF)	6,556	*(+1,668)* 8,224	*(+55)* 8,279	*(+114)* 8,393
O'SULLIVAN, Michael (SWP)	217	*(+10)* 227		
RYAN, Brendan (Lab)	3,282	*(+179)* 3,461	*(+48)* 3,509	*(+234)* 3,743
SINNOTT, Kathy (Ind)	4,984	*(+409)* 5,393	*(+98)* 5,491	*(+418)* 5,909
NON-TRANSFERABLE			16	157

	5th Count	6th Count	7th Count	8th Count	9th Count	10th Count
	Transfer of **Hanlon** Votes	Transfer of **Ryan** Votes	Transfer of **Clune** Votes	Transfer of **Coveney** Surplus	Transfer of **O'Keeffe** Surplus	Transfer of **Boyle** Surplus
	(+568) 6,334	*(+1,427)* 7,761	*(+543)* 8,304	*(+1,013)* 9,317		
	(+93) 6,075	*(+518)* 6,593				
	(+132) 6,038	*(+596)* 6,634	*(+4,939)* 11,573			
	(+364) 8,061	*(+220)* 8,281	*(+199)* 8,480	*(+204)* 8,684	*(+82)* 8,766	*(+23)* 8,789
	(+301) 8,694	*(+203)* 8,897	*(+215)* 9,112	*(+219)* 9,331		
	(+223) 3,966					
	(+541) 6,450	*(+765)* 7,215	*(+509)* 7,724	*(+930)* 8,654	*(+42)* 8,696	*(+87)* 8,783
	415	652	840	840	840	

Cork South-West

Elected

Voting by Party

1st Preference	Number	%	% 1997
Fianna Fáil	14,882	39.48	39.05
Fine Gael	12,189	32.33	44.18
Labour	3,442	9.13	6.75
Sinn Féin	2,207	5.85	—
Others	4,978	13.20	1.41

Statistics

Population	62,678	
Electorate	54,274	
Total Poll	38,132	70.26
Spoiled Votes	434	1.14
Valid Poll	37,698	69.46
Seats	3	
Quota	9,425	
Candidates	10	

Seats

FF	2
FG	1
FF gain from FG	

The Cork South-West constituency is unchanged from the 1997 General Election.

Denis O'Donovan (FF)

Home Address
Montrose House, Slip, Bantry, Co Cork
Constituency Office
New Street, Bantry
Telephone
Home (027) 51541; *Constituency office* (027) 53840; *Mobile* 087 543806
Birth Place/Date
Bantry. 23 July 1955
Married
Mary Murphy. 3 sons, 1 daughter
Education
Bantry Secondary School; Carrignavar Secondary College; University College, Cork (BCL)
Occupation
Public representative. Solicitor

Denis O'Donovan is a new Dáil deputy. He was a Senator (Industrial and Commercial Panel) 1997–2002. He was the only Fianna Fáil senator on the All-Party Committee on the Constitution. Senator, Taoiseach's nominee, 1989–93.

Member, Cork County Council since 1985 (Chairman 1989/90).

Joe Walsh (FF)

Home Address
5 Emmet Square, Clonakilty, Co Cork
Business Address
Department of Agriculture and Food, Kildare Street, Dublin 2
Telephone
Constituency Office (023) 33575;
Fax (023) 34267; *Business* (01) 6072884;
Fax (01) 6611013
Birth Place/Date
Ballineen, Co Cork. May 1943
Married
Marie Donegan. 3 sons, 2 daughters
Education
St Finbarr's College, Farranferris, Cork; University College, Cork (Dairy Science)
Occupation
Government Minister. Formerly dairy manager

Joe Walsh was re-appointed Minister for Agriculture and Food in June 2002. He held the portfolio of Minister for Agriculture, Food and Rural Development 1997–2002. He was Minister for Agriculture, Food and Forestry January 1993– December 1994. He was Minister for Agriculture and Food, February 1992–January 1993; Minister of State at the Department of Agriculture and Food 1987–February 1992 with special responsibility for the food industry. He has been a member of the Dáil since 1977 with the exception of the period June 1981 to February 1982. He was a candidate in the June 1981 general election. He was a Senator August 1981–February 1982.

He was a Fianna Fáil front bench spokesperson on Social Welfare 1995–March 1997 and on Agriculture March–June 1997.

Former member, Cork County Council; Cork County Committee of Agriculture (chairman 1976/77, 1985/86); Cork County Vocational Education Committee.

He was a member, Irish Creamery Managers' Association; Society of Dairy Technology.

Jim O'Keeffe (FG)

Home Address
Oldchapel, Bandon, Co Cork
Telephone
Home (023) 41399; *Mobile* 087 259 1694;
Fax (023) 41421
Birth Place/Date
Skibbereen, Co Cork. 31 March 1941
Married
Maeve O'Sullivan. 1 son, 7 daughters
Education
St Fachtna's High School, Skibbereen;
University College, Cork; University College,
Dublin; Law School of the Incorporated Law
Society of Ireland, Dublin
Occupation
Public representative. Solicitor and Notary
Public

Jim O'Keeffe was first elected to the Dáil for
Cork South West in 1977. He was Minister of
State at the Departments of Finance and the
Public Service February 1986–March 1987. He
was Minister of State at the Department of
Foreign Affairs with special responsibility for
Development Cooperation 1982–86 and June
1981–March 1982. He was at various times
front bench spokesperson on: Social,
Community and Family Affairs; Foreign
Affairs; Justice; Social Welfare; Agriculture;
Health; Security; and Law Reform. He was a
founding Chairman of the All-Party Committee
on the Constitution which began work in
1993.

Cork South-West

Seats 3 Quota 9,425	1st Count	2nd Count Transfer of **Butler** Votes	3rd Count Transfer of **Heaney** Votes
BUTLER, Edmund John (Ind)	621		
HEANEY, Theresa (Ind)	748	*(+116)* 864	
MCCARTHY, Michael (Lab)	3,442	*(+63)* 3,505	*(+131)* 3,636
O'DONOVAN, Denis (FF)	7,695	*(+79)* 7,774	*(+88)* 7,862
O'KEEFFE, Jim* (FG)	6,358	*(+118)* 6,476	*(+146)* 6,622
O'LEARY, Ann (SF)	899	*(+9)* 908	*(+37)* 945
O'SULLIVAN, Christy (Ind)	3,609	*(+75)* 3,684	*(+165)* 3,849
Ó SÚILLEABHÁIN, Cionnaith (SF)	1,308	*(+21)* 1,329	*(+43)* 1,372
SHEEHAN, PJ* (FG)	5,831	*(+33)* 5,864	*(+68)* 5,932
WALSH, Joe* (FF)	7,187	*(+84)* 7,271	*(+124)* 7,395
NON-TRANSFERABLE		23	85

4th Count	5th Count	6th Count	7th Count
Transfer of **Ó Súilleabháin, O'Leary** Votes	Transfer of **McCarthy** Votes	Transfer of **O'Sullivan** Votes	Transfer of **O'Donovan** Surplus
(+394) 4,030			
(+415) 8,277	*(+586)* 8,863	*(+1,316)* 10,179	
(+213) 6,835	*(+889)* 7,724	*(+772)* 8,496	*(+95)* 8,591
(+454) 4,303	*(+841)* 5,144		
(+224) 6,156	*(+831)* 6,987	*(+1,300)* 8,287	*(+269)* 8,556
(+311) 7,706	*(+413)* 8,119	*(+878)* 8,997	*(+390)* 9,387
391	861	1,739	1,739

Donegal North-East

Elected

James McDaid (FF)*	1st Count
Cecilia Keaveney (FF)*	4th Count
Niall Blaney (Ind)	6th Count

Voting by Party

1st Preference	Number	%	% 1997
Fianna Fáil	17,954	49.40	41.81
Fine Gael	7,637	21.01	18.87
Labour	1,021	2.81	—
Sinn Féin	3,611	9.93	8.11
Others	6,124	16.85	25.73

Statistics

Population	67,691	
Electorate	58,208	
Total Poll	36,896	63.39
Spoiled Votes	549	1.49
Valid Poll	36,347	62.44
Seats	3	
Quota	9,087	
Candidates	7	

Seats

FF	2
Ind	1
No change	

The Donegal North-East constituency is unchanged since the 1997 General Election.

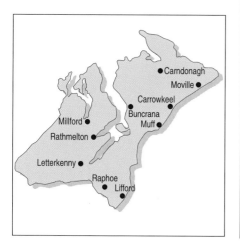

James McDaid (FF)

Home Address
Pearse Road, Letterkenny, Co Donegal
Business Address
Department of Transport, 25 Clare Street, Dublin 2
Telephone
Office (01) 6707444; *Lo-call* 1890 443311; *Fax* (01) 6041320
Birth Place/Date
Donegal. 3 October 1949
Married
Currently separated. 3 sons, 1 daughter
Education
Currin National School, Termon; St Eunan's College, Letterkenny; University College, Galway (MB, BCh, BAO) MRCGP
Occupation
Minister of State. Formerly medical doctor (GP)

James McDaid was appointed Minister of State at the Department of Transport with responsibility for Road traffic, including road haulage, in June 2002. He was first elected to the Dáil in 1989. This was the first time he was a candidate for public office. Minister for Tourism, Sport and Recreation 1997–2002. Party front bench spokesperson on Equality and Law Reform 1997. Spokesperson on North-South Development 1995–97.

He has served as a member of the All-Party Committees on Women's Rights and Public Accounts and the Committee on the Foreign Adoption Bill.

At university he was prominent in sporting activities and captain of the UCG soccer team that won three national titles and he captained two of these teams. He was medical officer to Donegal senior Gaelic Athletic Association team 1983–87.

Co-founder of Donegal Hospice (with Dr Tom McGinley, Foyle Hospice, Derry). He is currently President of the Donegal Hospice Movement, having served as Chairperson 1988–98.

Cecilia Keaveney (FF)

Home Address
Loreto, Moville, Co Donegal
Telephone
Constituency office (077) 82177; *Fax* (077) 82832
Birth Place/Date
Derry. November 1968
Education
Carndonagh Community School, Co Donegal; University of Ulster at Jordanstown (BMus, MPhil)
Occupation
Full-time public representative. Formerly music teacher

Cecilia Keaveney was first elected to the Dáil in a by-election in April 1996 in Donegal North-East caused by the death of Neil T. Blaney.

Member, Donegal County Council since July 1995 when she was co-opted in replacement of her late father, Paddy Keaveney. She was re-elected in 1999.

Cecilia Keaveney worked as a music teacher in Nigeria, England and Northern Ireland.

Her father, Paddy Keaveney, was an Independent Fianna Fáil deputy 1976–77.

Niall Blaney (Ind)

Home Address
Rossnakill, Letterkenny, Co Donegal
Constituency Office
Plunkett O'Boyle Terrace, Letterkenny
Telephone
Home (074) 59014; *Constituency office*
(074) 27754; *Fax* (074) 27783
Birth Place/Date
Letterkenny. 29 January 1974
Married
Roseleen Shovelin
Education
Mulroy College, Milford, Co Donegal;
Letterkenny Institute of Technology (Diploma
in Civil Engineering)
Occupation
Public representative. Formerly Civil
Engineering technician

Niall Blaney is a new Dáil deputy. He takes
over the Independent Fianna Fáil seat held by
his father, Harry, and before that by his uncle,
Neil T. Blaney.

Member, Donegal County Council and North-
Western Health Board.

Niall Blaney is a son of Harry Blaney who was
a Dáil deputy for Donegal North-East
1997–2002. He is a nephew of Neil T. Blaney,
Dáil deputy 1948–96 as a Fianna Fáil
representative up to 1971 and after that as
Independent. He held several ministerial posts
during his long career and was also a Member
of the European Parliament. Niall Blaney's
grandfather, Neil Blaney, was a Dáil deputy
1927–38 and 1943–48.

Donegal North-East

	1st Count	2nd Count Transfer of **McNair** Votes	3rd Count Transfer of **McDaid** Surplus	4th Count Transfer of **Mac Lochlainn** Votes	5th Count Transfer of **Keaveney** Surplus	6th Count Transfer of **McGuinness** Votes
Seats 3 **Quota 9,087**						
BLANEY, Niall (Ind)	6,124	(+137) 6,261	(+131) 6,392	(+1,275) 7,667	(+364) 8,031	(+758) 8,789
KEAVENEY, Cecilia* (FF)	8,340	(+123) 8,463	(+249) 8,712	(+1,012) 9,724		
MAC LOCHLAINN, Pádraig (SF)	3,611	(+103) 3,714	(+37) 3,751			
MALONEY, Seán (FG)	3,723	(+358) 4,081	(+100) 4,181	(+446) 4,627	(+53) 4,680	(+2,752) 7,432
MCDAID, James* (FF)	9,614					
MCGUINNESS, Bernard (FG)	3,914	(+187) 4,101	(+10) 4,111	(+265) 4,376	(+175) 4,551	
MCNAIR, Jackie (Lab)	1,021					
NON-TRANSFERABLE		113	0	753	45	1,041

If you're looking for property... to buy,
rent or to simply dream about, make

IrishTimesProperty.com

your homepage.

THE IRISH TIMES

Donegal South-West

Elected

Voting by Party

1st Preference	Number	%	% 1997
Fianna Fáil	14,997	42.09	38.04
Fine Gael	9,058	25.42	22.97
Labour	1,079	3.03	4.20
Sinn Féin	3,829	10.75	—
Others	6,672	18.72	30.58

Statistics

Population	62,303	
Electorate	54,789	
Total Poll	36,135	65.95
Spoiled Votes	500	1.38
Valid Poll	35,635	65.04
Seats	3	
Quota	8,909	
Candidates	10	

Seats

FF	2
FG	1
No change	

The constituency of Donegal South-West is unchanged since the 1997 General Election.

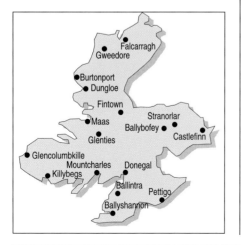

Pat the Cope Gallagher (FF)

Home Address
Dungloe, Co Donegal
Business Address
Department of the Environment and Local Government; Custom House, Custom House Quay, Dublin 1
Constituency Office
Dungloe
Telephone
Home (075) 21364; *Constituency office* (075) 21176; *Fax* (075) 21133; *Business* (01) 8882633
Birth Place/Date
Burtonport, Co Donegal. 10 March 1948
Married
Ann Gillespie
Education
Roshine National School; Dungloe; Luinneach National School, Gweedore; High School, Dungloe; St Enda's College, Galway; University College, Galway (BComm)
Occupation
Minister of State. Formerly fish exporter.

Pat the Cope Gallagher was appointed in June 2002 as Minister of State at the Department of the Environment and Local Government. He returns to the Dáil five years after he gave up his seat in Donegal South-West to remain as a Member of the European Parliament to which he had been elected in 1994. He was first elected to the Dáil on his first attempt in 1981 and at each subsequent election. He was Minister of State at the Department of the Marine 1987–89. He was also Minister of State for Arts, Culture and the Gaeltacht 1989–94. He served as a Member of the European Parliament 1994–2002.

Elected to Donegal County Council 1979 (Chairman 1985/86).

His grandfather, Paddy the Cope, was a leading figure in the co-operative movement early in the last century.

Mary Coughlan (FF)

Home Address
Ballybrillighan, Mount Charles PO, Co Donegal
Constituency Office
Cranny, Inver, Co Donegal
Business Address
Department of Social and Family Affairs, Áras Mhic Diarmada, Store Street, Dublin 2
Telephone
Office (01) 8748444; *Fax* (01) 7043869; *Constituency Office* (073) 36002/36535
Birth Place/Date
Donegal. May 1965
Married
David Charlton. 1 son, 1 daughter
Education
Ursuline Convent, Sligo; University College, Dublin (BSocSc).
Occupation
Government minister. Formerly social worker

Mary Coughlan was appointed Minister for Social and Family Affairs in June 2002.

She was first elected to the Dáil in 1987. Minister of State at the Department of Arts, Heritage, Gaeltacht and the Islands 2001–02. Was Vice-Chairperson of Oireachtas Committee on Tourism, Sport and Recreation and member of Committee on Justice, Equality and Law Reform. Member of British-Irish Inter-Parliamentary Body.

Member of Donegal County Council 1986–2001. North-Western Health Board 1987–2001. Donegal Vocational Education Committee 1986–99 (Chairperson 1991–92). Chairperson of Board of Management, Abbey Vocational School, Donegal Town. Member of Board of Management, Tourism College, Killybegs. Member, Comhchoiste na Gaeilge (Chairperson 1993–94). Elected Honorary Secretary of Fianna Fáil 1995. Secretary of the Fianna Fáil Agriculture Committee.

President of Killybegs Coast and Cliff Rescue Service.

She is daughter of the late Cathal Coughlan, Dáil deputy for Donegal South-West 1983–86, and niece of the late Clement Coughlan, Dáil deputy for the same constituency 1980–83.

Dinny McGinley (FG)

Home Address
Bunbeg, Co Donegal
Telephone
Home (075) 31719; *Constituency office* (075)
31025; *Mobile* 087 241 4809; *Fax* (075) 31025
Birth Place/Date
Gweedore, Co Donegal. 27 April 1945
Education
Coláiste Íosagáin, Ballyvourney, Co Cork; St
Patrick's Teachers' Training College,
Drumcondra, Dublin; University College,
Dublin (BA, HDipEd)
Occupation
Full time public representative. Formerly
principal national school teacher

Dinny McGinley was appointed front bench
spokesperson on Defence in June 2002. He
was spokesperson for Arts, Heritage and the
Islands February 2001–02. He was first
elected to the Dáil in February 1982.
Chairperson, Joint Oireachtas Committee on
the Irish Language 1995–97.

Member, British-Irish Parliamentary Body
1993–97.

Member, Donegal Vocational Education
Committee 1991–99.

Donegal South-West

Seats 3 Quota 8,909	1st Count	2nd Count Transfer of **Breslin** Votes	3rd Count Transfer of **Dignam** Votes
BRESLIN, Gwen (Ind)	951		
COUGHLAN, Mary* (FF)	7,257	*(+123)* 7,380	*(+85)* 7,465
DIGNAM, Tom (SF)	1,133	*(+15)* 1,148	
DOHERTY, Pearse (SF)	2,696	*(+75)* 2,771	*(+800)* 3,571
GALLAGHER, Pat the Cope (FF)	7,740	*(+103)* 7,843	*(+117)* 7,960
KELLY, Joe (Ind)	3,091	*(+83)* 3,174	*(+45)* 3,219
MCGINLEY, Dinny* (FG)	4,378	*(+106)* 4,484	*(+28)* 4,512
PRINGLE, Thomas (Ind)	2,630	*(+257)* 2,887	*(+21)* 2,908
RODGERS, Séamus (Lab)	1,079	*(+120)* 1,199	*(+6)* 1,205
WHITE, James (FG)	4,680	*(+40)* 4,720	*(+20)* 4,740
NON-TRANSFERABLE		29	26

4th Count	5th Count	6th Count	7th Count	8th Count
Transfer of **Rodgers** Votes	Transfer of **Pringle** Votes	Transfer of **Kelly** Votes	Transfer of **Gallagher** Surplus	Transfer of **Doherty** Votes
(+82) 7,547	*(+788)* 8,335	*(+422)* 8,757	*(+175)* 8,932	
(+149) 3,720	*(+446)* 4,166	*(+1,004)* 5,170	*(+99)* 5,269	
(+242) 8,202	*(+300)* 8,502	*(+779)* 9,281		
(+110) 3,329	*(+467)* 3,796			
(+285) 4,797	*(+419)* 5,216	*(+705)* 5,921	*(+81)* 6,002	*(+1,368)* 7,370
(+170) 3,078				
(+82) 4,822	*(+339)* 5,161	*(+224)* 5,385	*(+17)* 5,402	*(+528)* 5,930
85	319	662		3373

Dublin Central

Elected

Voting by Party

1st Preference	Number	%	% 1997
Fianna Fáil	13,472	39.59	42.83
Fine Gael	3,769	11.06	14.51
Labour	4,146	12.17	8.49
Green Party	1,469	4.31	3.51
Sinn Féin	4,972	14.61	6.65
Christian Solidarity	366	1.07	—
Others	5,850	17.19	22.59

Statistics

Population	88,900	
Electorate	62,180	
Total Poll	34,517	55.51
Spoiled Votes	436	1.26
Valid Poll	34,081	54.81
Seats	4	
Quota	6,817	
Candidates	10	

Seats

FF	2
Lab	1
Ind	1

Lab gain from FG

The Dublin Central constituency in the 1998 revision reverted to representing the north inner city and ceded parts south of the Liffey to Dublin South-Central while gaining areas from Dublin North-West. Its population size was reduced by 2,514.

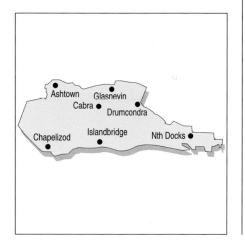

Bertie Ahern (FF)

Home Address
44 Beresford Avenue, Dublin 9
Business Address
Department of the Taoiseach, Government Buildings, Merrion Street, Dublin 2
Constituency Office
St Luke's, 161 Drumcondra Road, Dublin 9
Telephone
Constituency Office (01) 837 4129;
Office (01) 662 4888
Birth Place/Date
Dublin. 12 September 1951
Marital Status
Separated. 2 daughters
Education
St Aidan's CBS, Whitehall, Dublin; Rathmines College of Commerce, Dublin; University College, Dublin
Occupation
Full time public representative. Formerly accountant

Bertie Ahern was re-elected Taoiseach on 6 June 2002 following a general election which saw the Fianna Fáil–Progressive Democrats coalition returned to power. It was the first time an outgoing government was re-elected since 1969.

Bertie Ahern was Taoiseach from June 1997 to June 2002.

He was Tánaiste November–December 1994. Minister for Finance November 1991–94. Minister for Industry and Commerce January 1993. Minister for Arts, Culture and the Gaeltacht November–December 1994. Minister for Labour 1987–91. Minister of State at the Department of the Taoiseach and at the Department of Defence and Government Chief Whip March–December 1982. Assistant Government Whip 1980–81. Opposition Chief Whip December 1982–84. Fianna Fáil Front Bench spokesman on Labour 1984–87; on Youth 1981–82. He was first elected to the Dáil in 1977 for the constituency of Dublin-Finglas and has represented Dublin Central since 1981.

Leader of Fianna Fáil since 1994.

Member of Dublin City Council 1978–88 (Lord Mayor 1986/87).

Brother of Noel Ahern, Fianna Fáil deputy for Dublin North-West since 1992.

Tony Gregory (Ind)

Home Address
5 Sackville Gardens, Ballybough, Dublin 3
Telephone
Dáil Office (01) 618 3488
Birth Place/Date
Dublin. 5 December 1947
Education
St Canice's National School; Christian Brothers' O'Connell School, Dublin; University College, Dublin (BA, HDipEd)
Occupation
Full-time public representative. Formerly secondary school teacher

Tony Gregory has been a Dáil deputy since February 1982. Served on Oireachtas Committee on European Affairs 1997–2002.

Member, Dublin City Council since 1979. Former member, Dublin Port and Docks Board.

Chairman, North Centre City Community Action Project.

Former member Official Sinn Féin and the Irish Republican Socialist Party.

Member, Association of Secondary Teachers of Ireland.

In both March 1982 and March 1987, Tony Gregory's vote was a key factor in the election of Taoiseach. In 1982 he voted for Charles Haughey and in 1987 his abstention in the vote was crucial in the success of Mr Haughey.

Joe Costello (Lab)

Home Address
66 Aughrim Street, Dublin 1
Telephone
Home (01) 838 5355
Birth Place/Date
Sligo. July 1945
Education
Summerhill College, Sligo; St Patrick's
College, Maynooth; University College Dublin.
Occupation
Public representative. Formerly teacher

Joe Costello was appointed party spokesman on Education and Science in June 2002. He has returned to the Dáil after losing his seat there in 1997. He was first elected to the Dáil for Dublin Central in 1992. Senator, Administrative Panel, 1989–92. Party leader in Seanad 1997–2002. Spokesperson on Education, Science, Trade and Employment, Sport and Finance. Member, Joint Committee on Family, Community and Social Affairs.

Former vice-chairman, Parliamentary Labour Party. Member, British-Irish Inter-Parliamentary Body.

Member, Dublin City Council since 1991; City of Dublin Vocational Education Committee since 1991 (Chairman, 1993). Former President of Association of Secondary Teachers of Ireland. Prisoners' Rights Organisation 1973–87 (Chairman 1975–85). Member, Seán McDermott Street Community Association; Save Temple Street Children's Hospital Campaign; Amnesty International; Irish Council for Civil Liberties.

Dermot Fitzpatrick (FF)

Home Address
80 Navan Road, Dublin 7
Telephone
Home/Office (01) 838 7515
Birth Place/Date
Dublin. 12 April 1940
Married
Mary Wallace. 1 son, 3 daughters
Education
Phoenix Park National School; Coláiste Mhuire, Parnell Square, Dublin; University College, Dublin (Medical and dentistry degrees)
Occupation
Public representative. Doctor

Dermot Fitzpatrick was first elected to the Dáil in 1987 on his first attempt but lost his seat two years later in the 1989 general election. He was a Senator 1997–2002 as a Taoiseach's nominee.

Member, Dublin City Council since 1985. Former member, Eastern Health Board.

Dublin Central

	1st Count	2nd Count	3rd Count
Seats 4 **Quota 6,807**		Transfer of **Ahern** Surplus	Transfer of **O'Donnell,** **O'Loughlin,** **Prendeville** Votes
AHERN, Bertie* (FF)	10,882		
COSTELLO, Joe (Lab)	4,136	*(+363)* 4,499	*(+40)* 4,539
FITZPATRICK, Dermot (FF)	2,590	*(+2,265)* 4,855	*(+113)* 4,968
GREGORY, Tony* (Ind)	5,664	*(+813)* 6,477	*(+148)* 6,625
KEHOE, Nicky (SF)	4,972	*(+328)* 5,300	*(+43)* 5,343
MITCHELL, Jim* (FG)	3,769	*(+207)* 3,976	*(+87)* 4,063
O'DONNELL, Patrick Noel (Ind)	89	*(+6)* 95	
O'LOUGHLIN, Paul T (CSP)	366	*(+11)* 377	
PRENDEVILLE, Tom (Ind)	97	*(+6)* 103	
SIMPSON, Tom (GP)	1,469	*(+76)* 1,545	*(+107)* 1,652
NON-TRANSFERABLE		0	37

4th Count	5th Count	6th Count	7th Count
Transfer of **Simpson** Votes	Transfer of **Mitchell** Votes	Transfer of **Costello** Surplus	Transfer of **Gregory** Surplus
(+507) 5,046	(+2,824) 7,870		
(+76) 5,043	(+517) 5,560	(+704) 6,264	(+154) 6,418
(+617) 7,242			
(+144) 5,487	(+331) 5,818	(+359) 6,177	(+162) 6,339
(+205) 4,268			
104	596		119

Dublin Mid-West

Elected

John Curran (FF)	9th Count
Mary Harney (PD)*	9th Count
Paul Gogarty (GP)	10th Count

Voting by Party

1st Preference	Number	%	% 1997
Fianna Fáil	9,122	32.06	—
Fine Gael	3,276	11.51	—
Labour	2,563	9.01	—
Prog Democrats	5,706	20.05	—
Green Party	3,508	12.33	—
Sinn Féin	1,855	6.52	—
Workers' Party	393	1.38	—
Christian Solidarity	107	0.38	—
Others	1,926	6.77	—

Statistics

Population	67,192	
Electorate	55,184	
Total Poll	28,693	52.00
Spoiled Votes	237	0.82
Valid Poll	28,456	51.57
Seats	3	
Quota	7,115	
Candidates	13	

Seats

FF	1
PD	1
GP	1

Dublin Mid-West is a new constituency created under the 1998 revision from parts of Dublin South-West and Dublin West and covers the greater Clondalkin area.

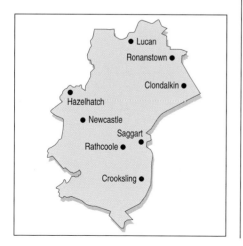

John Curran (FF)

Home Address
15 Knockmeenagh Road, Clondalkin, Dublin 22
Constituency Office
2A Main Street, Clondalkin
Telephone
Home/Office (01) 4592803
Birth Place/Date
Dublin. 17 June 1960
Married
Shauna O'Higgins. 2 sons, 1 daughter
Education
Moyle Park College, Clondalkin; University College, Dublin (BComm)
Occupation
Public representative. Former company director

John Curran is a new Dáil deputy.

Member of South Dublin County Council since 1999.

Member, Board of Management of Scoil Mhuire; Gaelic Athletic Association.

Mary Harney (PD)

Home Address
11 Serpentine Terrace, Ballsbridge, Dublin 4
Business Address
Department of Enterprise, Trade and Employment, Kildare Street, Dublin 2
Telephone
Business (01) 631 2172
Birth Place/Date
Ballinasloe, Co Galway. March 1953
Married
Brian Geoghegan
Education
Convent of Mercy, Goldenbridge, Inchicore, Dublin; Coláiste Bhríde, Clondalkin, Co Dublin; Trinity College, Dublin (BA [Mod])
Occupation
Tánaiste and Government Minister. Formerly research worker

Mary Harney was re-appointed Tánaiste and Minister for Enterprise, Employment and Trade in June 2002, again making history as the first woman to hold the title of Tánaiste and to serve a second successive term. She has been leader of the Progressive Democrats since 1993 and led them back to the Dáil with a doubling in their numbers from 4 to 8 ensuring a role for the party in the new Government. She ran this time in the new constituency of Dublin Mid-West but did not top the poll. She received the highest percentage vote of any Progressive Democrat candidate in the election.

She was Tánaiste and Minister for Enterprise, Employment and Trade 1997–2002. She was Minister of State at the Department of the Environment with responsibility for Environmental Protection 1989–92. She was first elected to the Dáil in 1981 as a Fianna Fáil candidate. She was a founder member of the Progressive Democrats with Desmond O'Malley in 1985. Senator, Taoiseach's nominee, 1977–81. When nominated by the Taoiseach, Jack Lynch, in August 1977, she became the youngest ever member of the Seanad. She had been a candidate in the 1977 general election in Dublin South-East.

Member, Dublin County Council 1979–91. Vice-chairperson, County Dublin Vocational Education Committee 1985.

Paul Gogarty (GP)

Home Address
34 Cherbury Park Road, Lucan, Co Dublin
Telephone
Mobile 087 275 28489
Birth Place/Date
Castlepollard, Co Westmeath. 20 December
1968
Education
St Mary's Boys' National School, Lucan;
Coláiste Phádraig, Lucan; College of
Commerce, Rathmines (Diploma in
Journalism)
Occupation
Full-time public representative. Former
editor/journalist

Paul Gogarty is a new Dáil deputy. He is
spokesperson for Education and Science,
Arts, Sports and Tourism, and Youth Affairs.

Member, South Dublin County Council since
1999 where he is the only Green Party
representative. Active in preservation of Liffey
Valley from land speculation.

Member, Lucan Sarsfields GAA club.

Dublin Mid-West

Seats 3 Quota 7,115	1st Count	2nd Count Transfer of **Callanan** Votes	3rd Count Transfer of **O'Mara** Votes	4th Count Transfer of **McGrath, McGuinness** Votes
CALLANAN, Colm (CSP)	107			
CURRAN, John (FF)	5,904	*(+24)* 5,928	*(+51)* 5,979	*(+133)* 6,112
CURRIE, Austin* (FG)	2,008	*(+9)* 2,017	*(+6)* 2,023	*(+28)* 2,051
FLANNERY, Tony (SF)	1,855	*(+6)* 1,861	*(+51)* 1,912	*(+119)* 2,031
GOGARTY, Paul Nicholas (GP)	3,508	*(+15)* 3,523	*(+18)* 3,541	*(+86)* 3,627
GREEN, David (Ind)	1,078	*(+14)* 1,092	*(+78)* 1,170	*(+143)* 1,313
HARNEY, Mary* (PD)	5,706	*(+13)* 5,719	*(+13)* 5,732	*(+80)* 5,812
KELLY, Des (FF)	3,218	*(+14)* 3,232	*(+5)* 3,237	*(+53)* 3,290
MCGRATH, Colm (Ind)	487	*(+1)* 488	*(+33)* 521	
MCGUINNESS, Andrew (WP)	393	*(+0)* 393	*(+14)* 407	
O'MARA, Michael (Ind)	361	*(+1)* 362		
RIDGE, Therese (FG)	1,268	*(+3)* 1,271	*(+43)* 1,314	*(+105)* 1,419
TUFFY, Joanna (Lab)	2,563	*(+3)* 2,566	*(+36)* 2,602	*(+142)* 2,744
NON-TRANSFERABLE		4	14	39

5th Count	6th Count	7th Count	8th Count	9th Count	10th Count
Transfer of **Green** Votes	Transfer of **Ridge** Votes	Transfer of **Flannery** Votes	Transfer of **Currie** Votes	Transfer of **Kelly** Votes	Transfer of **Curran** Surplus
(+180) 6,292	(+216) 6,508	(+401) 6,909	(+177) 7,086	(+2,264) 9,350	
(+49) 2,100	(+473) 2,573	(+114) 2,687			
(+213) 2,244	(+82) 2,326				
(+243) 3,870	(+77) 3,947	(+647) 4,594	(+666) 5,260	(+385) 5,645	(+700) 6,345
(+141) 5,953	(+243) 6,196	(+152) 6,348	(+576) 6,924	(+600) 7,524	
(+91) 3,381	(+53) 3,434	(+191) 3,625	(+112) 3,737		
(+117) 1,536					
(+147) 2,891	(+308) 3,199	(+395) 3,594	(+901) 4,495	(+313) 4,808	(+563) 5,371
132	84	426	255	175	972

Dublin North

Elected

Voting by Party

1st Preference	Number	%	% 1997
Fianna Fáil	16,803	38.24	38.65
Fine Gael	5,189	11.81	18.98
Labour	6,359	14.47	13.64
Green Party	7,294	16.60	13.64
Sinn Féin	1,350	3.07	—
Socialist Party	5,501	12.52	7.22
Christian Solidarity	247	0.56	1.62
Others	1,199	2.73	2.77

Statistics

Population	88,392	
Electorate	72,908	
Total Poll	43,942	60.27
Spoiled Votes	0	
Valid Poll	43,942	60.27
Seats	4	
Quota	8,789	
Candidates	12	

Seats

FF	2
Lab	1
GP	1

FF gain from FG. Seán Ryan (Lab) had won the seat in the by-election caused by the resignation of Ray Burke (FF) in 1997.

The Dublin North constituency lost 2,147 population in the 1998 revision due to an adjustment of its southern boundary. It was one of the three constituencies where electronic voting was used for the first time.

Trevor Sargent (GP)

Home Address
37 Tara Cove, Balbriggan, Co Dublin
Constituency Office
35 Main Street, Swords, Co Dublin
Telephone
Home (01) 841 2371; *Fax* (01) 841 2371;
Office (01) 890 0360; *Fax* (01) 890 0361;
Mobile 087 2547836
Birth Place/Date
Dublin. July 1960
Education
The High School, Dublin; Church of Ireland College, Rathmines, Dublin; Trinity College, Dublin (BEd)
Occupation
Full-time public representative. Formerly national school teacher and principal

Trevor Sargent was elected the first Leader of the Green Party in October 2001. He was first elected to the Dáil in 1992. He contested the general election of 1987 as a Green Alliance candidate in the old 3-seat constituency of Dublin North, and the 1989 general election as a Green Party candidate in the same constituency.

Member, Dublin County Council 1991–93. Cathaoirleach, Fingal Area 1991–92 and of Coiste Stiúrtha na Gaeilge. Resigned from Council 1993 in opposition to dual mandate of Oireachtas and local council.

Former chairman, Tara Cove Residents' Association; Fingal Council Against Blood Sports. Member, Fingal Committee of An Taisce; Amnesty International; Irish Wildbird Conservancy; Greenpeace; Irish Organic Society; Dublin Food Cooperative; Alternative Technology Association. Director of Sonairte (Ecology Centre). Member, Earthwatch.

Cathaoirleach, Craobh Shéamuis Ennis, Conradh na Gaeilge. Member, Balbriggan Rugby Club.

Seán Ryan (Lab)

Home Address
1 Burrow Road, Portrane, Co Dublin
Telephone
Home (01) 8436254
Birth Place/Date
Dublin. January 1943
Married
Patricia Brehony
Education
North Strand Vocational School; College of Technology, Bolton Street; College of Industrial Relations; School of Management, Rathmines
Occupation
Full-time public representative. Formerly CIÉ Production Controller

Seán Ryan was re-appointed party spokesperson on Older People's Issues in June 2002. He was first elected to the Dáil in 1989 and re-elected in 1992. He was defeated in the 1997 general election and was elected to the Seanad. He returned to the Dáil in 1998 when he won the by-election in Dublin North caused by the resignation of Fianna Fáil Minister Ray Burke.

Member, Dublin County Council 1983–93. Member, Fingal County Council since 1993. Member, Transport Salaried Staffs Association. Former member, Amalgamated Transport and General Workers' Union.

Jim Glennon (FF)

Home Address
96 Strand Street, Skerries
Constituency Office
Thomas Hand Street, Skerries
Telephone
Home (01) 8492377; *Constituency office* (01)
8491577; *Fax* (01) 8492856
Birth Place/Date
Skerries. 7 July 1953
Married
Helen Crinion. 1 daughter, 2 sons
Education
Holy Faith School, Skerries; Mount St
Joseph's, Roscrea, Co Tipperary
Occupation
Public representative. Formerly Chief
Executive of Medisec Ireland.

Jim Glennon is a new Dáil deputy. He served
in the Seanad, Industrial and Commercial
Panel, June 2000–2002. He served on the
Oireachtas Committee on Tourism, Sport and
Recreation.

He is a former rugby international and was
capped six times for Ireland. He was coach
and manager to the Leinster senior team. He
was also a manager to the Ireland under-19
and under-21 teams.

G.V. Wright (FF)

Home Address
58 The Moorings, Malahide, Co Dublin
Constituency Office
1 Church Road, Malahide
Telephone
Home (01) 845 2642; *Constituency Office* (01)
845 0710; *Fax* (01) 845 5545
Birth Place/Date
Malahide. 3 August 1947
Married
Monica Kane. 2 sons, 1 daughter
Education
Chanel College, Coolock, Co Dublin.
Occupation
Full-time public representative. Formerly
businessman, fresh food.

G.V. Wright and his running mate, Jim
Glennon, had to fight off a strong challenge
from Clare Daly of the Socialist Party to win
two Fianna Fáil seats in Dublin North. G.V.
Wright was first elected to the Dáil in 1987
after standing unsuccessfully in the general
elections of February and November 1982. He
lost his seat in 1989 but re-entered the
Seanad as a Taoiseach's nominee where he
served from 1989 to 1997. He had previously
been a Senator from May 1982 to January
1983.

He was Assistant Government Chief Whip in
the Dáil 1989, Chief Whip in the Seanad
1990–91 and Leader of the House 1991–94.
Fianna Fáil Leader, Seanad, 1994–97.

Member, Fingal County Council since 1993
(Leader of the Fianna Fáil Group); Dublin
County Council 1985–92.

He served as a director of Bord Iascaigh
Mhara, 1980–85.

He played Gaelic football with Dublin County
and was an international basketball coach.

Dublin North

Seats 4 Quota 8,789	1st Count	2nd Count Transfer of **Quinn, Walshe** Votes	3rd Count Transfer of **Goulding** Votes
BOLAND, Cathal (FG)	1,177	*(+12)* 1,189	*(+27)* 1,216
DALY, Clare (SP)	5,501	*(+50)* 5,551	*(+179)* 5,730
DAVIS, Mick (SF)	1,350	*(+32)* 1,382	*(+42)* 1,424
GLENNON, Jim (FF)	5,892	*(+53)* 5,945	*(+83)* 6,028
GOULDING, Ciaran (Ind)	914	*(+95)* 1,009	
KENNEDY, Michael (FF)	5,253	*(+56)* 5,309	*(+59)* 5,368
OWEN, Nora* (FG)	4,012	*(+18)* 4,030	*(+102)* 4,132
QUINN, Eamon (Ind)	285		
RYAN, Seán* (Lab)	6,359	*(+48)* 6,407	*(+128)* 6,535
SARGENT, Trevor* (GP)	7,294	*(+86)* 7,380	*(+298)* 7,678
WALSHE, David Henry (CSP)	247		
WRIGHT, GV* (FF)	5,658	*(+49)* 5,707	*(+32)* 5,739
NON-TRANSFERABLE		33	59

4th Count	5th Count	6th Count	7th Count	8th Count
Transfer of **Boland** Votes	Transfer of **Davis** Votes	Transfer of **Owen** Votes	Transfer of **Sargent** Surplus	Transfer of **Kennedy** Votes
(+66) 5,796	(+448) 6,244	(+346) 6,590	(+182) 6,772	(+751) 7,523
(+16) 1,440				
(+124) 6,152	(+142) 6,294	(+217) 6,511	(+85) 6,596	(+2,044) 8,640
(+54) 5,422	(+110) 5,532	(+200) 5,732	(+69) 5,801	
(+588) 4,720	(+43) 4,763			
(+130) 6,665	(+182) 6,847	(+1,731) 8,578	(+550) 9,128	
(+140) 7,818	(+300) 8,118	(+1,667) 9,785		
(+38) 5,777	(+91) 5,868	(+271) 6,139	(+110) 6,249	(+2,368) 8,617
60	124	331		638

Dublin North-Central

Elected

Voting by Party

1st Preference	Number	%	% 1997
Fianna Fáil	20,043	50.05	46.44
Fine Gael	6,809	17.00	26.03
Labour	4,203	10.49	6.60
Green Party	2,275	5.68	3.82
Sinn Féin	2,299	5.74	—
Socialist Workers' Party	638	1.59	1.62
Others	3,781	9.44	9.43

Statistics

Population	86,954	
Electorate	65,583	
Total Poll	40,475	61.72
Spoiled Votes	427	1.05
Valid Poll	40,048	61.06
Seats	4	
Quota	8,010	
Candidates	10	

Seats

FF	2
FG	1
Ind	1
Ind gain from Labour	

The Dublin North-Central constituency lost 602 population in the 1998 revision to Dublin Central.

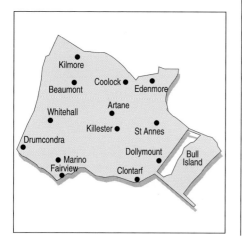

Seán Haughey (FF)

Home Address
Chapelfield Lodge, Baskin Lane, Kinsealy, Dublin 17
Constituency Office
5 Mornington Park, Malahide Road, Artane, Dublin 5
Telephone
Home (01) 8464004; *Fax* (01) 845 1444; *Constituency Office* (01) 8450111
Birth Place/Date
Dublin. 8 November 1961
Married
Orla O'Brien. 2 sons, 1 daughter
Education
St Paul's College, Raheny, Dublin; Trinity College, Dublin (BA [Mod])
Occupation
Full-time public representative

Seán Haughey was first elected a Dáil deputy in 1992. Was Senator, Administrative Panel, 1987–92. Was candidate in Dublin North-East in the general elections of 1987 and 1989. Served on Oireachtas Committees on the Environment and Local Government (vice-chairman) and European Affairs in last Dáil. National chairman Ógra Fianna Fáil 1995–97.

Member of the Beaumont Hospital Board; Board of Governors of the Incorporated Orthopaedic Hospital of Ireland, Clontarf; Board of the Northside Partnership Ltd; National Economic and Social Forum; Commissioners of Irish Lights; Irish Council of the European Movement.

Alderman, Dublin City Council since 1985. Lord Mayor 1989–90.

He is a son of Charles J. Haughey, Taoiseach, December 1979–June 1981, March–December 1982, March 1987–June 1989; Acting Taoiseach June–July 1989; Taoiseach July 1989–February 1992. Dáil deputy 1957–92.

He is a grandson of Seán Lemass, Taoiseach, 1959–66.

Richard Bruton (FG)

Home Address
210 Griffith Avenue, Drumcondra, Dublin 9
Telephone
Home (01) 836 8185; *Fax* (01) 836 8185
Website www.richardbruton.net
Birth Place/Date
Dublin. 15 March 1953
Married
Susan Meehan. 2 sons, 2 daughters
Education
Belvedere College, Dublin; Clongowes Wood College, Co Kildare; University College, Dublin; Nuffield College, Oxford (BA, MA, MPhil [Oxon] Economics)
Occupation
Full-time public representative. Formerly economist

Richard Bruton was appointed Deputy Leader of Fine Gael and spokesperson on Finance in June 2002 after he unsuccessfully contested the leadership following the resignation of Michael Noonan.

He was first elected to the Dáil in February 1982. He was Minister for Enterprise and Employment 1994–97. He was Minister of State at the Department of Industry and Commerce 1986–87. Director of Policy 2000–02. Front Bench spokesperson on Education and Science 1997–2002; on Enterprise and Employment 1993–94; Director of Policy 1994; Spokesperson on Employment 1992–93; Health 1990–92; Energy and Natural Resources 1989–90; Energy and Communications 1987–89. He was a Senator, Agricultural Panel, August 1981–February 1982.

Committees in last Dáil: Education and Science; Public Enterprise.

Member, Dublin City Council 1991–94. Re-elected 1999.

Member, Meath County Council 1979–82.

Richard Bruton is a brother of John Bruton, Taoiseach 1994–97, Dáil deputy for Meath since 1969, Leader of Fine Gael 1990–2001 and former Minister.

Ivor Callely (FF)

Home Address
Lansdale House, 7 St Lawrence Road,
Clontarf, Dublin 3
Business Address
Department of Health and Children, Hawkins
House, Dublin 2
Constituency Office
191 Howth Road, Killester, Dublin 3
Telephone
Home (01) 8330350; *Constituency Office*
(01) 8334331; *Office* (01) 6711175
Birth Place/Date
Dublin. 6 May 1958
Married
Jennifer Foley. 2 sons, 1 daughter
Education
St Paul's College, Raheny, Dublin; Fairview
College, Dublin (Diplomas in Business
Studies, Accountancy and Sales and
Marketing)
Occupation
Minister of State. Formerly medical
representative

Ivor Callely was appointed Minister of State at
the Department of Health and Children with
responsibility for Services for Older People in
June 2002.

He was first elected to the Dáil in 1989. In last
Dáil he was Chairman of the Enterprise and
Small Business Committee 1997–2002.
Convenor of Committee on Legislation and
Security 1993–95.

Member, Dublin City Council and Eastern
Health Board 1985–2002; appointed chairman
of the new Eastern Regional Health Authority
in 2000.

Member, Raheny Gaelic Athletic Association,
Clontarf Tennis Club and Killester Sports and
Social Club.

Finian McGrath (Ind)

Home Address
342 Charlemont, Griffith Avenue, Dublin 9
Telephone
Home/Office (01) 837 8028; *Mobile*
087 673 8041
Birth Place/Date
Tuam. 9 April 1953
Married
Anne Russell. 2 daughters
Education
Tuam CBS; St Patrick's Training College,
Drumcondra, Dublin
Occupation
Public representative. Formerly school
principal and full-time worker with the Simon
Community

Finian McGrath is a new Dáil deputy. He
campaigned as a member of the Independent
Health Alliance calling for improved health
services. He contested the 1997 general
election.

Member, Dublin City Council since 1999.
Chairperson of the Council's Committee for
the Elderly; Board member of Northside
Centre for the Unemployed, Coolock; Board
member of the Orthopaedic Hospital, Clontarf.

Member, Irish National Teachers
Organisation.

Dublin North-Central

Seats 4 Quota 8,010	1st Count	2nd Count Transfer of **Browne** Votes	3rd Count Transfer of **Breen** Votes	4th Count Transfer of **McCole** Votes	5th Count Transfer of **Maher** Votes	6th Count Transfer of **McDowell** Votes
BREEN, Gerry (FG)	1,650	*(+11)* 1,661				
BROWNE, Ritchie (SWP)	638					
BRUTON, Richard* (FG)	5,159	*(+36)* 5,195	*(+1,052)* 6,247	*(+115)* 6,362	*(+388)* 6,750	*(+2,295)* 9,045
CALLELY, Ivor* (FF)	6,896	*(+41)* 6,937	*(+98)* 7,035	*(+178)* 7,213	*(+225)* 7,438	*(+395)* 7,833
HAUGHEY, Seán* (FF)	7,614	*(+41)* 7,655	*(+63)* 7,718	*(+310)* 8,028		
HENEY, Deirdre (FF)	5,533	*(+31)* 5,564	*(+63)* 5,627	*(+175)* 5,802	*(+299)* 6,101	*(+426)* 6,527
MAHER, Bronwen (GP)	2,275	*(+128)* 2,403	*(+83)* 2,486	*(+572)* 3,058		
MCCOLE, Frances (SF)	2,299	*(+146)* 2,445	*(+14)* 2,459			
MCDOWELL, Derek* (Lab)	4,203	*(+82)* 4,285	*(+146)* 4,431	*(+288)* 4,719	*(+829)* 5,548	
MCGRATH, Finian (Ind)	3,781	*(+112)* 3,893	*(+128)* 4,021	*(+677)* 4,698	*(+1,058)* 5,756	*(+1,882)* 7,638
NON-TRANSFERABLE		10	14	144	259	550

The Leader of the Progressive Democrats, Mary Harney, taking a horse and carriage ride through the village of Ballycommon in Co Offaly with local candidate Tom Parlon.

Dublin North-East

Elected

Michael J. Woods (FF)*	5th Count
Tommy Broughan (Lab)*	6th Count
Martin Brady (FF)*	6th Count

Voting by Party

1st Preference	Number	%	% 1997
Fianna Fáil	11,761	40.12	40.61
Fine Gael	4,504	15.36	18.90
Labour	4,758	16.23	17.25
Prog Democrats	1,219	4.16	7.80
Green Party	1,656	5.65	3.57
Sinn Féin	3,003	10.24	5.93
Others	2,417	8.24	1.82

Statistics

Population	68,637	
Electorate	52,105	
Total Poll	29,634	56.87
Spoiled Votes	316	1.07
Valid Poll	29,318	56.27
Seats	3	
Quota	7,330	
Candidates	10	

Seats

FF	2
Lab	1

The Dublin North-East constituency was reduced from 4 seats to 3 in this General Election, losing 11,666 population mainly to Dublin North-Central. Fine Gael lost the seat it won in 1997.

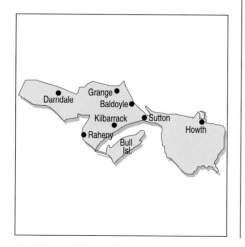

Michael J. Woods (FF)

Home Address
13 Kilbarrack Grove, Raheny, Dublin 5
Telephone
Home (01) 832 3357
Birth Place/Date
Bray, Co Wicklow. December 1935
Married
Margaret Maher. 3 sons, 2 daughters
Education
Synge Street CBS, Dublin; University College, Dublin (BAgrSc, MAgrSc, PhD, DSc); Institute of Public Administration (Diploma in Central Administrtion and Fellowship in Public Administration); Harvard Business School (Diploma in Marketing)
Occupation
Full-time public representative. Formerly Principal Officer and Head of Glasshouse Crops and Mushroom Department, An Foras Talúntais

Michael Woods was first elected to the Dáil in 1977. After re-election in 2002, he was not re-appointed to a post in Cabinet where he had served 14 years in various portfolios. Minister for Education 2000–2002. Minister for the Marine and Natural Resources 1997–2000. Minister for Social Welfare 1993–December 1994 and Minister for Health November–December 1994. He was Minister for the Marine 1992–93; Minister for Agriculture and Food 1991–92; Minister for Social Welfare 1987–91. He was Minister for Health and Minister for Social Welfare March–December 1982 and 1979–81. He was Minister of State at the Department of the Taoiseach and the Department of Defence and Government Chief Whip in 1979. Party spokesperson on Justice 1982–87, on Equality and Law Reform 1993–94; on Social Welfare 1994.

Former member, Dublin City Council.

He is the author of *Research in Ireland, Key to Economic and Social Development* and numerous technical and scientific papers.

Tommy Broughan (Lab)

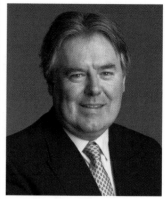

Home Address
23 Riverside Road, Coolock, Dublin 17
Telephone
Home (01) 847 7634; *Office* (01) 6183557
Birth Place/Date
Clondalkin, Co Dublin. August 1947
Married
Carmel Healy
Education
Moyle Park College, Clondalkin; University College, Dublin (BA, HDipEd); London University (BSc, MSc [Econ])
Occupation
Full-time public representative. Formerly teacher

Tommy Broughan was re-appointed party spokesperson on Enterprise, Trade and Employment in June 2002. In the last Dáil he was vice-chairperson of the Oireachtas Committee on Family, Community and Social Affairs and member, Committee on Enterprise and Small Business. He was first elected to the Dáil in 1992. He was an unsuccessful candidate in Dublin North-East in the 1989 election.

Member, Dublin City Council since 1991; Leader of the Labour Group.

Founding secretary, Community Enterprise, Donaghmede and Artane. Founding chairman of Coolock Development Council. Director, Northside Centre for the Unemployed.

Member of several north-side Gaelic football and soccer clubs.

Martin Brady (FF)

Home Address
37 Grangemore Drive, Dublin 13
Telephone
Home (01) 848 4509
Birth Place/Date
Virginia, Co Cavan. 7 May 1947
Married
Veronica Brady. 3 daughters
Education
Franciscan Brothers College, Clara, Co Offaly
Occupation
Full-time public representative. Formerly
Telecom Éireann executive

Martin Brady was first elected to the Dáil in
1997. He was a candidate in the Dublin North-
East constituency in the 1992 general
election. In the 28th Dáil he was Government
Whip on the Oireachtas Committee on Public
Enterprise and Transport and a member of the
Committees on Health and Children and
Heritage and the Irish Language.

He has been a member of Dublin City Council
since 1991.

Dublin North-East

Seats 3 Quota 7,330	1st Count	2nd Count Transfer of **Jenkinson, Ryan** Votes	3rd Count Transfer of **Healy** Votes	4th Count Transfer of **Cosgrave** Votes	5th Count Transfer of **Harrold** Votes	6th Count Transfer of **O'Toole** Votes
BRADY, Martin* (FF)	5,304	*(+227)* 5,531	*(+126)* 5,657	*(+119)* 5,776	*(+279)* 6,055	*(+854)* 6,909
BROUGHAN, Tommy* (Lab)	4,758	*(+173)* 4,931	*(+495)* 5,426	*(+450)* 5,876	*(+949)* 6,825	*(+1,601)* 8,426
COSGRAVE, Michael Joe* (FG)	2,349	*(+105)* 2,454	*(+92)* 2,546			
DOYLE, Gavin (FG)	2,155	*(+218)* 2,373	*(+202)* 2,575	*(+1,510)* 4,085	*(+563)* 4,648	*(+289)* 4,937
HARROLD, Mark (Ind)	2,116	*(+205)* 2,321	*(+485)* 2,806	*(+106)* 2,912		
HEALY, David (GP)	1,656	*(+200)* 1,856				
JENKINSON, Thomas (Ind)	301					
O'TOOLE, Larry (SF)	3,003	*(+80)* 3,083	*(+203)* 3,286	*(+87)* 3,373	*(+347)* 3,720	
RYAN, Noelle (PD)	1,219					
WOODS, Michael J* (FF)	6,457	*(+285)* 6,742	*(+169)* 6,911	*(+227)* 7,138	*(+414)* 7,552	
NON-TRANSFERABLE		27	84	47	360	976

Dublin North-Central candidate Bronwen Maher arriving for the Green Party Manifesto Launch in Dublin.

Dublin North-West

Elected

Noel Ahern (FF)*	1st Count
Pat Carey (FF)*	6th Count
Róisín Shortall (Lab)*	6th Count

Voting by Party

1st Preference	Number	%	% 1997
Fianna Fáil	12,435	47.54	47.04
Fine Gael	2,082	7.96	15.60
Labour	4,391	16.79	11.13
Green Party	607	2.32	4.16
Sinn Féin	4,781	18.28	—
Workers' Party	608	2.32	1.33
Christian Solidarity	154	0.59	—
Others	1,100	4.21	10.66

Statistics

Population	67,129	
Electorate	47,641	
Total Poll	26,543	55.71
Spoiled Votes	385	1.45
Valid Poll	26,158	54.91
Seats	3	
Quota	6,540	
Candidates	9	

Seats

FF	2
Lab	1

The Dublin North-West constituency was reduced from 4 seats to 3 for this General Election, losing 16,237 population in the Cabra and Drumcondra areas to Dublin Central. The fourth seat in the 1997 election was held by Democratic Left which has now merged with Labour.

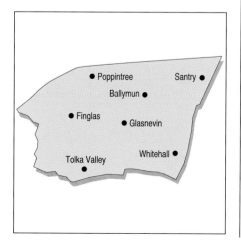

Noel Ahern (FF)

Home Address
25 Church Avenue, Drumcondra, Dublin 9
Office
Department of Environment and Local Government, Custom House, Dublin 1
Telephone
Home (01) 832 5911; *Fax* (01) 832 5911.
Office (01) 8882000
Birth Place/Date
Dublin. December 1944
Married
Helen Marnane. 2 sons, 1 daughter
Education
Christian Brothers' O'Connell School, Dublin; University College, Dublin; College of Commerce, Rathmines, Dublin (DPA, MCIT)
Occupation
Minister of State. Formerly official with CIÉ

Noel Ahern was appointed in June 2002 as Minister of State at the Department of Environment and Local Government, with responsibility for Housing and Urban Renewal, and at the Department of Community, Rural and Gaeltacht Affairs, with responsibility for Drugs Strategy and Community Affairs. Member of the Cabinet Committee on Social Inclusion. He was first elected to the Dáil in 1992. Party spokesperson on the Environment with special responsibility for Housing 1994–97. Chairperson, Oireachtas Committee on Social, Community and Family Affairs 1997–2002.

Member, Dublin City Council 1985–2002. Former chairperson of Housing and Traffic Committees and chairperson of the North-West Area Committee 2001–2002.

Former branch officer and member of National Executive of the Transport Salaried Staffs Association.

He is brother of Bertie Ahern, Taoiseach since 1997, Leader of the Fianna Fáil party since 1994, former Minister and Dáil deputy since 1977.

Pat Carey (FF)

Home Address
69 Bourne View, Ashbourne, Co Meath
Constituency Office
2 Finglas Town Centre, Dublin 11
Telephone
Home (01) 8350544; *Fax* (01) 8350430;
Mobile 087 2574393; *Constituency Office*
(01) 8644118; *Fax* (01) 8644199
Birth Place/Date
Castlemaine, Co Kerry. 9 November 1947
Education
Presentation Brothers' College, Milltown, Co Kerry; St Patrick's Teacher's Training College, Drumcondra, Dublin; University College, Dublin; Trinity College, Dublin (BA HDipEd)
Occupation
Full-time public representative. Formerly primary school teacher, vice-principal

Pat Carey was first elected as a Dáil deputy in 1997. He was a candidate in the 1992 general election. Served in last Dáil on Oireachtas Committees for Education and Science; Language and Heritage and European Affairs (Government convenor).

Member of Dublin City Council since 1985. Member of the Strategic Policy Committee on Arts and Leisure. Member of City of Dublin Vocational Education Committee since 1985 (Chairman 1988–91). Chairman, Council of Technology, Bolton Street, Dublin (1985–91). Member, Council of College of Catering, Cathal Brugha Street, Dublin (1985–91). Governing Body of Dublin Institute of Technology (1985–94). Co-chairman TCD-DIT Liaison Council (1988–91).

Chairman, School Committee of Coláiste Éoin and Coláiste Íde, Finglas, since 1985; Plunkett College, Whitehall 1985–91. Member, Sports Advisory Council, City of Dublin VEC and City of Dublin Youth Service Board. Former Chairman, Catholic Youth Council. Council member, NCEA 1991–96.

Róisín Shortall (Lab)

Home Address
12 Iveragh Road, Gaeltacht Park, Dublin 9
Telephone
Home (01) 837 0563; *Dáil Office*
(01) 6183593; *Fax* (01) 6184380
Birth Place/Date
Dublin. 25 April 1954
Married
Seamus O'Byrne. 3 daughters
Education
Dominican College, Eccles Street, Dublin;
University College, Dublin; St Mary's College
of Education, Marino, Dublin (BA, NTDip
Teacher of the Deaf)
Occupation
Full-time public representative. Formerly
primary school teacher for the deaf at St
Joseph's School, Cabra, Dublin

Róisín Shortall was critical of the leadership of
Ruairí Quinn and refused a position on the
party front bench following the 2002 election.

She has been a Dáil deputy since 1992. Party
spokesperson on Education and Children
1997–2002.

Member in last Dáil of Oireachtas Committee
on Education and Science.

Member, Dublin City Council since 1991;
Eastern Health Board since 1991 (chairperson
1997). Board member, Ballymun Housing
Task Force; Finglas Vocational Education
Committee; Finglas Area Partnership;
Ballymun Local Drugs Task Force; Finglas
Local Drugs Task Force.

Dublin North-West

Seats 3 Quota 6,540	1st Count	2nd Count Transfer of **Larkin** Votes	3rd Count Transfer of **Ahern** Surplus	4th Count Transfer of **Ó Cionnaith** Votes	5th Count Transfer of **O'Brien** Votes	6th Count Transfer of **Tormey, Brady** Votes
AHERN, Noel* (FF)	6,912					
BRADY, Brendan (FG)	2,082	(+18) 2,100	(+20) 2,120	(+25) 2,145	(+58) 2,203	
CAREY, Pat* (FF)	5,523	(+42) 5,565	(+262) 5,827	(+79) 5,906	(+62) 5,968	(+631) 6,599
ELLIS, Dessie (SF)	4,781	(+18) 4,799	(+26) 4,825	(+168) 4,993	(+105) 5,098	(+504) 5,602
LARKIN, Michael (CSP)	154					
O'BRIEN, Eugene (GP)	607	(+22) 629	(+6) 635	(+69) 704		
Ó CIONNAITH, Seán (WP)	608	(+6) 614	(+6) 620			
SHORTALL, Róisín* (Lab)	4,391	(+9) 4,400	(+43) 4,443	(+186) 4,629	(+286) 4,915	(+2,017) 6,932
TORMEY, Bill (Ind)	1,100	(+28) 1,128	(+9) 1,137	(+68) 1,205	(+146) 1,351	
NON-TRANSFERABLE		11		25	47	402

Dublin South

Elected

Voting by Party

1st Preference	Number	%	% 1997
Fianna Fáil	20,250	36.64	38.62
Fine Gael	10,931	19.78	29.09
Labour	5,247	9.49	10.60
Prog Democrats	8,288	15.00	9.39
Green Party	5,222	9.45	6.10
Sinn Féin	2,172	3.93	—
Socialist Party	1,063	1.92	1.08
Others	2,090	3.78	4.92

Statistics

Population	114,491	
Electorate	92,645	
Total Poll	55,690	60.11
Spoiled Votes	427	0.77
Valid Poll	55,263	59.65
Seats	5	
Quota	9,211	
Candidates	11	

Seats

FF	2
FG	1
PD	1
GP	1
GP gain from FG	

The Dublin South constituency lost 2,636 population in the 1998 revision mainly to Dublin South-West.

Séamus Brennan (FF)

Home Address
31 Finsbury Park, Churchtown, Dublin 14
Business Address
Department of Transport, Transport House, 44 Kildare Street, Dublin 2
Telephone
Constituency Office (01) 2957171; *Office* (01) 604 1074; *Fax* (01) 296 2628/676 3533
Birth Place/Date
Galway. 16 February 1948
Married
Ann O'Shaughnessy. 2 sons, 4 daughters
Education
St Joseph's Secondary School, Galway; University College, Galway (BA, BComm); University College, Dublin (MComm)
Occupation
Full-time public representative. Formerly accountant and management consultant

Séamus Brennan was appointed Minister for Transport in June 2002. He served as Minister of State for Public Enterprise 6 to 18 June 2002. He was Minister of State at the Department of the Taoiseach and at the Department of Defence and Chief Whip 1997–2002.

He was Minister of State at the Department of the Taoiseach with special responsibility as Government Chief Whip, and Minister of State at the Department of Defence 1997–2002. He was Minister of State at the Department of Enterprise and Employment, with special responsibility for Commerce and Technology, 1993–94. Minister for Education 1992–93. Minister for Tourism, Transport and Communications 1991–92. Minister for Tourism and Transport 1989–91. Minister of State at the Department of Industry and Commerce with special responsibility for Trade and Marketing 1987–89.

He was party spokesperson on Transport, Energy and Communications 1995–97. He was first elected to the Dáil in 1981. He was a Senator, Taoiseach's nominee, 1977–81. He was general secretary of Fianna Fáil 1973–80.

Member, Dublin County Council 1985–87.

Tom Kitt (FF)

Home Address
3 Pine Valley, Rathfarnham, Dublin 16
Business Address
Department of Foreign Affairs, Bishop's Square, Redmond's Hill, Dublin 2
Constituency Office
4 Ashgrove Terrace, Dundrum, Dublin 16
Telephone
Home (01) 493 8200; *Fax* (01) 493 2207; *Constituency Office* (01) 298 2304; *Office* (01) 478 0822; *Fax* (01) 298 2460
Website www.tomkitttd.ie
Birth Place/Date
Galway. 11 July 1952
Married
Jacinta Burke-Walsh. 3 sons, 1 daughter
Education
St Jarlath's College, Tuam, Co Galway; St Patrick's Teachers' Training College, Drumcondra, Dublin
Occupation
Minister of State. Formerly national school teacher

Tom Kitt was appointed Minister of State at the Department of Foreign Affairs with responsibility for Overseas Development and Human Rights in June 2002.

He was first elected to the Dáil in 1987. Minister of State at the Department of Enterprise, Trade and Employment with special responsibility for Labour Affairs, Consumer Rights and International Trade 1997–2002. Minister of State at the Department of the Taoiseach and the Department of Foreign Affairs with special responsibility for European Affairs and Overseas Development Aid 1993–94. Minister of State at the Department of the Taoiseach with special responsibility for Arts and Culture, Women's Affairs and European Affairs 1992–93. Party spokesman on Labour Affairs 1995–97.

Member of the British-Irish Inter-Parliamentary Body 1991–92. Member of Dublin County Council 1979–92. Chairman, Dún Laoghaire-Rathdown District Committee 1986–87.

He is son of Michael F. Kitt, Dáil deputy for Galway constituencies 1948–51, 1957–75, and brother of Michael Kitt TD, Galway East, 1981–2002.

Liz O'Donnell (PD)

Home Address
23 Temple Gardens, Dublin 6
Telephone
Home (01) 491 0363; *Fax* (01) 491 0369;
Constituency Office (01) 408 2212
Birth Place/Date
Dublin. July 1956
Married
Michael T. Carson. 1 son, 1 daughter
Education
Salesian Convent, Fernbank, Limerick; Trinity
College, Dublin (BA [Mod] Legal Science)
Occupation
Public representative. Formerly lawyer

Liz O'Donnell following her re-election in Dublin South returned to the back benches for family reasons.

She has been a Dáil deputy since 1992. In 1997 she was appointed Minister of State at the Department of Foreign Affairs with special responsibility for Overseas Development Assistance and Human Rights. She helped negotiate the Fianna Fáil/Progressive Democrats Programme for Government. She was a member of the Government team at the multi-party talks leading to the Good Friday Agreement in 1998. Was a member of the Cabinet sub-committee on Abortion and of the sub-committee on Asylum, Immigration and related issues. Chaired an independent committee to review the Irish Overseas Aid Programme as part of the Government decision to expand the ODA budget to reach the UN target of 0.7 per cent of GNP by 2007. Member of National Executive of Progressive Democrats.

Was party spokesperson on Health and Social Welfare and Justice and party Chief Whip 1993–97. Chairperson of the party Policy Development Committee.

Member, Dublin City Council 1991–94. Member, Local Authority Committee Dublin Transport Initiative.

Member, Executive Committee of the Women's Political Association 1989–91. Vice-chairwoman and delegate to Council for the Status of Women 1990–91.

Olivia Mitchell (FG)

Home Address
18 Ballawley Court, Dundrum, Dublin 16
Telephone
Home (01) 295 3033; *Fax* (01) 295 3033
Birth Place/Date
Birr, Co Offaly. 31 July 1947
Married
James Mitchell. 2 sons, 1 daughter
Education
Dominican Convent, Eccles Street, Dublin;
Trinity College, Dublin (BA, HDipEd)
Occupation
Full-time public representative. Formerly secondary school teacher

Olivia Mitchell was appointed party spokesperson on Health and Children in June 2002.

She was first elected as a Dáil deputy in 1997. She was a candidate in Dublin South in the 1989 and 1992 general elections. Party spokesperson on Local Development, National Drugs strategy and Dublin Traffic (1997–Feb 2001); on Local Government and Housing (2001–02).

Member in last Dáil of Oireachtas Committees on Heritage and the Irish Language and on Environment and Local Government.

Member, Dublin County Council 1985–93 and of Dún Laoghaire-Rathdown County Council since 1994 (Cathaoirleach 1995–96).

Member, Eastern Health Board; Dublin Regional Authority; Dublin Transport Office Steering Committee.

She was a member of the Fine Gael delegation to the Forum for Peace and Reconciliation. Member, Co-ordinating Committee of the European Sustainable Cities and Towns Campaign.

Eamon Ryan (GP)

Home Address
9 Ashfield Road, Ranelagh, Dublin 6
Telephone
Home (01) 496 0944; *Constituency office*
(01) 6183000; *Mobile* 087 829 4429
Birth Place/Date
Dublin. 28 July 1963
Married
Victoria White. 3 sons
Education
Holy Cross National School, Dundrum;
Gonzaga College, Ranelagh, Dublin; University
College, Dublin (BComm)
Occupation
Public representative. Formerly tour operator and founder of activity holiday company

Eamon Ryan is a new Dáil deputy.

Member of Dublin City Council since 1998 when co-opted. Elected in 1999.

Founding chairman of the Dublin Cycling Campaign. Member of the Dublin Transportation Office Advisory Committee. Editor of Lord Mayor's Commission Report on Cycling in Dublin, 1996. Special interest in Dublin domestic re-cycling system and planning and housing issues.

Dublin South

	1st Count	2nd Count	3rd Count	4th Count
Seats 5 **Quota 9,211**		Transfer of **Maher** Votes	Transfer of **Brennan** Surplus	Transfer of **Canning** Votes
BRENNAN, Séamus* (FF)	9,326	*(+0)* 9,326		
CANNING, Karen (Ind)	2,090	*(+117)* 2,207	*(+2)* 2,209	
CORRIGAN, Maria (FF)	3,180	*(+40)* 3,220	*(+25)* 3,245	*(+173)* 3,418
FITZGERALD, Eithne (Lab)	5,247	*(+153)* 5,400	*(+4)* 5,404	*(+319)* 5,723
KITT, Tom* (FF)	7,744	*(+113)* 7,857	*(+60)* 7,917	*(+200)* 8,117
MAHER, Lisa (SP)	1,063			
MITCHELL, Olivia* (FG)	5,568	*(+61)* 5,629	*(+4)* 5,633	*(+211)* 5,844
O'DONNELL, Liz* (PD)	8,288	*(+56)* 8,344	*(+12)* 8,356	*(+291)* 8,647
RYAN, Eamonn (GP)	5,222	*(+260)* 5,482	*(+3)* 5,485	*(+676)* 6,161
SHATTER, Alan* (FG)	5,363	*(+47)* 5,410	*(+3)* 5,413	*(+155)* 5,568
WHELAN, Deirdre (SF)	2,172	*(+173)* 2,345	*(+2)* 2,347	*(+127)* 2,474
NON-TRANSFERABLE		43		57

Dublin South

5th Count	6th Count	7th Count	8th Count	9th Count
Transfer of **Whelan** Votes	Transfer of **Corrigan** Votes	Transfer of **Kitt** Surplus	Transfer of **Shatter** Votes	Transfer of **Mitchell** Surplus
(+230) 3,648				
(+354) 6,077	(+155) 6,232	(+251) 6,483	(+625) 7,108	(+1,155) 8,263
(+379) 8,496	(+2,430) 10,926			
(+84) 5,928	(+214) 6,142	(+398) 6,540	(+4,508) 11,048	
(+169) 8,816	(+499) 9,315			
(+963) 7,124	(+195) 7,319	(+700) 8,019	(+527) 8,546	(+682) 9,228
(+85) 5,653	(+40) 5,693	(+140) 5,833		
210	115	226	173	

Dublin South-Central

Elected

Voting by Party

1st Preference	Number	%	% 1997
Fianna Fáil	15,106	34.32	34.43
Fine Gael	7,456	16.94	24.95
Labour	8,679	19.72	10.41
Prog Democrats	1,377	3.13	5.01
Green Party	2,299	5.22	3.95
Sinn Féin	5,591	12.70	4.77
Socialist Workers' Party	617	1.40	0.54
Workers' Party	823	1.87	0.73
Others	2,068	4.70	2.88

Statistics

Population	114,383	
Electorate	86,161	
Total Poll	44,768	51.96
Spoiled Votes	752	1.68
Valid Poll	44,016	51.09
Seats	5	
Quota	7,337	
Candidates	15	

Seats

FF	2
FG	1
Lab	1
SF	1

The Dublin South-Central constituency was enlarged and had one seat added for this General Election. It gained 27,293 population mainly from Dublin Central.

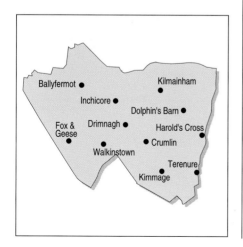

Gay Mitchell (FG)

Home Address
192 Upper Rathmines Road, Dublin 6
Telephone
Home (01) 490 3744
Birth Place/Date
Dublin. December 1951
Married
Norma O'Connor. 1 son, 3 daughters
Education
St Michael's CBS, Inchicore, Dublin; Emmet Road Vocational School; Rathmines College of Commerce; Queen's University, Belfast (MSocSc, FSCA, FCIS, AITI)
Occupation
Full-time public representative. Formerly company accountant and chartered secretary and administrator

Gay Mitchell was appointed party spokesperson on Foreign Affairs in June 2002. He had been an unsuccessful candidate in the leadership contest following the resignation of Michael Noonan.

He was first elected to the Dáil in 1981. In 1994–97 was Minister of State at the Department of the Taoiseach with special responsibility for IFSC and Local Government initiatives, and Minister of State at the Department of Foreign Affairs with special responsibility for European Affairs. Front bench spokesperson on Foreign Affairs 1997–2002; Justice 1993–94; Public Service and Constitutional Reform 1991–92; Tourism and Transport 1989–91; European integration 1988–89; Urban Renewal 1987–88; Health Board Reform 1981–82.

Chairman, Dáil Committee of Public Accounts 1987–93. Former vice-chairman, Dáil Committee on Crime, Lawlessness and Vandalism; chairman of Sub-Committee on Motor Insurance. Chaired the Advisory Group on Public Financial Accountability 1987–88.

Member of Dublin City Council 1979–95 and re-elected 1999. Lord Mayor 1992–93 and introduced the concept of Lord Mayor's commissions. Founder Dublin International Sports Council 1992 and President until 1997. He was a co-founder of the International IMPAC Dublin Literary Award.

Seán Ardagh (FF)

Home Address
168 Walkinstown Road, Dublin 12
Constituency Office
168 Walkinstown Road, Dublin 12
Telephone
Home/Office (01) 456 8736; *Fax* (01) 4080436
Birth Place/Date
Dublin. 25 November 1947
Married
Marie Bhreathnach. 2 sons, 1 daughter
Education
Marian College, Sandymount, Dublin; University College, Dublin (BSc); University of Toronto (Chartered Accountant)
Occupation
Public representative. Partner, Ardagh Horan, Chartered Accountants

Seán Ardagh was first elected to the Dáil in 1997. He was member of the Public Accounts Committee and Chairperson, Oireachtas Committee on Justice, Equality, Defence and Women's Rights in the 28th Dáil

Member, Dublin City Council since 1999.
Member, Dublin County Council 1985–1991.
Member South Dublin County Council 1985–99.

Member, St Jude's GAA Club.

Michael Mulcahy (FF)

Home Address
3 Beechwood Road, Ranelagh, Dublin 6
Telephone
Home (01) 4972758
Website www.michaelmulachy.ie
Birth Place/Date
Dublin. 23 June 1960
Married
Veronica Gates
Education
St Conleth's College, Dublin 4; Trinity College, Dublin, 1977–81 (Degree in Mental and Moral Science); Trinity College 1981–83 (Degree in legal science); Kings Inns, Dublin
Occupation
Public representative. Barrister-at-Law

Michael Mulcahy is a new Dáil deputy. He contested the Dublin South-Central constituency in the general elections of 1992 and 1997 and by-elections in the constituency in 1994 and 1999. Senator, 1994–97 (Party spokesperson on Justice).

Member of Fianna Fáil National Executive 1990–92.

Member, Dublin City Council since 1985. Lord Mayor of Dublin 2001–02.

Chairman of Dublin Regional Authority 1999.

Member of the Board, Hugh Lane Muncipal Gallery of Modern Art, Dublin.

Aengus Ó Snodaigh (SF)

Constituency Office
Unit 14, The Maltings Business Centre, Marrowbone Lane, Dublin 8
Telephone
Constituency Office (01) 454 1868;
Fax (01) 618 4324
Birth Place/Date
Dublin. 31 July 1964
Married
Aisling Ó Dálaigh. 2 sons
Education
Scoil Lorcain, Monkstown, Co Dublin; Coláiste Eoin, Booterstown, Co Dublin; University College, Dublin (BA, HDipEd)
Occupation
Full-time public representative. Formerly officer, Bord na Gaeilge

Aengus Ó Snodaigh is a new Dáil deputy. He was appointed Sinn Féin whip in June 2002. He is also responsible for Justice and Equality, Culture, Gaeilge and Gaeltacht, International Affairs and Defence. He contested the constituency of Dublin South-East in the general election of 1987 and the by-election in Dublin South-Central in 1999.

Member, Sinn Féin Ard Comhairle since 1999; National Forum on Europe; Sinn Féin delegation in talks with the British Government at Lancaster House in 2000 and Weston Park 2001.

Mary Upton (Lab)

Home Address
38 Highfield Park, Dundrum, Dublin 14
Telephone
Dáil Office (01) 6183756
Birth Place/Date
Derrylough, Kilrush, Co Clare. 30 May 1946
Education
Coláiste Mhuire, Ennis; University College, Galway (MSc in Microbiology); University College, Dublin (PhD)
Occupation
Public representative. University lecturer

Mary Upton was appointed party spokesperson for Food Safety, Consumer Affairs and Health Promotion in June 2002. She was first elected to the Dáil in October 1999 in the by-election caused by the death of her brother, Pat Upton, who was the Labour TD in Dublin South Central 1992–1999.

She is a former chairperson of the National Council for Educational Awards and a former chairperson of the Radiological Protection Institute of Ireland.

Dublin South-Central

Seats 5 Quota 7,337	1st Count	2nd Count Transfer of **Kelly** Votes	3rd Count Transfer of **Smith** Votes	4th Count Transfer of **Kavanagh** Votes	5th Count Transfer of **Ní Chonaill** Votes
ARDAGH, Seán* (FF)	6,031	*(+2)* 6,033	*(+14)* 6,047	*(+19)* 6,066	*(+65)* 6,131
BYRNE, Catherine (FG)	2,012	*(+3)* 2,015	*(+10)* 2,025	*(+34)* 2,059	*(+32)* 2,091
BYRNE, Eric (Lab)	4,159	*(+29)* 4,188	*(+77)* 4,265	*(+100)* 4,365	*(+71)* 4,436
JACKSON, Vincent Ballyfermot (Ind)	1,142	*(+5)* 1,147	*(+56)* 1,203	*(+120)* 1,323	*(+88)* 1,411
KAVANAGH, Linda (WP)	553	*(+139)* 692	*(+90)* 782		
KELLY, Shay (WP)	270				
MCGENNIS, Marian* (FF)	4,085	*(+0)* 4,085	*(+25)* 4,110	*(+50)* 4,160	*(+39)* 4,199
MCELROY, Kristina (GP)	2,299	*(+12)* 2,311	*(+89)* 2,400	*(+91)* 2,491	*(+84)* 2,575
MITCHELL, Gay* (FG)	5,444	*(+12)* 5,456	*(+13)* 5,469	*(+38)* 5,507	*(+105)* 5,612
MULCAHY, Michael (FF)	4,990	*(+4)* 4,994	*(+13)* 5,007	*(+17)* 5,024	*(+78)* 5,102
NÍ CHONAILL, Áine (Ind)	926	*(+4)* 930	*(+19)* 949	*(+17)* 966	
QUINN, Bob (PD)	1,377	*(+4)* 1,381	*(+14)* 1,395	*(+10)* 1,405	*(+67)* 1,472
SMITH, Bríd (SWP)	617	*(+16)* 633			
Ó SNODAIGH, Aengus (SF)	5,591	*(+28)* 5,619	*(+140)* 5,759	*(+120)* 5,879	*(+220)* 6,099
UPTON, Mary* (Lab)	4,520	*(+9)* 4,529	*(+64)* 4,593	*(+84)* 4,677	*(+72)* 4,749
NON-TRANSFERABLE		3	9	82	45

Dublin South-Central

6th Count	7th Count	8th Count	9th Count	10th Count	11th Count
Transfer of **Jackson** Votes	Transfer of **Quinn** Votes	Transfer of **Byrne, C** Votes	Transfer of **McElroy** Votes	Transfer of **McGennis** Votes	Transfer of **Ardagh** Surplus
(+71) 6,202	*(+197)* 6,399	*(+73)* 6,472	*(+123)* 6,595	*(+1,612)* 8,207	
(+55) 2,146	*(+113)* 2,259				
(+132) 4,568	*(+91)* 4,659	*(+180)* 4,839	*(+599)* 5,438	*(+220)* 5,658	*(+186)* 5,844
(+224) 4,423	*(+158)* 4,581	*(+95)* 4,676	*(+151)* 4,827		
(+196) 2,771	*(+203)* 2,974	*(+141)* 3,115			
(+96) 5,708	*(+233)* 5,941	*(+1,339)* 7,280	*(+429)* 7,709		
(+63) 5,165	*(+177)* 5,342	*(+49)* 5,391	*(+106)* 5,497	*(+1,867)* 7,364	
(+62) 1,534					
(+277) 6,376	*(+55)* 6,431	*(+91)* 6,522	*(+370)* 6,892	*(+390)* 7,282	*(+241)* 7,523
(+114) 4,863	*(+247)* 5,110	*(+222)* 5,332	*(+954)* 6,286	*(+389)* 6,675	*(+288)* 6,963
121	60	69	383	349	155

Dublin South-East

Elected

John Gormley (GP)*	4th Count
Michael McDowell (PD)	4th Count
Eoin Ryan (FF)*	5thCount
Ruairí Quinn (Lab)*	6th Count

Voting by Party

1st Preference	Number	%	% 1997
Fianna Fáil	8,767	27.03	25.79
Fine Gael	5,210	16.06	27.38
Labour	4,032	12.43	16.67
Prog Democrats	6,093	18.79	10.97
Green Party	5,264	16.23	11.71
Sinn Féin	2,398	7.39	—
Socialist Workers	286	0.88	1.12
Workers' Party	284	0.88	1.89
Others	99	0.31	0.65

Statistics

Population	89,621	
Electorate	59,896	
Total Poll	32,720	54.63
Spoiled Votes	287	0.88
Valid Poll	32,433	54.15
Seats	4	
Quota	6,487	
Candidates	11	

Seats

FF	1
Lab	1
PD	1
GP	1
PD gain from FG	

The Dublin South-East constituency lost 5,845 population in the 1998 revision to Dublin South-Central, Dublin South and Dun Laoghaire.

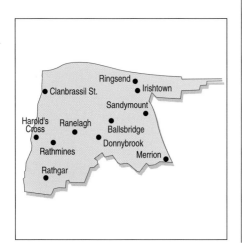

John Gormley (GP)

Home Address
119 Ringsend, Dublin 4
Telephone
Home (01) 2815134; *Constituency Office*
(01) 6183019
Website: www.johngormley.com
Birth Place/Date
Dublin. 4 August 1959
Married
Penny Stuart. 1 son, 1 daughter
Education
St Munchin's College, Limerick; University College, Dublin; Freiburg University, Germany (BA)
Occupation
Full-time public representative. Formerly director of Academy of European Languages

John Gormley was appointed party spokesperson on Foreign Affairs, Health and Defence in June 2002. He is the first chairperson of the Green Party. He was first elected to the Dáil in June 1997. During the last Dáil he was party spokesperson on Foreign Affairs and a member of the Oireachtas Committee on Health and Children. He introduced a number of Private Members' Bills including the Energy Conservation Bill and the Road Traffic Reduction Bill. He contested the Dublin South-East constituency in 1992 and 1989.

Member of Dublin City Council since 1991. He was Lord Mayor 1994–95.

Author of the *Green Guide for Ireland* (Wolfhound Press 1990). Member of Earthwatch, Amnesty International and the Chartered Institute of Water Management. He was the first elected representative to have an e-mail address (johngormley@eircom.ie). His hobbies are theatre, photography and computers.

Michael McDowell (PD)

Home Address
40 Charleston Road, Dublin 6
Business Address
Department of Justice, Equality and Law Reform, 72–76 St Stephen's Green, Dublin 2
Telephone
Private Office (01) 6028321; *Constituency Office* (01) 602 8325/8504/8363; *Local Call* 1890 221227
Website www.michaelmcdowell.ie
Birth Place/Date
Dublin. May 1951
Married
Niamh Brennan. 3 sons
Education
Pembroke School; Gonzaga College; University College, Dublin (BA Economics and Politics); King's Inns, Dublin (Barrister-at-Law)
Occupation
Full-time public representative. Senior Counsel and former practising barrister

Michael McDowell was appointed Minister for Justice, Equality and Law Reform in June 2002. He served as Attorney General to the Fianna Fáil-Progressive Democrats Coalition 1999–2002.

He was first elected to the Dáil for Dublin South East in 1987. He lost his seat in 1989 but regained it in 1992. He lost it again in 1997 but topped the poll in the May 2002 election. Party spokesperson successively on Foreign Affairs, Northern Ireland, Trade and Tourism and Finance 1992–97.

He was appointed President of the Progressive Democrats in February 2002. Served as chairman of the party 1989–92.

He chaired the Working Group on Company Law Enforcement and Compliance which reported in November 1998. In 1999 he was appointed to chair the Implementation Advisory Group on the Establishment of the Single Regulatory Authority for the Financial Services Industry.

Michael McDowell is a grandson of Eoin McNeill, co-founder of the Gaelic League and founder of the Irish Volunteers who served as Minister for Finance and Education in the First Dáil and Second Dáil.

Eoin Ryan (FF)

Home Address
19 Vavasour Square, Sandymount, Dublin 4
Telephone
Home (01) 6673790. *Mobile* 087 6685277
Birth Place/Date
Dublin. 24 February 1953
Married
Sheila McKeever. 1 son, 2 daughters
Education
St Joseph's, Roscrea, Co. Tipperary; St
Mary's College, Rathmines, Dublin; College of
Commerce, Rathmines; Kildalton Horticultural
College, Co Kilkenny
Occupation
Public representative. Formerly retailer and
restaurateur

Eoin Ryan has been a Dáil deputy since 1992.
Minister of State for Local Development and
National Drugs Strategy 2000–2002. Party
spokesman on Ecology and Urban Renewal
1995–97. He contested the general elections
of 1987 and 1989 in Dublin South-East
constituency. Senator, Taoiseach's nominee,
1989–92 and Government Whip in the Seanad
February–November 1992.

Member, Dublin City Council 1985–2000
Planning and Development Committee and
Youth Committee. Member, Dublin Ports and
Docks Board.

Member of Lansdowne Tennis Club and
Shamrock Rovers' Football Club.

Son of former Senator Eoin Ryan and
grandson of Dr Jim Ryan, a Minister in the
Governments of Éamon de Valera and Seán
Lemass.

Ruairí Quinn (Lab)

Home Address
23 Strand Road, Sandymount, Dublin 4
Telephone
Office (01) 6183434; *Fax* (01) 6184153
Birth Place/Date
Dublin. 2 April 1946
Married
Liz Allman. 1 son and 1 son, 1 daughter by
previous marriage
Education
Blackrock College, Dublin; University College,
Dublin (BArch); Athens Centre of Ekistics,
Greece (HCE)
Occupation
Public representative. Architect and town
planner

Ruairí Quinn announced his intention to retire
as Leader of the Labour Party on 27 August
2002. He was elected Leader in November
1997. Deputy leader 1989–97. He was
Minister for Finance 1994–97; Minister for
Enterprise and Employment 1993–94;
Minister for Labour December 1983–January
1987; Minister for the Public Service February
1986–January 1987; Minister of State at the
Department of the Environment with special
responsibility for Urban Affairs and Housing
1982–83. He was first elected to the Dáil in
Dublin South-East in 1977 but lost his seat in
the 1981 general election. He regained his
seat in February 1982, having served as a
Senator, Industrial and Commercial Panel,
August 1981–February 1982. He was also a
Senator in 1976–77 when selected to fill a
vacancy in the Taoiseach's nominees.

Member, Dublin City Council 1974–77 and
1991–93 (Leader, Labour Group; Leader, Civic
Alliance).

Member, Royal Institute of Architects in
Ireland; Royal Institute of British Architects;
Irish Planning Institute; An Taisce; World
Society of Ekistics; Amnesty International.

Dublin South-East

Seats 4	1st Count	2nd Count	3rd Count	4th Count	5th Count	6th Count
Quota 6,487		Transfer of **Gray, Crilly, Ryan S** Votes	Transfer of **Mac Eochaidh** Votes	Transfer of **Doolan** Votes	Transfer of **Andrews** Votes	Transfer of **Ryan, E** Surplus
ANDREWS, Chris (FF)	3,449	*(+24)* 3,473	*(+27)* 3,500	*(+324)* 3,824		
CRILLY, Tom (WP)	284					
DOOLAN, Dáithí (SF)	2,398	*(+157)* 2,555	*(+23)* 2,578			
FITZGERALD, Frances* (FG)	3,337	*(+21)* 3,358	*(+1,013)* 4,371	*(+72)* 4,443	*(+225)* 4,668	*(+587)* 5,255
GORMLEY, John* (GP)	5,264	*(+219)* 5,483	*(+310)* 5,793	*(+1,051)* 6,844		
GRAY, Norman (Ind)	99					
MCDOWELL, Michael (PD)	6,093	*(+28)* 6,121	*(+297)* 6,418	*(+91)* 6,509		
MAC EOCHAIDH, Colm (FG)	1,873	*(+32)* 1,905				
QUINN, Ruairí* (Lab)	4,032	*(+95)* 4,127	*(+191)* 4,318	*(+356)* 4,674	*(+477)* 5,151	*(+709)* 5,860
RYAN, Eoin* (FF)	5,318	*(+54)* 5,372	*(+36)* 5,408	*(+415)* 5,823	*(+2,819)* 8,642	
RYAN, Shay (SWP)	286					
NON-TRANSFERABLE		39	8	269	303	859

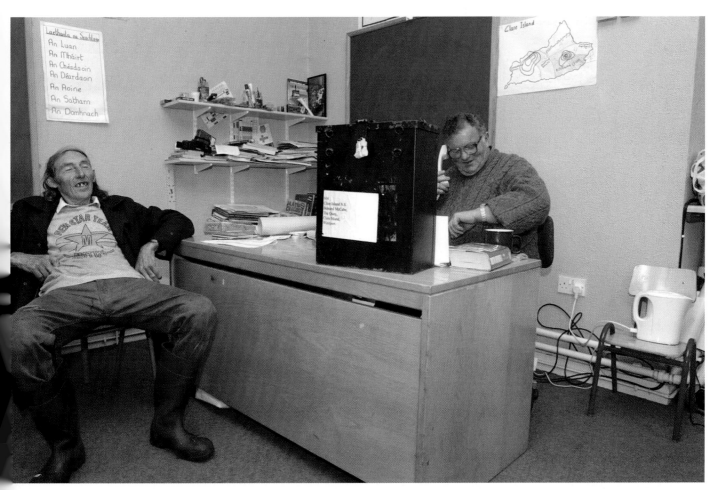

Presiding officers Bernard Winters and Bernard McCabe waiting for voters on Clare Island, Co Mayo.

Dublin South-West

Elected

Voting by Party

1st Preference	Number	%	% 1997
Fianna Fáil	14,235	38.68	29.94
Fine Gael	4,654	12.65	15.50
Labour	7,285	19.80	9.72
Green Party	1,157	3.14	3.14
Sinn Féin	7,466	20.29	8.90
Socialist Party	954	2.59	4.84
Christian Solidarity	760	2.07	—
Others	291	0.79	2.15

Statistics

Population	90,594	
Electorate	64,947	
Total Poll	37,216	57.30
Spoiled Votes	414	1.11
Valid Poll	36,802	56.66
Seats	4	
Quota	7,361	
Candidates	10	

Seats

FF	2
Lab	1
SF	1

SF gain from FG

The Dublin South-West constituency was reduced from 5 seats to 4 for this General Election, losing 20,756 population mainly to the new Dublin Mid-West constituency. Democratic Left which won a seat in 1997 later merged with Labour.

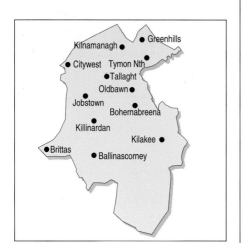

Seán Crowe (SF)

Home Address
16 Raheen Green, Tallaght, Dublin 24
Telephone
Home (01) 4524950
Birth Place/Date
Dublin. 7 March 1957
Married
Pamela Kane
Education
De La Salle, Churchtown, Co Dublin; Dundrum Technical School, Co Dublin
Occupation
Full-time public representative. Formerly party officer

Seán Crowe is a new Dáil deputy. He was a candidate in the 1989, 1992 and 1997 general elections. He contested the European elections in Dublin in 1999.

Member, Sinn Féin Ard Comhairle; secretary of party delegation to Forum for Peace and Reconciliation. Member, Sinn Féin negotiating team with the British Government; committee on confidence-building measures in the negotiation of the Good Friday Agreement 1998. Formerly Sinn Féin Youth Officer.

Member, South Dublin County Council since 1999.

Charlie O'Connor (FF)

Home Address
622 Virginia Heights, Springfield, Tallaght, Dublin 24
Telephone
Home (01) 525409
Birth Place/Date
Dublin. 9 April 1946
Married
Separated. 3 sons
Education
Synge Street CBS; Drimnagh Castle CBS; Irish Marketing Institute; Industrial Relations Institute
Occupation
Full-time public representative. Formerly Press Officer for National Youth Federation

Charlie O'Connor is a new Dáil deputy.

Member, Dublin County Council 1991–94; South Dublin County Council 1994 to date (Chairperson 1999–2000). Former member, Dublin Vocational Education Committee. Member, Tallaght Hospital Board. Founder Chairman of the South-Western Area Health Board. Member, Tallaght Partnership and Tallaght Welfare Society.

Conor Lenihan (FF)

Home Address
44 Templeogue Village, Dublin 6W
Constituency Office
Above First Active House, Tallaght Village
Telephone
Constituency Office (01) 4596285; *Fax*
(01) 2443363
Birth Place/Date
Dublin. 3 March 1963
Married
Denise Russell. 2 sons
Education
Belvedere College, Dublin; University College,
Dublin (BA); Dublin City University (Diploma in
Journalism); European Business School,
INSEAD
Occupation
Full-time public representative. Advises a
number of Irish-based companies. Formerly
journalist, political correspondent, programme
manager with Esat Digifone

Conor Lenihan was elected to the Dáil in 1997
on his first attempt. Served on Committee of
Public Accounts and Joint Committee on
Enterprise and Small Business. Member of
British-Irish Inter-Parliamentary Body.

He is a son of Brian Lenihan, a former
Tánaiste, Minister for Foreign Affairs; Minister
for Agriculture; Minister for Defence; Minister
for Forestry and Fisheries; Minister for
Transport and Power; Minister for Education;
Minister for Justice; and a Dáil deputy for
Roscommon-Leitrim 1961–73 and Dublin
West 1977–95. He is a brother of Brian
Lenihan, Dáil deputy for Dublin West since
1996 and now Minister of State at the
Departments of Health and Children, Justice,
Equality and Law Reform, and Education and
Science. He is a nephew of Mary O'Rourke, a
Dáil deputy 1982–2002 and a former Minister
in various portfolios. He is grandson of Patrick
Lenihan, Dáil deputy 1965–70.

Pat Rabbitte (Lab)

Home Address
56 Monastery Drive, Clondalkin, Dublin 22
Telephone
Home (01) 459 3191
Birth Place/Date
Claremorris, Co Mayo. 18 May 1949
Married
Derry McDermott. 3 daughters
Education
St Colman's College, Claremorris, Co Mayo;
University College, Galway (BA, HDipEd, LLB)
Occupation
Full-time public representative. Formerly trade
union official

Pat Rabbitte was appointed party Chief Whip
and spokesperson on Justice in June 2002.
He was spokesperson on Enterprise, Trade
and Employment 1999–2002. He was first
elected to the Dáil in 1989 for the Workers'
Party. During the 26th Dáil, six of the party's
TDs formed the Democratic Left Party. During
the 28th Dáil 1999, Democratic Left
merged with the Labour Party and the four DL
deputies became part of the Labour group. In
2002, Pat Rabbitte who had been a member
of the Labour Party until 1976, was re-elected
in Dublin South-West as a Labour deputy.
He was Minister of State to the Government
and at the Department of Enterprise and
Employment with special responsibility for
Commerce, Science and Technology and
Consumer Affairs, 1994–97. As the so-called
'Super Minister of State', he also had the right
to attend Cabinet meetings.

Member, Dublin County Council 1985–95 and
last chairperson before it became three
separate administrative counties. Elected to
South Dublin County Council 1999.

Member, Irish Transport and General
Workers' Union (now SIPTU). Formerly
National Secretary. President, UCG Students'
Union 1970/71. President, Union of Students
in Ireland 1972/74.

Dublin South-West

Seats 4 Quota 7,361	1st Count	2nd Count Transfer of **Kelly** Votes	3rd Count Transfer of **O'Reilly** Votes	4th Count Transfer of **Crowe** Surplus	5th Count Transfer of **Walsh** Votes	6th Count Transfer of **Murphy** Votes
CROWE, Seán (SF)	7,466					
HAYES, Brian* (FG)	4,654	*(+27)* 4,681	*(+122)* 4,803	*(+12)* 4,815	*(+95)* 4,910	*(+174)* 5,084
KELLY, Ray (Ind)	291	*(+0)* 291				
LENIHAN, Conor* (FF)	7,080	*(+36)* 7,116	*(+116)* 7,232	*(+18)* 7,250	*(+111)* 7,361	
MURPHY, Mick (SP)	954	*(+40)* 994	*(+61)* 1,055	*(+14)* 1,069	*(+35)* 1,104	
O'CONNOR, Charlie (FF)	7,155	*(+34)* 7,189	*(+153)* 7,342	*(+19)* 7,361		
O'REILLY, Darragh (CSP)	760	*(+19)* 779				
QUINN, Patrick (GP)	1,157	*(+57)* 1,214	*(+120)* 1,334	*(+14)* 1,348	*(+60)* 1,408	*(+279)* 1,687
RABBITTE, Pat* (Lab)	6,314	*(+50)* 6,364	*(+135)* 6,499	*(+24)* 6,523	*(+667)* 7,190	*(+458)* 7,648
WALSH, Eamonn (Lab)	971	*(+13)* 984	*(+20)* 1,004	*(+4)* 1,008		
NON-TRANSFERABLE		15	52		40	193

Sinn Féin's Martin Ferris celebrates with Northern Ireland Education Minister and party colleague Martin McGuinness after being elected for North Kerry.

Dublin West

Elected

Brian Lenihan (FF)*	1st Count
Joe Higgins (SP)*	4th Count
Joan Burton (Lab)	6th Count

Voting by Party

1st Preference	Number	%	% 1997
Fianna Fáil	10,386	34.63	33.19
Fine Gael	3,694	12.32	16.94
Labour	3,810	12.71	12.11
Socialist Party	6,442	21.48	16.21
Prog Democrats	2,370	7.90	7.61
Green Party	748	2.49	4.32
Sinn Féin	2,404	8.02	5.00
Christian Solidarity	134	0.45	—
Others			

Statistics

Population	67,297	
Electorate	52,676	
Total Poll	29,988	56.93
Spoiled Votes	0	
Valid Poll	29,988	56.93
Seats	3	
Quota	7,498	
Candidates	9	

Seats

FF	1
Lab	1
SP	1

The Dublin West constituency was reduced from 4 seats to 3 for this General Election, losing 33,943 population in the creation of Dublin Mid-West. Fine Gael had won a seat here in the 1997 election. It was one of the three constituencies where electronic voting was used for the first time.

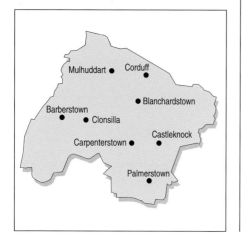

Brian Lenihan (FF)

Home Address
Longwood, Somerton Road, Strawberry Beds, Dublin 20
Local Office
Laurel Lodge Shopping Centre, Dublin 15
Business Address and Constituency Office
Department of Health and Children, Hawkins House, Dublin 2
Telephone
Ministerial Office (01) 6718142/6771618;
Constituency Office (01) 6354550/6354761;
Local Office (01) 8220970
Birth Place/Date
Dublin. 21 May 1959
Married
Patricia Ryan. 1 son, 1 daughter
Education
Belvedere College, Dublin; Trinity College Dublin (BA [Mod]); Cambridge University (LLB); King's Inns
Occupation
Minister of State. Senior Counsel

Brian Lenihan was appointed Minister of State with responsibility for Children at the Departments of Health and Children; Justice, Equality and Law Reform; and Education and Science in June 2002.

He was first elected to the Dáil in April 1996 in the by-election caused by the death of his father, Brian who had been a deputy in Dublin West since 1977. During the 28th Dáil, Brian Lenihan was chairperson of the All-Party Oireachtas Committee on the Constitution which considered changes in the abortion laws. He was also a member of the Committee on Procedure and Privileges.

He is a son of Brian Lenihan, former Tánaiste and a Minister in various portfolios who was a Dáil deputy for Roscommon-Leitrim 1961–73 and for Dublin West 1977–95. He is a brother of Conor Lenihan, Dáil deputy for Dublin South-West and a nephew of Mary O'Rourke who was a Dáil deputy 1982–2002 and who held various ministerial posts. He is a grandson of Patrick Lenihan, Dáil deputy 1965–70.

Joe Higgins (SP)

Home Address
155 Briarwood Close, Mulhuddart, Dublin 15
Telephone
Home (01) 820 1753
Birth Place/Date
Dingle, Co Kerry. May 1949
Education
Christian Brothers' School, Dingle. University College, Dublin (BA, HDipEd)
Occupation
Full-time public representative. Formerly second level teacher

Joe Higgins was first elected to the Dáil in 1997. He contested the 1992 general election in Dublin West and a by-election in the constituency in 1996 as a Militant Labour candidate. Founded the Socialist Party in 1997 and became its first TD.

Was member of the Enterprise and Small Business Committee in the last Dáil.

He was elected to Dublin County Council in 1991 and is now a member of Fingal County Council.

Joan Burton (Lab)

Home Address
81 Old Cabra Road, Dublin 7
Telephone
Home (01) 8388711
Website www.joanburton.ie
Birth Place/Date
Dublin. 1 February 1949
Married
Pat Carroll. 1 daughter
Education
Sisters of Charity, Stanhope Street, Dublin;
University College, Dublin (BComm); Fellow of
Institute of Chartered Accountants
Occupation
Full-time public representative. Accountant
and on leave of absence as senior lecturer,
Dublin Institute of Technology

Joan Burton was appointed party
spokesperson on Transport in June 2002. She
was first elected to the Dáil in 1992. Minister
of State at the Department of Social Welfare
1992–94; Minister of State at the Department
of Foreign Affairs with responsibility for
Overseas Development and at the
Department of Justice 1995–97. She lost her
Dáil seat in the 1997 general election.

She is vice-chairperson of the Labour Party.

Elected to Dublin County Council in 1991.
Elected to Fingal County Council 1999; Leader
of the Labour Party Group.

Chair of Steering Committee of
Blanchardstown Women's Refuge. Board
member of Centre for Independent Living
campaigning for transport rights of wheelchair
users.

Dublin West

	1st Count	2nd Count Transfer of **Smyth, Bonnie** Votes	3rd Count Transfer of **Lenihan** Surplus	4th Count Transfer of **McDonald** Votes	5th Count Transfer of **Morrissey** Votes	6th Count Transfer of **Doherty** Votes
Seats 3 Quota 7,498						
BONNIE, Robert (GP)	748					
BURTON, Joan (Lab)	3,810	*(+210)* 4,020	*(+59)* 4,079	*(+296)* 4,375	*(+750)* 5,125	*(+1,175)* 6,300
DOHERTY RYAN, Deirdre (FF)	2,300	*(+86)* 2,386	*(+312)* 2,698	*(+358)* 3,056	*(+672)* 3,728	
HIGGINS, Joe* (SP)	6,442	*(+218)* 6,660	*(+71)* 6,731	*(+1,122)* 7,853		
LENIHAN, Brian* (FF)	8,086					
MCDONALD, Mary Lou (SF)	2,404	*(+94)* 2,498	*(+26)* 2,524			
MORRISSEY, Tom (PD)	2,370	*(+110)* 2,480	*(+74)* 2,554	*(+108)* 2,662		
SMYTH, John T (CSP)	134					
TERRY, Sheila (FG)	3,694	*(+89)* 3,783	*(+46)* 3,829	*(+153)* 3,982	*(+881)* 4,863	*(+806)* 5,669
NON-TRANSFERABLE		75		487	359	1,747

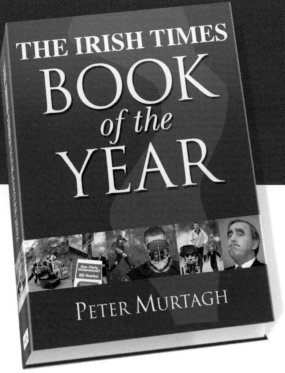

Dún Laoghaire

Elected

Mary Hanafin (FF)*	4th Count
Eamon Gilmore (Lab)*	8th Count
Fiona O'Malley (PD)	11th Count
Barry Andrews (FF)	11th Count
Ciarán Cuffe (GP)	11th Count

Voting by Party

1st Preference	Number	%	% 1997
Fianna Fáil	16,243	30.29	25.83
Fine Gael	8,069	15.04	30.96
Labour	12,164	22.68	8.66
Prog Democrats	7,166	13.36	8.55
Green Party	5,002	9.33	5.09
Sinn Féin	2,159	4.03	—
Socialist Workers' Party	876	1.63	—
Christian Solidarity	265	0.49	3.69
Others	1,689	3.15	3.34

Statistics

Population	114,674	
Electorate	91,522	
Total Poll	54,071	59.08
Spoiled Votes	438	0.81
Valid Poll	53,633	58.60
Seats	5	
Quota	8,939	
Candidates	17	

Seats

FF	2
Lab	1
PD	1
GP	1

PD and GP gain seats from FG

The Dun Laoghaire constituency lost 1,861 population in the 1998 revision mainly to Dublin South-East.

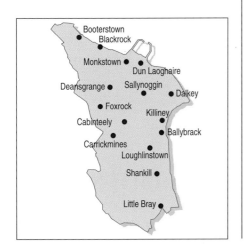

Mary Hanafin (FF)

Home Address
7 Oaklands Drive, Rathgar, Dublin 6
Business Address and Constituency Office
Department of the Taoiseach, Government Buildings, Dublin 2
Telephone
Constituency Office (01) 619 4350/619 4496; *Fax* (01) 676 3533
Birth Place/Date
Thurles, Co Tipperary. June 1959
Married
Eamon Leahy
Education
Presentation Convent, Thurles; St Patrick's College, Maynooth (BA, HDipEd); Dublin Institute of Technology (Diploma in Legal Studies)
Occupation
Minister of State. Formerly secondary school teacher

Mary Hanafin was appointed Minister of State at the Department of the Taoiseach, with responsibility as Government Chief Whip and for the Information Society, and Minister of State at the Department of Defence in June 2002. She served as Minister of State at the Departments of Health and Children; Justice, Equality and Law Reform; and Education and Science, with special responsibility for Children 2000–2002. She was first elected to the Dáil in 1997. She was a candidate in Dublin South-East constituency in the 1989 general election.

Joint Honorary Treasurer of Fianna Fáil since 1993. Awarded Stagiaire scholarship to European Parliament and Robert Schuman silver medal for services towards European unity.

Member of Dublin City Council and of City of Dublin Vocational Education Committee 1985–91.

She is daughter of Des Hanafin, Senator 1969–93 and 1997–2002, and sister of Senator John Hanafin, elected in 2002.

Eamon Gilmore (Lab)

Home Address
1 Corbawn Close, Shankill, Co Dublin
Telephone
Office (01) 6183566
Birth Place/Date
Galway. 24 April 1955
Married
Carol Hanney. 2 sons, 1 daughter
Education
Garbally College, Ballinasloe, Co Galway; University College, Galway (BA)
Occupation
Full-time public representative. Formerly trade union official

Eamon Gilmore was appointed party spokesperson on Communications and Natural Resources in June 2002. He helped negotiate the merger of Democratic Left with the Labour Party during the 28th Dáil. He was Minister of State at the Department of the Marine, with special responsibility for Port Development, Pollution and Nuclear Hazards 1994–97. He was first elected to the Dáil in 1989 as a Workers' Party deputy. He had contested the general elections in November 1982 and 1987 for the Workers' Party, six of whose seven deputies in the 26th Dáil formed Democratic Left. He was Democratic Left spokesperson on Education, Environment, Justice, Transport, Energy and Communications 1993–94. He was spokesperson on the Environment, Marine, Agriculture and Public Enterprise 1997–2002.

Member, Dublin County Council and Dún Laoghaire Borough Corporation 1985–95. Elected to the new Dún Laoghaire-Rathdown County Council 1999.

President, UCG Students' Union 1974/75; President, Union of Students in Ireland 1976–78. Member, Irish Transport and General Workers' Union (now SIPTU) since 1978. Union official 1978–89.

Member, CND; Greenpeace; Irish Council Against Blood Sports.

Dún Laoghaire

Fiona O'Malley (PD)

Home Address
4 Banna Ville, Dublin 6
Telephone
Home (01) 497 9948
Website www.voteno1.com
Birth Place/Date
Limerick. 19 January 1968
Education
Laurel Hill, Limerick; Trinity College, Dublin (BA French and the History of Western Art and Architecture); City University, London (MA Museum and Gallery Management)
Occupation
Public representative. Former arts administrator

Fiona O'Malley is a new Dáil deputy.

She has been a member of Dún Laoghaire Rathdown County Council since 1999. Member, Housing Committee and of the County Development Board.

She is a daughter of Desmond O'Malley, founder of the Progressive Democrats and a former Minister for Justice, Industry and Commerce, and Trade, Commerce and Tourism in various governments since 1969. He retired from the Dáil before the last general election.

She is a cousin of Tim O'Malley who was elected in Limerick East.

Barry Andrews (FF)

Home Address
43 Temple Road, Blackrock, Co Dublin
Constituency Office
43 Temple Road, Blackrock, Co Dublin
Telephone
Home/Office (01) 2880099; *Mobile* 086 836 1396
Birth Place/Date
Dublin. 16 May 1967
Education
Willow Park, Blackrock College, Co Dublin; University College, Dublin (MA History); Kings Inns, Dublin (Barrister-at-law)
Occupation
Public representative. Barrister. Former teacher.

Barry Andrews is a new Dáil deputy.

He has been a member of Dún Laoghaire Rathdown County Council since 1999. Member, Dún Laoghaire Vocational Education Committee. Director of Dalkey Irish Heritage Town Company. Governor of the Royal Academy of Music.

He is a son of David Andrews who was a TD for Dún Laoghaire 1965–2002 and a Minister for Foreign Affairs and for the Marine.

Ciarán Cuffe (GP)

Home Address
Quarry Road, Shankill, Co Dublin
Telephone
Home (01) 6773372; *Mobile* 087 265 2075
Birth Place/Date
Dublin. 3 April 1963
Education
Gonzaga College, Dublin; University College, Dublin (BArch); School of Architecture, Venice, Italy
Occupation
Public representative. Former Lecturer in Urban Planning

Ciarán Cuffe is a new Dáil deputy. He is party spokesperson for the Environment, Local Government and Justice, Equality and Law Reform.

Member of Dublin City Council since 1991. Commissioner of Irish Lights. Former member, Council of Dublin Docklands Authority; Former member, Dublin Transportation Initiative's Local Authority Committee. Member, Amnesty International and An Taisce.

Dún Laoghaire

Seats 5
Quota 8,939

	1st Count	2nd Count Transfer of **Hyland** Votes	3rd Count Transfer of **Redmond** Votes	4th Count Transfer of **Williams** Votes	5th Count Transfer of **Ó Buachalla** Votes
ANDREWS, Barry (FF)	7,425	*(+6)* 7,431	*(+18)* 7,449	*(+10)* 7,459	*(+24)* 7,483
BAILEY, John (FG)	1,705	*(+1)* 1,706	*(+6)* 1,712	*(+8)* 1,720	*(+15)* 1,735
BOYD BARRETT, Richard (SWP)	876	*(+2)* 878	*(+2)* 880	*(+10)* 890	*(+26)* 916
BHREATHNACH, Niamh (Lab)	*3,893*	*(+6)* 3,899	*(+1)* 3,900	*(+35)* 3,935	*(+35)* 3,970
COSGRAVE, Liam T. (FG)	3,135	*(+2)* 3,137	*(+16)* 3,153	*(+14)* 3,167	*(+14)* 3,181
CUFFE, Ciaran (GP)	5,002	*(+10)* 5,012	*(+21)* 5,033	*(+75)* 5,108	*(+69)* 5,177
GILMORE, Eamon* (Lab)	8,271	*(+13)* 8,284	*(+13)* 8,297	*(+46)* 8,343	*(+32)* 8,375
HANAFIN, Mary* (FF)	8,818	*(+9)* 8,827	*(+93)* 8,920	*(+30)* 8,950	
HYLAND, Barbara (Ind)	86				
KEOGH, Helen (FG)	3,229	*(+1)* 3,230	*(+3)* 3,233	*(+19)* 3,252	*(+20)* 3,272
MCDOWELL, Vincent (Ind)	345	*(+9)* 354	*(+15)* 369	*(+25)* 394	*(+24)* 418
O'BRIEN, Michael (SF)	2,159	*(+1)* 2,160	*(+13)* 2,173	*(+3)* 2,176	*(+16)* 2,192
Ó BUACHALLA, Denis (Ind)	346	*(+7)* 353	*(+8)* 361	*(+19)* 380	
O'KEEFE, Patrick (Ind)	593	*(+3)* 596	*(+18)* 614	*(+14)* 628	*(+56)* 684
O'MALLEY, Fiona (PD)	7,166	*(+5)* 7,171	*(+17)* 7,188	*(+29)* 7,217	*(+43)* 7,260
REDMOND, Michael (CSP)	265	*(+2)* 267			
WILLIAMS, Heather Elizabeth (Ind)	319	*(+4)* 323	*(+15)* 338		
NON-TRANSFERABLE		5	8	1	6

6th Count	7th Count	8th Count	9th Count	10th Count	11th Count
Transfer of **McDowell** Votes	Transfer of **Boyd Barrett, O'Keefe** Votes	Transfer of **Bailey** Votes	Transfer of **O'Brien** Votes	Transfer of **Keogh** Votes	Transfer of **Bhreathnach** Votes
(+36) 7,519	*(+157)* 7,676	*(+66)* 7,742	*(+547)* 8,289	*(+78)* 8,367	*(+551)* 8,918
(+10) 1,745	*(+50)* 1,795				
(+16) 932					
(+32) 4,002	*(+100)* 4,102	*(+145)* 4,247	*(+303)* 4,550	*(+540)* 5,090	
(+24) 3,205	*(+67)* 3,272	*(+639)* 3,911	*(+85)* 3,996	*(+2,330)* 6,326	*(+1,204)* 7,530
(+129) 5,306	*(+389)* 5,695	*(+104)* 5,799	*(+800)* 6,599	*(+319)* 6,918	*(+1,752)* 8,670
(+39) 8,414	*(+348)* 8,762	*(+180)* 8,942			
(+16) 3,288	*(+54)* 3,342	*(+527)* 3,869	*(+47)* 3,916		
(+13) 2,205	*(+200)* 2,405	*(+16)* 2,421			
(+40) 724					
(+49) 7,309	*(+189)* 7,498	*(+79)* 7,577	*(+130)* 7,707	*(+552)* 8,259	*(+1,005)* 9,264
14	102	39	509	97	578

Galway East

Elected

Voting by Party

1st Preference	Number	%	% 1997
Fianna Fáil	23,117	46.77	48.60
Fine Gael	15,576	31.52	31.17
Green Party	1,022	2.07	—
Sinn Féin	1,828	3.70	—
Christian Solidarity	93	0.19	—
Others	7,786	15.75	4.67

Statistics

Population	84,945	
Electorate	73,659	
Total Poll	49,874	67.71
Spoiled Votes	452	0.91
Valid Poll	49,422	67.01
Seats	4	
Quota	9,885	
Candidates	9	

Seats

FF	2
FG	1
Ind	1
Ind gain from FG	

The Galway East constituency gained 5,217 population from Galway West in the 1998 revision.

Paul Connaughton (FG)

Home Address
Mount Bellew, Ballinasloe, Co Galway
Telephone
Home (0905) 79249
Birth Place/Date
Mount Bellew. 6 June 1944
Married
Bernadette Keating. 2 sons, 5 daughters
Education
St Mary's Secondary School, Ballygar, Co Galway; St Jarlath's Vocational School, Mount Bellew; Mount Bellew Agricultural College; Athenry Agricultural College; IMI Management Course
Occupation
Public representative. Farmer. Formerly general manager, Tuam Livestock Mart

Paul Connaughton was appointed spokesperson on Regional Development in June 2002.

He was first elected to the Dáil in 1981. He contested the 1977 general election as a Fine Gael candidate in Galway East and a by-election in the old Galway North-East constituency in 1975. Senator, Agricultural Panel, 1977–81. Was deputy spokesperson on Agriculture and Food and Rural Development in the last Dáil. Was Minister of State at the Department of Agriculture with special responsibility for Land Structure and Development 1982–87. Party spokesperson on Energy and Western Development 1993–94. Also served as spokesperson on Agriculture, Social Welfare, Regional Development, Defence, and as deputy spokesperson on Tourism.

Member Galway County Council 1979–85 and since 1991; Galway County Committee of Agriculture 1979–85.

Member, Macra na Feirme; Irish Farmers' Association; Mount Bellew Town Development Association; Tuam Chamber of Commerce; Gaelic Athletic Association.

Joe Callanan (FF)

Home Address
Calla, Kilconnell, Ballinasloe, Co Galway
Constituency Office
Westbridge, Loughrea, Co Galway
Telephone
Home (0905) 86695; *Constituency office* (091) 870 642; *Fax* (091) 870 643
Birth Place/Date
Ballinasloe. 30 January 1949
Married
Noreen Kilroy. 2 sons, 4 daughters
Education
Kilconnell National School; St Killian's Vocational School, New Inn, Co Galway
Occupation
Public representative. Farmer

Joe Callanan is a new Dáil deputy. He contested Galway East in 1997.

Member, Galway County Council since 1982 and Western Health Board (Chairperson 1990/92). Member, Irish Farmers' Association and Irish Creamery Milk Suppliers' Association. Involved in GAA, sporting and cultural organisations.

He is a nephew of the late Johnny Callanan, a Fianna Fáil TD for Galway East 1977–82.

Paddy McHugh (Ind)

Home Address
Shop Street, Tuam, Co Galway
Constituency Office
Chapel Lane, Tuam
Telephone
Home (093) 24924; *Constituency Office*
(093) 26455; *Fax* (093) 28419
Birth Place/Date
Tuam. 23 January 1953
Married
Teresa Connelly. 2 daughters, 1 son
Education
Caherlistrane National School; Tuam
Vocational School; Athlone Institute of
Technology; Waterford Institute of
Technology (Diploma in Architecture)
Occupation
Full-time public representative. Formerly
architect

Paddy McHugh is a new Dáil deputy. He ran
as an Independent after failing to win a Fianna
Fáil nomination.

Member, Galway County Council since 1985.
Member, Tuam Town Commissioners since
1999. Member, Tuam Chamber of
Commerce; Gaelic Athletic Association.

Noel Treacy (FF)

Home Address
Gurteen, Ballinasloe, Co Galway
Constituency Office
Cross Street, Athenry, Co Galway
Business Address
Department of Agriculture and Food,
Agriculture House, Kildare Street, Dublin 2
Telephone
Home (0905) 77094; *Constituency Office*
(091) 844360; *Office* (01) 607 2000; *Fax*
(01) 6763947
Birth Place/Date
Ballinasloe. 18 December 1951
Married
Mary Cloonan. 3 daughters, 1 son
Education
St Joseph's College, Garbally Park, Ballinasloe
Occupation
Public representative. Formerly auctioneer

Noel Treacy was appointed Minister of State
at the Department of Agriculture and Food in
June 2002. He has responsibility for Food and
Horticulture. He was Minister of State at the
Department of Enterprise, Trade and
Employment and at the Department of
Education with special responsibility for
Science and Technology 1997–2002. He was
Minister of State at the Departments of the
Taoiseach, Finance and Transport, Energy and
Communications with special responsibility
for Energy 1993–94. He was Minister of State
at the Department of Finance with special
responsibility for the Office of Public Works
and the Central Development Committee
1992–93. He was Minister of State at the
Department of Health 1989–91 and at the
Department of Justice 1990. He was
previously Minister of State at the
Department of Finance 1987–89 with
responsibility for the Office of Public Works,
and Minister of State at the Department of
the Taoiseach 1988–89 with responsibility for
Heritage Affairs. He was first elected to the
Dáil in May 1982 in a by-election. Was party
deputy spokesperson on Defence 1983–87.

Galway East

Seats 4 Quota 9,885	1st Count	2nd Count Transfer of **Mac Meanmain, Ní Bhroin** Votes	3rd Count Transfer of **Mac an Bhaird** Votes	4th Count Transfer of **Burke** Votes	5th Count Transfer of **Connaughton** Surplus
BURKE, Ulick* (FG)	6,941	*(+211)* 7,152	*(+293)* 7,445		
CALLANAN, Joe (FF)	7,898	*(+65)* 7,963	*(+352)* 8,315	*(+1,099)* 9,414	*(+952)* 10,366
CONNAUGHTON, Paul* (FG)	8,635	*(+131)* 8,766	*(+218)* 8,984	*(+4,987)* 13,971	
KITT, Michael P* (FF)	7,454	*(+59)* 7,513	*(+198)* 7,711	*(+239)* 7,950	*(+293)* 8,243
MAC MEANMAIN, Manus (CSP)	93				
MCHUGH, Paddy (Ind)	7,786	*(+256)* 8,042	*(+539)* 8,581	*(+244)* 8,825	*(+1,056)* 9,881
MAC AN BHAIRD, Dáithí (SF)	1,828	*(+240)* 2,068			
NÍ BHROIN, Una (GP)	1,022				
TREACY, Noel* (FF)	7,765	*(+82)* 7,847	*(+244)* 8,091	*(+635)* 8,726	*(+527)* 9,253
NON-TRANSFERABLE		71	224	241	1258

Nora Owen and Seán Ryan at the City West Hotel, after results from the electronic voting count for Dublin North.

Galway West

Elected

Voting by Party

1st Preference	Number	%	% 1997
Fianna Fáil	20,442	41.33	45.94
Fine Gael	8,359	16.90	22.21
Labour	5,213	10.54	10.07
Prog. Democrats	6,192	12.52	12.27
Green Party	2,193	4.43	3.44
Sinn Féin	2,779	5.62	2.51
Others	4,288	8.67	1.14

Statistics

Population	103,909	
Electorate	82,213	
Total Poll	50,146	61.00
Spoiled Votes	680	1.36
Valid Poll	49,466	60.17
Seats	5	
Quota	8,245	
Candidates	17	

Seats

FF	2
FG	1
Lab	1
PD	1
No change	

The Galway West constituency lost 5,217 population to Galway East in the 1998 revision.

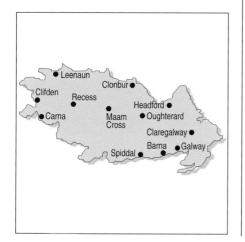

Éamon Ó Cuív (FF)

Home Address
Corr na Móna, Co na Gaillimhe
Constituency Office
3 Plás Victoria, Gaillimh
Business Office
Department of Community, Rural and Gaeltacht Affairs; Dun Aimhirgin, 43–49 Mespil Road, Dublin 4
Telephone
Home (092) 48021; *Constituency Office* (091) 562846; *Fax* (091) 562846; *Office* (01) 6473000; *Fax* (01) 6473101
Birth Place/Date
Dublin. June 1950
Married
Áine Ní Choincheannain. 3 sons, 1 daughter
Education
Oatlands College, Mount Merrion, Dublin; University College, Dublin (BSc)
Occupation
Formerly Gaeltacht co-operative manager

Éamon Ó Cuív was appointed Minister for Community, Rural and Gaeltacht Affairs in June 2002.

He was first elected to the Dáil in 1992. He had been Minister of State at the Department of Agriculture, Food and Rural Development with responsibility for Rural Development 2001–2002. He was Minister of State at the Department of Arts, Heritage, Gaeltacht and the Islands with responsibility for the Gaeltacht areas, the Irish Language and for Island Development 1997–2001. He was party spokesperson for Rural Development and the Islands 1995–97. Senator, Cultural and Educational Panel, 1989–92. Member of Forum for Peace and Reconciliation.

Member, Galway County Council 1991–97 and of a number of subsidiary committees.

He is grandson of Éamon de Valera, President 1959–73; Taoiseach 1937–48, 1951–54, 1957–59; President of Executive Council, Irish Free State, 1932–37; President First Dáil 1919–21; President Second Dáil 1921–January 1922.

He is a nephew of Major Vivion de Valera, Dáil deputy for Dublin North City and Central City constituencies 1945–81.

He is cousin of Síle de Valera, Dáil deputy for Clare, Minister of State at the Department of Education and Science and a former Minister for Arts, Heritage, the Gaeltacht and the Islands.

Frank Fahey (FF)

Home Address
4 Carraig Bán, Menlo, Co Galway
Constituency Office
Ballybane Industrial Estate, Galway
Telephone
Constituency office (091) 771020; *Fax* (091) 771040
Birth Place/Date
Dublin. June 1951
Married
Ethelle Griffin. 2 sons, 1 daughter
Education
St Mary's College, Galway; Our Lady's College, Gort; University College, Galway (BA, HDipEd)
Occupation
Minister of State. Formerly secondary school teacher

Frank Fahey was appointed Minister of State at the Department of Enterprise, Trade and Employment with responsibility for Labour Affairs June 2002.

He was Minister for the Marine and Natural Resources January 2000–June 2002. Minister of State at the Department of Health and Children with special responsibility for Children 1997–2000. He was Minister of State at the Department of Education with special responsibility for Youth and Sport 1987–92 and also at the Department of Tourism, Transport and Communications with special responsibility for Sports Tourism. He was first elected to the Dáil in February 1982 and continued until he lost his seat in 1992. Senator, Labour Panel, 1993–97.

He was Fianna Fáil deputy spokesperson on Youth Affairs and Sport 1982–87.

Former member, Galway County Council; Galway County Vocational Education Committee; Western Health Board; Galway Regional Development Organisation.

Pádraic McCormack (FG)

Home Address
3 Renmore Park, Galway
Constituency Office
114 Bohermore, Galway
Telephone
Home (091) 753992; *Office* (091) 568686; *Fax* (091) 569204; *Dáil* (01) 6183767; *Fax* (01) 6184513
Birth Place/Date
Longford. May 1942
Married
Eilish King. 2 sons, 2 daughters
Education
Ballymahon Secondary School; Multyfarnham Agricultural College (DipAgrSc)
Occupation
Full-time public representative. Formerly auctioneer and company director

Pádraic McCormack was appointed deputy party spokesperson for Environment and Local Government in June 2002.

He has been a Dáil deputy since 1989. Contested the elections of 1977, 1981 and February 1982. Senator, Agricultural Panel 1987–89. Chairman of Fine Gael Parliamentary Party. Member in last Dáil of Public Accounts Committee and Environment Committee.

Member of Galway County Council 1974–1999; Galway City Council since 1985; He was the first Fine Gael councillor elected on the same day to a county and a county borough council. Mayor of Galway 1992–93. Member of Galway Harbour Board 1979–1995 (chairman 1990). General Council of County Councils 1979–87 (vice-chairman 1984–85).

Member, Gaelic Athletic Association.

Michael D. Higgins (Lab)

Home Address
Letteragh, Circular Road, Rahoon, Galway
Telephone
Home (091) 524513; *Fax* (091) 528501
Birth Place/Date
Limerick. 18 April 1941
Married
Sabina Coyne. 3 sons, 1 daughter
Education
St Flannan's College, Ennis, Co Clare; University College, Galway (BA, BComm); Indiana University (MA); Manchester University.
Occupation
Public representative. University lecturer

Michael D. Higgins was appointed party spokesperson on International Affairs in June 2002.

He was party spokesperson on Foreign Affairs 1997–2002. He was Minister for Arts, Culture and the Gaeltacht 1993–97. In the last Dáil he was a member of the Committee on Foreign Affairs and the Committee on Heritage and the Irish Language.

He was first elected to the Dáil in 1981. He lost his seat in the general election of November 1982 and regained it in 1987. Senator, NUI constituency, 1982–87 and Taoiseach's nominee 1973–77. Labour Party candidate in Galway West in the general elections of 1969, 1973 and 1977. He also contested the European Parliament elections in the Connacht-Ulster constituency in 1979 and 1985.

Member of the Parliamentary Assembly of the Council of Europe 2000–2002. At different periods he has been party spokesperson on European and International Affairs, Overseas Development, Education and the Gaeltacht.

Member Galway City Council 1985–93 (Mayor 1982/83 and 1991/92). Member, Galway County Council 1974–85; Western Health Board; Governing Body, University College, Galway.

Chairman of the Labour Party 1978–87. First recipient of the MacBride International Peace Prize 1992.

Author of several collections of poems. Writer and presenter of TV documentaries on Montserrat and Dr Noel Browne.

Noel Grealish (PD)

Home Address
Carnmore, Oranmore, Co Galway
Telephone
Constituency Office (091) 764 807; *Fax* (091) 764 974; *Mobile* 087 264 8607
Birth Place/Date
Carnmore. 16 December 1965
Education
Carnmore National School; St Mary's College, Galway
Occupation
Public representative. Company director

Noel Grealish is a new Dáil deputy. He won the Progressive Democrat seat in Galway West vacated by the senior party figure, Bobby Molloy, on the eve of the general election.

Member, Galway County Council.

Member, Carnmore Hurling Club.

Galway West

Seats 5 Quota 8,245	1st Count	2nd Count Transfer of Ó Cuív Surplus	3rd Count Transfer of Manning, Nulty Votes	4th Count Transfer of Healy Eames Votes	5th Count Transfer of Ac Coistealbha Votes	6th Count Transfer of McDonnell Votes	7th Count Transfer of Scallon Votes
AC COISTEALBHA, Seán (SF)	1,311	*(+62)* 1,373	*(+10)* 1,383	*(+14)* 1,397			
CALLANAN, Daniel Joseph (SF)	1,468	*(+17)* 1,485	*(+13)* 1,498	*(+11)* 1,509	*(+657)* 2,166	*(+34)* 2,200	*(+106)* 2,306
COX, Margaret (FF)	3,269	*(+428)* 3,697	*(+7)* 3,704	*(+48)* 3,752	*(+49)* 3,801	*(+69)* 3,870	*(+212)* 4,082
FAHEY, Frank* (FF)	7,226	*(+676)* 7,902	*(+2)* 7,904	*(+89)* 7,993	*(+127)* 8,120	*(+198)* 8,318	
GREALISH, Noel (PD)	2,735	*(+52)* 2,787	*(+4)* 2,791	*(+67)* 2,858	*(+18)* 2,876	*(+245)* 3,121	*(+112)* 3,233
HEALY EAMES, Fidelma (FG)	1,320	*(+20)* 1,340	*(+7)* 1,347				
HIGGINS, Michael D* (Lab)	5,213	*(+102)* 5,315	*(+28)* 5,343	*(+167)* 5,510	*(+136)* 5,646	*(+126)* 5,772	*(+323)* 6,095
LYONS, Donal (PD)	1,995	*(+22)* 2,017	*(+9)* 2,026	*(+32)* 2,058	*(+10)* 2,068	*(+477)* 2,545	*(+168)* 2,713
MANNING, Eileen (Ind)	96	*(+1)* 97					
MCCORMACK, Pádraic* (FG)	4,760	*(+90)* 4,850	*(+9)* 4,859	*(+401)* 5,260	*(+58)* 5,318	*(+184)* 5,502	*(+363)* 5,865
MCDONAGH, Michael (FG)	2,279	*(+21)* 2,300	*(+6)* 2,306	*(+313)* 2,619	*(+13)* 2,632	*(+38)* 2,670	*(+78)* 2,748
MCDONNELL, Declan (PD)	1,462	*(+17)* 1,479	*(+5)* 1,484	*(+15)* 1,499	*(+7)* 1,506		
NULTY, Joseph (Ind)	76	*(+1)* 77					
Ó BROLCHÁIN, Niall (GP)	2,193	*(+23)* 2,216	*(+25)* 2,241	*(+67)* 2,308	*(+108)* 2,416	*(+34)* 2,450	*(+201)* 2,651
Ó CUÍV, Éamon* (FF)	9,947						
SCALLON, Dana Rosemary (Ind)	1,677	*(+50)* 1,727	*(+13)* 1,740	*(+72)* 1,812	*(+60)* 1,872	*(+48)* 1,920	
WALSH, Seamus (Ind)	2,439	*(+120)* 2,559	*(+38)* 2,626	*(+38)* 2,626	*(+116)* 2,742	*(+32)* 2,774	*(+170)* 2,944
NON-TRANSFERABLE			7	13	38	21	187

8th Count	9th Count	10th Count	11th Count	12th Count	13th Count	14th Count	15th Count
Transfer of **Callanan** Votes	Transfer of **Fahey** Surplus	Transfer of **Lyons** Votes	Transfer of **McDonagh** Votes	Transfer of **Walsh** Votes	Transfer of **McCormack** Surplus	Transfer of **Ó Brolcháin** Votes	Transfer of **Higgins** Surplus
(+215) 4,297	*(+17)* 4,314	*(+309)* 4,623	*(+159)* 4,782	*(+462)* 5,244	*(+29)* 5,273	*(+312)* 5,585	*(+321)* 5,906
(+82) 3,315	*(+8)* 3,323	*(+1,221)* 4,544	*(+554)* 5,098	*(+227)* 5,325	*(+27)* 5,352	*(+332)* 5,684	*(+531)* 6,215
(+569) 6,664	*(+18)* 6,682	*(+489)* 7,171	*(+327)* 7,498	*(+653)* 8,151	*(+93)* 8,244	*(+2,336)* 10,580	
(+74) 2,787	*(+11)* 2,798						
(+136) 6,001	*(+11)* 6,012	*(+273)* 6,285	*(+1,338)* 7,623	*(+797)* 8,420			
(+60) 2,808	*(+4)* 2,812	*(+76)* 2,888					
(+457) 3,108	*(+3)* 3,111	*(+156)* 3,267	*(+124)* 3,391	*(+358)* 3,749	*(+26)* 3,775		
(+210) 3,154	*(+1)* 3,155	*(+79)* 3,234	*(+94)* 3,328				
503	–	195	292	831	–	795	1,483

Kerry North

Elected

Voting by Party

1st Preference	Number	%	% 1997
Fianna Fáil	11,811	30.15	26.31
Fine Gael	8,652	22.09	24.29
Labour	8,773	22.40	29.90
Sinn Féin	9,496	24.24	15.91
Others	441	1.13	—

Statistics

Population	63,024	
Electorate	55,476	
Total Poll	39,524	71.25
Spoiled Votes	351	0.89
Valid Poll	39,173	70.61
Seats	3	
Quota	9,794	
Candidates	7	

Seats

FF	1
FG	1
SF	1
SF gain from Labour	

The Kerry North constituency is unchanged from the 1997 General Election.

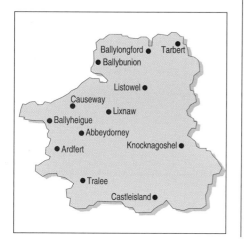

Tom McEllistrim (FF)

Home Address
Ahane, Ballymacelligott, Tralee, Co Kerry
Telephone
Home/Office (066) 713 7127
Birth Place/Date
Tralee. 24 October 1968
Education
Presentation Convent, Tralee; St Patrick's College, Castleisland, Co Kerry; St Brendan's College, Killarney; St Patrick's College, Maynooth (BA, HDipEd)
Occupation
Public representative. Formerly secondary school teacher

Tom McEllistrim is a new Dáil deputy. His win brings the McEllistrim name back into national politics following the defeat of his father in Kerry North in 1992. Tom junior contested the 1997 general election.

Member of Kerry County Council since 1999 where he became the youngest councillor and the fourth generation of the family to serve in local politics.

Member, Kerry County Enterprise Board; Fenit Harbour Board; Partnership Tra Lí; Ballyseedy Wood Committee; Kerry County Rural Water Company; Housing and Social Support Strategic Policy Committee.

He is the son of Tom McEllistrim who was a Dáil deputy 1969–92; grandson of Tom McEllistrim who was a Dáil deputy 1923–69.

Martin Ferris (SF)

Home Address
18 Casement View, Ardfert, Co Kerry
Constituency Office
2 Moyderwell, Tralee, Co Kerry; Market Street, Listowel, Co Kerry
Telephone
Constituency Office (066) 7129545; *Fax* (066) 7129572 (Tralee); (068) 24949 (Listowel)
Birth Place/Date
Tralee. 28 March 1952
Married
Marie Hoare. 3 sons, 3 daughters
Education
Barrow National School, Ardfert; CBS Tralee
Occupation
Full-time public representative. Formerly fisherman

Martin Ferris is a new Dáil deputy. He was a candidate in the general election of 1997.

He first became a member of the Sinn Féin Ard Comhairle in 1983. He was arrested on board the gun-running ship, *Marita Ann*, in 1984 and convicted for possession of explosive substances for unlawful purpose and for possession of firearms and ammunition with intent to endanger life. He was imprisoned in Portlaoise Jail 1984–94. Member, Sinn Féin Ard Comhairle since 1995; Sinn Féin delegation to the Forum for Peace and Reconciliation; party delegation in direct talks with the British Prime Minister, Tony Blair, in 1997; negotiating team for Good Friday Agreement 1998.

Member of Kerry County Council since 1999.

Jimmy Deenihan (FG)

Home Address
Finuge, Lixnaw, Co Kerry
Telephone
Home (068) 40235/40154
Birth Place/Date
Listowel, Co Kerry. September 1952
Married
Mary Dowling
Education
St Michael's College, Listowel; National
College of Physical Education, Limerick (BEd)
Occupation
Full-time public representative. Formerly
teacher

Jimmy Deenihan was appointed party
spokesperson on Arts, Sports and Tourism in
June 2002. He has been a Dáil deputy since
1987. He was Minister of State at the
Department of Agriculture, Food and Forestry
with special responsibility for Rural
Development, the LEADER programme and
monitoring the activities of An Bord Bia and
the food industry 1994–97. He was a
candidate in the general election of November
1982 and a Senator, Taoiseach's nominee,
1982–87. Spokesperson on the Office of
Public Works 1997–2002.

Member, Kerry County Council 1985–94;
Kerry County Vocational Educational
Committee; Library Committee 1985–94.

Member, Gaelic Athletic Association. He won
All-Ireland football medals in 1975, 1978,
1979, 1980 and 1981 and was captain of the
1981 team. He also won four National League
medals and five Railway Cup medals. GAA All-
Star Award 1981.

Seats 3
Quota 9,794

	1st Count	2nd Count Transfer of **O'Connor, Kennedy, Kiely** Votes	3rd Count Transfer of **McEllistrim** Surplus
DEENIHAN, Jimmy* (FG)	8,652	*(+886)* 9,538	*(+304)* 9,842
FERRIS, Martin (SF)	9,496	*(+520)* 10,016	
KENNEDY, James (Ind)	233		
KIELY, Dan (FF)	3,927		
MCELLISTRIM, Tom (FF)	7,884	*(+2,401)* 10,285	
O'CONNOR, Anthony (Ind)	208		
SPRING, Dick* (Lab)	8,773	*(+393)* 9,166	*(+187)* 9,353
NON-TRANSFERABLE		168	

Kerry South

Elected

John O'Donoghue (FF)*   1st Count
Breda Moynihan-Cronin (Lab)*   6th Count
Jackie Healy-Rae (Ind)*   7th Count

Voting by Party

1st Preference	Number	%	% 1997
Fianna Fáil	16,357	44.64	31.79
Fine Gael	6,473	17.66	13.77
Labour	5,307	14.48	14.05
Others	8,509	23.22	40.39

Statistics

Population	63,106	
Electorate	51,761	
Total Poll	37,022	71.52
Spoiled Votes	376	1.02
Valid Poll	36,646	70.80
Seats	3	
Quota	9,162	
Candidates	8	

Seats

FF	1
Lab	1
Ind	1
No change	

The Kerry South constituency is unchanged since the 1997 General Election.

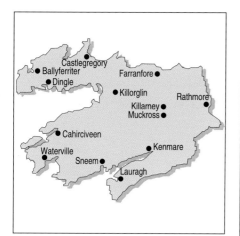

John O'Donoghue (FF)

Home Address
Garranearagh, Cahirciveen, Co Kerry
Business Address
Department of Arts, Sport and Tourism, Kildare Street, Dublin 2
Telephone
Home (066) 94 72413/94 72631; *Fax* (066) 94 72667; *Office* (01) 6313804
Birth Place/Date
Cahirciveen. May 1956
Married
Kate Ann Murphy. 2 sons, 1 daughter
Education
CBS, Cahirciveen; University College, Cork; Incorporated Law Society of Ireland, Dublin (BCL, LLB)
Occupation
Full-time public representative. Formerly solicitor

John O'Donoghue was appointed Minister for the Arts, Sport and Tourism in June 2002.

He was first elected to the Dáil in 1987. He was Minister for Justice, Equality and Law Reform 1997–2002; Minister of State at the Department of Finance, with special responsibility for the Office of Public Works, November 1991–February 1992. He was party spokesperson on Justice 1995–97. Member, British-Irish Inter-Parliamentary Body 1993–97.

Member, Kerry County Council 1985–91 (chairperson 1990–91) and 1993–1997; Southern Health Board and the Psychiatric Services Committee 1982–97 (chairperson 1992–93); Kerry County Committee of Agriculture (1985–88); Kerry County Fisheries Committee 1989–91 (chairperson 1989–90); Kerry County Library Committee 1991–97.

Member, St Mary's Gaelic Athletic Association Club and Cahirciveen Social Services Committee.

Breda Moynihan-Cronin (Lab)

Home Address
10 Muckross Grove, Killarney, Co Kerry
Telephone
Constituency Office (064) 34993; *Fax* (064) 34993
Birth Place/Date
Killarney. 31 March 1953
Married
Daniel C. Cronin
Education
St Brigid's Secondary School, Killarney; Sion Hill College, Blackrock, Co Dublin; Skerry's College, Cork
Occupation
Full-time public representative. Formerly bank official

Breda Moynihan-Cronin was appointed spokesperson on Social and Family Affairs in June 2002.

She was first elected to the Dáil in 1992 when she won the Labour seat previously held by her father Michael. She was party spokesperson on Tourism and Recreation 1999–2002; on Social, Community and Family Affairs 1998–99, and on Justice, Equality and Law Reform 1997–98. Was Chairperson of Joint Committee on Tourism, Sport and Recreation in the last Dáil. Former member of the Council of Europe.

Member of Kerry County Council since 1991. Member, County Kerry Vocational Education Committee and Kerry County Enterprise Board.

She was involved in amateur dramatics and won many awards. She helped form the Ivy Leaf Theatre Company in Castleisland and was instrumental in setting up the Ivy Leaf Centre there.

She is daughter of Michael Moynihan, Labour deputy in Kerry South in 1981–87 and 1989–92. He was Minister of State at the Department of Trade, Commerce and Tourism 1983–87 and was a Senator in 1973–77.

Jackie Healy-Rae (Ind)

Home Address
Main Street, Kilgarvan, Co Kerry
Business Address
Main Street, Kilgarvan
Telephone
Home (064) 85315; *Constituency office*
(064) 37376
Birth Place/Date
Kilgarvan. March 1931
Married
Separated. 4 sons, 2 daughters
Occupation
Full-time public representative. Formerly
farmer, publican, plant-hire business

Jackie Healy-Rae was first elected to the Dáil
in 1997 when he stood as an Independent
after he failed to get a Fianna Fáil nomination.
He voted for Bertie Ahern as Taoiseach in
1997 and supported the minority Fianna Fáil-
Progressive Democrat Coalition whenever
necessary. He claimed that as a result he
helped secure many benefits for his
constituency.

Fianna Fáil member of Kerry County Council
1974–97 and since then as as Independent.
Chairman of County Council 1995/96. Served
for many years on the Southern Health Board
(Chairperson 1981/82).

Chairperson for seven years of Comhaltas
Ceoltóirí Chiarraí.

Kerry South

Seats 3 Quota 9,162	1st Count	2nd Count Transfer of **Barry** Votes	3rd Count Transfer of **Grady** Votes
BARRY, Donal (Ind)	934		
CASEY, Sheila (FG)	1,934	(+99) 2,033	(+183) 2,216
GRADY, Donal (Ind)	1,346	(+103) 1,449	
FITZGERALD, Seamus (FG)	4,539	(+193) 4,732	(+59) 4,791
FLEMING, Tom (FF)	6,912	(+83) 6,995	(+260) 7,255
HEALY-RAE, Jackie* (Ind)	6,229	(+226) 6,455	(+364) 6,819
MOYNIHAN-CRONIN, Breeda* (Lab)	5,307	(+173) 5,480	(+466) 5,946
O'DONOGHUE, John* (FF)	9,445		
NON-TRANSFERABLE		57	117

4th Count	5th Count	6th Count	7th Count
Transfer of **O'Donoghue** Surplus	Transfer of **Casey** Votes	Transfer of **Fitzgerald** Votes	Transfer of **Moynihan-Cronin** Surplus
(+4) 2,220			
(+20) 4,811	*(+1,272)* 6,083		
(+152) 7,407	*(+186)* 7,593	*(+683)* 8,276	*(+105)* 8,381
(+74) 6,893	*(+254)* 7,147	*(+1,262)* 8,409	*(+175)* 8,584
(+33) 5,979	*(+453)* 6,432	*(+3,010)* 9,442	
	55	1128	

Kildare North

Elected

Charlie McCreevy (FF)*	1st Count
Emmet Stagg (Lab)*	4th Count
Bernard Durkan (FG)*	5th Count

Voting by Party

1st Preference	Number	%	% 1997
Fianna Fáil	14,250	43.21	34.86
Fine Gael	5,786	17.54	26.19
Labour	7,051	21.38	19.00
Prog. Democrats	3,919	11.88	6.69
Green Party	1,974	5.99	4.47

Statistics

Population	68,259	
Electorate	60,094	
Total Poll	33,271	55.36
Spoiled Votes	291	0.87
Valid Poll	32,980	54.88
Seats	3	
Quota	8,246	
Candidates	6	

Seats

FF	1
FG	1
Lab	1
No change	

The Kildare North constituency lost 4,399 population to Kildare South in the 1998 revision.

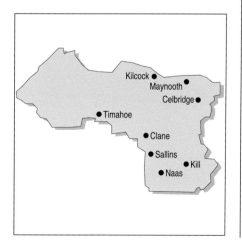

Charlie McCreevy (FF)

Home Address
Sallins, Co Kildare
Constituency Office
Hillview House, Kilcullen Road, Naas,
Co Kildare
Business Address
Department of Finance, Upper Merrion Street,
Dublin 2
Telephone
Constituency office (045) 876816;
Fax (045) 876092; *Business* (01) 676 7571;
Fax (01) 676 1951
Birth Place/Date
Sallins, Co Kildare. September 1949
Married
Noeleen Halligan. 3 sons. 1 son, 3 daughters
from previous marriage
Education
Naas CBS; Franciscan College, Gormanston,
Co Meath; University College, Dublin
(BComm); Institute of Chartered Accountants
Occupation
Government Minister. Formerly chartered
accountant

Charlie McCreevy was re-appointed Minister
for Finance in June 2002. He was first
appointed to that post in June 1997. He was
Minister for Tourism and Trade 1993–94. He
was Minister for Social Welfare February
1992–January 1993. He was first elected to
the Dáil in 1977 for the then 3-seat
constituency of Kildare.

Party front bench spokesman on Finance
1995–97.

Member, Kildare County Council 1979–85.
Member of various Oireachtas committees;
Kill Club GAA; Institute of Chartered
Accountants.

Emmet Stagg (Lab)

Home Address
736 Lodge Park, Straffan, Co Kildare
Telephone
Home (01) 627 2149
Birth Place/Date
Mayo. October 1944
Married
Mary Morris. 1 son, 1 daughter
Education
Ballinrobe CBS; College of Technology, Kevin
Street, Dublin; member, Institute of Medical
Laboratory Sciences
Occupation
Full-tme public representative. Formerly
medical laboratory technologist

Emmet Stagg appointed party Chief Whip in
June 2002. He was Minister of State at the
Department of the Environment, with special
responsibility for Housing and Urban Renewal
1993–94; Minister of State at the Department
of Transport, Energy and Communications,
with special responsibility for Nuclear Safety,
Renewable Energy, Gas and Oil Industry, Air
Safety, Road Haulage and Bus Regulation
1994–97. He was first elected to the Dáil in
1987. He was a candidate in the 1981 general
election.

Labour Party spokesperson on Public
Enterprise since 1997; on Social Welfare
1989–92; on Agriculture 1987–89. Vice-
chairman of the Labour Party 1987–89.

Member, Kildare County Council 1978–93
(chairperson 1981/82) and since 1999; Kildare
County Vocational Education Committee
1985–93; Eastern Health Board 1978–85;
Kildare County Library Committee 1975–89.

Member, SIPTU.

Member, Gaelic Athletic Association and
president of Celbridge Soccer Club. President,
Maynooth Soccer Club.

Bernard Durkan (FG)

Home Address
Timard, Maynooth, Co Kildare
Telephone
Home (01) 628 6063/628 5215
Birth Place/Date
Killasser, Swinford, Co Mayo. 26 March 1945
Married
Hilary Spence. 2 sons
Education
St John's National School, Carramore, Co Mayo
Occupation
Full-time public representative. Formerly agricultural contractor

Bernard Durkan was appointed Chief Whip in June 2002. He was first elected to the Dáil in 1981, lost his seat in February 1982 and regained it in November 1982. He has since been re-elected in successive general elections. He served as Minister of State at the Department of Social Welfare, with special responsibility for Information and Customer Services and the Integration of the Tax and Social Welfare Codes 1994–97. Spokesperson on Overseas Development Assistance and Human Rights in 28th Dáil. Spokesperson on Health 1994; on the Office of the Tánaiste and on the National Development Plan 1993–94; on the Insurance Industry 1991–92; on Trade and Marketing 1989–91; on the Food Industry 1987–89. Assistant Whip 1986–87.

Member, Kildare County Council 1976–94 (Chairperson 1986/87). He has served on the Eastern Regional Development Organisation and various Dáil committees including Public Accounts and Foreign Affairs.

Kildare North

Seats 3 Quota 8,246	1st Count	2nd Count Transfer of **McCreevy** Surplus	3rd Count Transfer of **Kelly-McCormack** Votes	4th Count Transfer of **Walsh** Votes	5th Count Transfer of **Stagg** Surplus
DURKAN, Bernard J* (FG)	5,786	(+73) 5,859	(+318) 6,177	(+1,164) 7,341	(+684) 8,025
KELLY, Paul (FF)	5,168	(+513) 5,681	(+242) 5,923	(+1,459) 7,382	(+508) 7,890
KELLY-MCCORMACK, Anne (GP)	1,974	(+25) 1,999			
MCCREEVY, Charlie* (FF)	9,082				
STAGG, Emmet* (Lab)	7,051	(+117) 7,168	(+837) 8,005	(+1,467) 9,472	
WALSH, Kate (PD)	3,919	(+108) 4,027	(+446) 4,473		
NON-TRANSFERABLE		0	156	383	34

An Taoiseach Bertie Ahern with former government minister Pádraig Flynn and Fianna Fáil general election candidate Beverly Cooper-Flynn during a walkabout in Castlebar, Co. Mayo.

Kildare South

Elected

Seán Power (FF)*	4th Count
Seán O'Fearghail (FF)	4th Count
Jack Wall (Lab)*	6thCount

Voting by Party

1st Preference	Number	%	% 1997
Fianna Fáil	15,152	46.43	37.59
Fine Gael	5,795	17.76	26.49
Labour	6,043	18.52	20.25
Prog Democrats	3,887	11.91	13.5
Green Party	1,208	3.70	—
Others	546	1.67	2.15

Statistics

Population	66,733	
Electorate	58,354	
Total Poll	33,132	56.78
Spoiled Votes	501	1.51
Valid Poll	32,631	55.92
Seats	3	
Quota	8,158	
Candidates	8	

Seats

FF	2
Lab	1
FF gain from FG	

The Kildare South constituency received a transfer of 4,399 population from Kildare North in the 1998 revision.

Seán Power (FF)

Home Address
Caragh, Naas, Co Kildare
Business Address
Main Street, Newbridge, Co Kildare
Telephone
Office (045) 432289; *Fax* (045) 435380
Birth Place/Date
Caragh, Naas. 14 October 1960
Married
Deirdre Malone. 3 sons, 1 daughter
Education
Caragh National School; Naas CBS
Occupation
Public representative. Publican

Seán Power was first elected to the Dáil in 1989. Was Assistant Government Whip in last Dáil. Served on following committees: Environment and Local Government; European Affairs; Public Enterprise and Transport.

Member of Kildare County Council.

Member of Raheen and Éire Óg Gaelic Football Clubs.

Son of Paddy Power, Dáil deputy for Kildare 1969–89; Minister for Defence March–December 1982; Minister for Fisheries 1979–81; Member of European Parliament 1977–79.

Seán O'Fearghail (FF)

Address
Fennor House, Kildare
Constituency Office
Stanhope Street, Athy, Co Kildare
Telephone
Home (045) 522966; *Constituency Office* and *Fax* (0507) 34805
Birth Place/Date
Dublin. 17 April 1960
Married
Maryclare Meaney. 1 son, 2 daughters
Education
De La Salle primary school, Kildare; St Joseph's Academy, Kildare
Occupation
Public representative. Farmer

Seán O'Fearghail is a new Dáil deputy. He contested the previous four general elections in 1987, 1989, 1992 and 1997.

Member, Kildare County Council since 1985; Eastern Health Board; Eastern Regional Health Authority. Chairperson, County Kildare Vocational Education Committee since 1989. Member, Board of Management of Blanchardstown Institute of Technology. Director and/or Chairperson of a number of voluntary housing associations in the constituency.

Jack Wall (Lab)

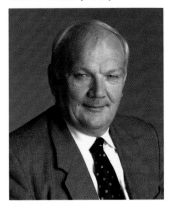

Home Address
Castlemitchell, Athy, Co Kildare
Telephone
Home/Office (0507) 31495; *Fax* (0507) 31798;
Mobile 088 257 0275
Birth Place/Date
Castledermot, Co Kildare. July 1945
Married
Ann Byrne. 2 sons, 2 daughters
Education
Castledermot Vocational School; Kevin Street
College of Technology
Occupation
Full-time public representative. Formerly
electrician

Jack Wall was appointed party spokesperson
on Agriculture in June 2002. He was first
elected to the Dáil in 1997, the only new
Labour deputy to be elected to the 28th Dáil.
He contested the 1992 election for the old
Kildare constituency. Senator, Taoiseach's
nominee, 1993–97. Party spokesperson on
Defence in 28th Dáil. Spokesperson in the
Seanad on Social Welfare.

Member, Kildare County Council since 1999.
Member, Athy Urban District Council since
1993 (Chairperson 1994/95).

Chairperson, Kildare GAA County Board since
1989. Director, Athy Credit Union.

Kildare South

Seats 3 Quota 8,158	1st Count	2nd Count Transfer of **Fitzgibbon** Votes	3rd Count Transfer of **Hendy** Votes	4th Count Transfer of **Dardis; Power, JJ** Votes	5th Count Transfer of **Power, S** Surplus	6th Count Transfer of **O'Fearghail** Surplus
DARDIS, John (PD)	3,887	*(+59)* 3,946	*(+112)* 4,058			
DUKES, Alan* (FG)	4,967	*(+73)* 5,040	*(+506)* 5,546	*(+1,624)* 7,170	*(+480)* 7,650	*(+140)* 7,790
FITZGIBBON, Gerald (Ind)	546					
HENDY, Rainsford (FG)	828	*(+22)* 850				
O'FEARGHAIL, Seán (FF)	7,370	*(+88)* 7,458	*(+43)* 7,501	*(+925)* 8,426		
POWER, J J (GP)	1,208	*(+127)* 1,335	*(+16)* 1,351			
POWER, Seán* (FF)	7,782	*(+35)* 7,817	*(+43)* 7,860	*(+1,309)* 9,169		
WALL, Jack* (Lab)	6,043	*(+105)* 6,148	*(+116)* 6,264	*(+1,179)* 7,443	*(+406)* 7,849	*(+128)* 7,977
NON-TRANSFERABLE		37	14	372	125	

EUROPEAN COMMISSION
REPRESENTATION IN IRELAND

18 Dawson Street, Dublin 2
Tel: (01) 634 1111 _ Fax: (01) 634 1112

Need to know more ...

- about the EU?

- about Enlargement?

- about EU Policies?

- about the Future of Europe?

For general information about the EU as it
relates to Ireland, latest news, citizens' rights,
information providers, schools facilities,
etc ...
www.euireland.ie

or call to or phone our **PUBLIC
INFORMATION CENTRE** at **18 Dawson Street,
Dublin 2**

Laois-Offaly

Elected

Brian Cowen (FF)*	1st Count
Tom Parlon (PD)	5th Count
Olwyn Enright (FG)	6th Count
John Moloney (FF)*	6th Count
Seán Fleming (FF)*	6th Count

Voting by Party

1st Preference	Number	%	% 1997
Fianna Fáil	32,432	51.30	49.85
Fine Gael	14,553	23.02	28.38
Labour	1,600	2.53	11.61
Prog Democrats	9,088	14.38	—
Green Party	520	0.82	—
Sinn Féin	2,600	4.11	—
Christian Solidarity	142	0.22	—
Others	2,282	3.61	1.54

Statistics

Population	112,062	
Electorate	95,373	
Total Poll	63,888	66.99
Spoiled Votes	671	1.05
Valid Poll	63,217	66.28
Seats	5	
Quota	10,537	
Candidates	14	

Seats

FF	3
FG	1
PD	1
PD gain from FG	

The constituency of Laois-Offaly is unchanged since the 1997 General Election.

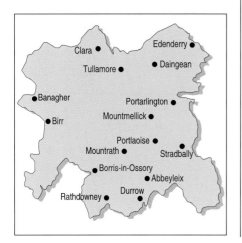

Brian Cowen (FF)

Home Address
Ballard, Tullamore, Co Offaly
Business Address
Department of Foreign Affairs, Iveagh House, 80 St Stephen's Green, Dublin 2
Telephone
Constituency Office (0506) 219 76; *Business* (01) 478 0822
Birth Place/Date
Tullamore. January 1960
Married
Mary Molloy. 2 daughters
Education
Ardscoil Naomh Ciaran, Clara, Co Offaly; Mount St Joseph's College, Roscrea, Co Tipperary; University College, Dublin (BCL); Incorporated Law Society of Ireland, Dublin
Occupation
Government Minister. Formerly solicitor

Brian Cowen was re-appointed Minister of Foreign Affairs in June 2002. He was first appointed to the post in January 2000. He was Minister for Health and Children June 1997–January 2000; Minister for Transport, Energy and Communications January 1993–December 1994; Minister for Labour February 1992–January 1993. He was first elected to the Dáil in a by-election in June 1984 caused by the death of his father, Bernard Cowen. That was the first time he had contested an election for public office.

Party front bench spokesperson on Agriculture, Food and Forestry December 1994–March 1997 and on Health March to June 1997.

Member, Offaly County Council 1984–92; Offaly County Vocational Education Committee 1989–92; British-Irish Inter-Parliamentary Body 1991–92.

He is a son of the late Bernard Cowen, Fianna Fáil deputy for Laois-Offaly 1969–73 and 1977–84; Senator 1973–77 and Minister of State at the Department of Agriculture March–December 1982.

Tom Parlon (PD)

Home Address
Coolderry, Birr, Co Offaly
Constituency Office
Hamilton House, Emmet Street, Birr
Business Address
Office of Public Works, 51 St Stephen's Green, Dublin 2
Telephone
Constituency office (0509) 23737; *Office* (01) 6476000
Birth Place/Date
Roscrea, Co Tipperary. 19 August 1953
Married
Martha Loughnane. 3 daughters, 2 sons
Education
Coolderry National School; Roscrea CBS; Gurteen Agricultural College
Occupation
Minister of State. Formerly farmer

Tom Parlon was appointed Minister of State at the Department of Finance with responsibility for the Office of Public Works in June 2002. He is a new Dáil deputy who joined the Progressive Democrats shortly before the general election and won the first seat for the party in Laois-Offaly. He was a member of the Progressive Democrats' negotiating team for the Programme of Government.

President, Irish Farmers' Association 1997–2001; Treasurer 1994–97; Deputy President 1991–93. Played minor hurling for Offaly.

Olwyn Enright (FG)

Home Address
John's Place, Birr, Co Offaly
Constituency Office
1 John's Place, Birr
2 Cormac Street, Tullamore
Telephone
Home (0509) 23893; *Birr Office* (0509) 22326;
Fax (0509) 20802; *Tullamore Office*
(0506) 29870
Website www.olwynenright.com
Birth Place/Date
Birr. 1 July 1974
Education
St Brendan's Community School, Birr;
University College, Dublin (BCL); Law Society
of Ireland; University College, Galway (Dip
Community Development Practice)
Occupation
Solicitor

Olwyn Enright is a new Dáil deputy. She was
appointed front bench spokesperson for
Education and Science.

She has been a member of Offaly County
Council since 1999. Member, Midland
Regional Authority. Chairperson, Birr Vintage
Week.

She is a daughter of Tom Enright, former TD
1969–92 and 1997–2002, Senator 1993–97.

John Moloney (FF)

Home Address
27 Patrick Street, Mountmellick, Co Laois
Constituency Office
26 Patrick Street, Mountmellick
Telephone
Home/Office (0502) 24391;
Mobile 087 277 0147
Birth Place/Date
Port Laoise, Co Laois. 12 June 1953
Married
Patricia McEvoy. 2 sons, 1 daughter
Education
Patrician Brothers, Ballyfin, Co Laois
Occupation
Full-time public representative. Formerly air
traffic controller, publican and undertaker

John Moloney was first elected to the Dáil in
June 1997. He had been a candidate in the
1992 general election. In the 28th Dáil he was
Government Whip on the Oireachtas
Committee on Education and Science;
member of Committees on Tourism, Sport
and Recreation and Family, Community and
Social Affairs.

Member, Laois County Council since 1981
(Chairperson 1989/90). Member, Midlands
Health Board; Chairperson, Mountmellick
Community Employment Scheme;
Mountmellick Tidy Towns Committee;
Kyletelisha Environmental Group.

John Moloney represents the third generation
of his family to serve on Laois County Council.

Seán Fleming (FF)

Home Address
Silveracre, Castletown, Port Laoise, Co Laois
Telephone
Home (0502) 32692
Birth Place/Date
The Swan, Co Laois. February 1958
Married
Mary O'Gorman. 1 son
Education
Salesian College, Ballinakill; University
College, Dublin (BComm); Fellow of the
Institute of Chartered Accountants
Occupation
Full-time public representative. Formerly
accountant and Financial Director of Fianna
Fáil at national level

Seán Fleming was first elected to the Dáil in
1997 at his first attempt in a general election.
He was vice-chairperson, Oireachtas
Committee on Finance in 28th Dáil.

Member, Laois County Council since 1999.

Laois-Offaly

Seats 5 Quota 10,537	1st Count	2nd Count Transfer of **Cowen** Surplus	3rd Count Transfer of **Fettes, Redmond, McCormack, Kelly** Votes	4th Count Transfer of **Dwyer** Votes	5th Count Transfer of **Buckley, Stanley** Votes	6th Count Transfer of **Killally** Votes
BUCKLEY, Molly (Ind)	1,695	*(+88)* 1,783	*(+183)* 1,966	*(+390)* 2,356		
COWEN, Brian* (FF)	12,529					
DWYER, John (Lab)	1,600	*(+75)* 1,675	*(+134)* 1,809			
FETTES, Christopher (GP)	520	*(+9)* 529				
ENRIGHT, Olwyn (FG)	8,053	*(+202)* 8,255	*(+148)* 8,403	*(+494)* 8,897	*(+1,308)* 10,205	*(+800)* 11,005
FLANAGAN, Charles* (FG)	6,500	*(+30)* 6,530	*(+116)* 6,646	*(+219)* 6,865	*(+519)* 7,384	*(+222)* 7,606
FLEMING, Seán* (FF)	7,091	*(+439)* 7,530	*(+112)* 7,642	*(+86)* 7,728	*(+633)* 8,361	*(+2,092)* 10,453
KELLY, John (Ind)	236	*(+1)* 237				
KILLALLY, Gerard (FF)	4,719	*(+668)* 5,387	*(+50)* 5,437	*(+93)* 5,530	*(+532)* 6,062	
MCCORMACK, Joe (Ind)	351	*(+2)* 353				
MOLONEY, John* (FF)	8,093	*(+167)* 8,260	*(+83)* 8,343	*(+41)* 8,384	*(+464)* 8,848	*(+2,124)* 10,972
PARLON, Tom (PD)	9,088	*(+270)* 9,358	*(+173)* 9,531	*(+158)* 9,689	*(+883)* 10,572	
REDMOND, Michael (CSP)	142	*(+2)* 144				
STANLEY, Brian (SF)	2,600	*(+39)* 2,639	*(+181)* 2,820	*(+197)* 3,017		
NON-TRANSFERABLE		0	83	131	1034	824

Michael Noonan gets a custard pie in the face, minutes after arriving in Boyle, Co Roscommon.

Limerick East

Elected

Willie O'Dea (FF)*	1st Count
Michael Noonan (FG)*	1st Count
Peter Power (FF)	10th Count
Tim O'Malley (PD)	11th Count
Jan O'Sullivan (Lab)*	11th Count

Voting by Party

1st Preference	Number	%	% 1997
Fianna Fáil	19,973	39.95	39.72
Fine Gael	13,919	27.84	26.51
Labour	4,629	9.26	9.19
Prog Democrats	4,885	9.77	12.42
Green Party	917	1.83	1.61
Christian Solidarity	86	0.17	—
Others	5,677	11.18	0.61

Statistics

Population	105,548	
Electorate	80,593	
Total Poll	50,513	62.68
Spoiled Votes	513	1.02
Valid Poll	50,000	62.04
Seats	5	
Quota	8,334	
Candidates	15	

Seats

FF	2
FG	1
Lab	1
PD	1
No change	

The Limerick East constituency lost 2,097 population to Limerick West in the 1998 revision.

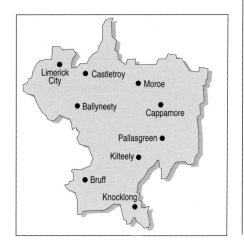

Willie O'Dea (FF)

Home Address
Milltown, Kilteely, Co Limerick
Constituency Office
2 Glenview Gardens, Farranshore, Limerick
Business Address
Department of Justice, Equality and Law Reform, Dún Aimhirgin, 43–49 Mespil Road, Dublin 4
Telephone
Home (061) 454488; *Business* (01) 663 2659
Birth Place/Date
Limerick. November 1952
Married
Geraldine Kennedy
Education
Patrician Brothers, Ballyfin, Co Laois; University College, Dublin; King's Inns, Dublin; Institute of Certified Accountants (BCL, LLM, BL, Certified Accountant)
Occupation
Minister of State. Formerly accountant

Willie O'Dea was appointed Minister of State at the Department of Justice, Equality and Law Reform in June 2002 with responsibility for equality issues including disability issues. He served as Minister of State at the Department of Education, Science and Technology, with special responsibility for Adult Education, Youth Affairs and School Transport 1997–2002. He was Minister of State at the Departments of Justice and Health 1993–94; Minister of State at the Department of Justice February 1992–January 1993. He was first elected to the Dáil in February 1982. He contested Limerick East unsuccessfully in the 1981 general election.

Michael Noonan (FG)

Home Address
18 Gouldavoher Estate, Father Russell Road, Limerick
Telephone
Home (061) 229350
Birth Place/Date
Limerick. 21 May 1943
Married
Florence Knightly. 3 sons, 2 daughters
Education
St Patrick's Secondary School, Glin, Co Limerick; St Patrick's Teachers' Training College, Drumcondra, Dublin; University College, Dublin (BA, HDipEd)
Occupation
Full-time public representative. Formerly teacher

Michael Noonan was first elected to the Dáil in 1981. He was elected leader of Fine Gael in February 2001 but resigned in June 2002 after what was regarded as a disastrous general election for the party with a loss of 23 seats. He was party spokesperson for Northern Ireland while leader. Party spokesperson on Finance 1997–2001. He was Minister for Health 1994–97; Minister for Energy January–March 1987; Minister for Industry and Commerce 1986–87; Minister for Justice 1982–86.

Member, Limerick County Council 1974–82 and 1991–94; Mid-Western Health Board, 1974–82 and 1991–94.

Member, Association of Secondary Teachers of Ireland (ASTI).

Peter Power (FF)

Home Address
Kilfeara, Ennis Road, Limerick
Telephone
Home (061) 452800
Birth Place/Date
Limerick. 26 January 1966
Married
Lorraine Power. 1 daughter
Education
John F. Kennedy, Ennis Road, Limerick; Ard
Scoil Rís, Ennis Road; University College, Cork
(BCL); Blackhall Place (Diploma in Property
Taxation)
Occupation
Public representative. Solicitor

Peter Power is a new Dáil deputy. He
contested the 1997 general election.

Member, Fianna Fáil National Executive
1989–91.

Elected as Alderman to Limerick Corporation
in 1999. Deputy Mayor 2000–2001.
Chairperson, Limerick Inner City Renewal
Committee. Member, Limerick City Enterprise
Board. Member of numerous community,
cultural and sporting organisations.

Tim O'Malley (PD)

Home Address
Milltown Ballysimon, Co Limerick
Constituency Office
Regional Pharmacy, Dooradoyle, Limerick
Business Address
Department of Health and Children, Hawkins
House, Dublin 2
Telephone
Constituency office (061) 229 401;
Fax (061) 228 718; *Office* (01) 635 4000
Website www.Timomalley.ie
Birth Place/Date
Limerick. 3 July 1944
Married
Peg Kelly. 2 sons, 2 daughters
Education
Model School, Limerick; Crescent College,
Limerick; University College, Dublin (BSc
Pharm, MPSI, FPSI)
Occupation
Minister of State. Former pharmacist

Tim O'Malley was appointed Minister of State
at the Department of Health and Children with
responsibility for Disability, Mental Health
Services and Food Safety in June 2002. He is
a new Dáil deputy. He won the seat held by
his cousin Desmond O'Malley until his
retirement from the Dáil at this election.

He contested the by-election caused by the
death of Jim Kemmy in 1997.

Member, Limerick County Council
1991–2002. Member, Limerick County
Enterprise Board; Bruff Area Committee;
Limerick Chamber of Commerce; Mid-
Western Health Board; Associations of Health
Boards of Ireland; Former President of the
Irish Pharmaceutical Union.

Jan O'Sullivan (Lab)

Home Address
7 Lanahone Avenue, Corbally, Limerick
Constituency Office
Mechanics Institute, Hartstonge Street,
Limerick
Telephone
Home (061) 346522; *Constituency Office*
(061) 312316; *Fax* (061) 313707
Mobile 087 243 0299
Birth Place/Date
Limerick. 6 December 1950
Married
Dr Paul O'Sullivan. 1 son, 1 daughter
Education
Villiers School, Limerick. Trinity College,
Dublin
Occupation
Full-time public representative. Formerly pre-
school teacher

Jan O'Sullivan was first elected to the Dáil in
1998 in a by-election caused by the death of
Jim Kemmy. Served on Oireachtas
Committee on Justice, Equality, Defence and
Women's Rights in last Dáil. Party
spokesperson on Equality and Law Reform.

She was elected to the Seanad in 1993 and
was leader of the Labour Group there
1993–97. Was member of Forum for Peace
and Reconciliation and the National Economic
and Social Forum.

Member, Democratic Socialist Party until the
merger with the Labour Party.

Member, Limerick City Council since 1985.
Mayor of Limerick 1993–94. Leader of Labour
group. Member, Mid-Western Health Board.
Former member of City of Limerick Vocational
Education Committee.

Member of Board of the Island Theatre
Company. Chairperson CARA (Ireland)
Housing Association; Chairperson, Limerick-
Quimper Twinning Committee; on the Board
of Rape Crisis Centre, Red Ribbon Project.
Member of Amnesty International.

Limerick East

Seats 5 Quota 8,334	1st Count	2nd Count Transfer of **O'Dea** Surplus	3rd Count Transfer of **Noonan** Surplus	4th Count Transfer of **Bennis, Ryan A, O'Donoghue** Votes	5th Count Transfer of **Kelly** Votes
BENNIS, Nora (Ind)	479	*(+57)* 536	*(+9)* 545		
GILLIGAN, John (Ind)	1,176	*(+139)* 1,315	*(+18)* 1,333	*(+46)* 1,379	*(+197)* 1,576
HOURIGAN, Timothy Edward (GP)	917	*(+53)* 970	*(+15)* 985	*(+68)* 1,053	*(+24)* 1,077
JACKMAN, Mary (FG)	4,468	*(+244)* 4,712	*(+697)* 5,409	*(+88)* 5,497	*(+32)* 5,529
KELLY, Michael John (Ind)	677	*(+59)* 736	*(+15)* 751	*(+13)* 764	
KENNEDY, Pat (Ind)	2,092	*(+221)* 2,313	*(+53)* 2,366	*(+68)* 2,434	*(+133)* 2,567
NOONAN, Michael* (FG)	9,451				
O'DEA, Willie* (FF)	13,174				
O'DONOGHUE, Conor (CSP)	86	*(+9)* 95	*(+1)* 96		
O'MALLEY, Tim (PD)	4,885	*(+442)* 5,327	*(+88)* 5,415	*(+75)* 5,490	*(+16)* 5,506
O'SULLIVAN, Jan* (Lab)	4,629	*(+419)* 5,048	*(+145)* 5,193	*(+62)* 5,255	*(+101)* 5,356
POWER, Peter (FF)	3,881	*(+1,957)* 5,838	*(+41)* 5,879	*(+90)* 5,969	*(+38)* 6,007
RYAN, Aidan (Ind)	19	*(+8)* 27	*(+2)* 29		
RYAN, Tom (Ind)	1,148	*(+121)* 1,269	*(+20)* 1,289	*(+72)* 1,361	*(+44)* 1,405
WADE, Eddie* (FF)	2,918	*(+1,111)* 4,029	*(+13)* 4,042	*(+42)* 4,084	*(+21)* 4,105
NON-TRANSFERABLE		0		46	158

6th Count	7th Count	8th Count	9th Count	10th Count	11th Count
Transfer of **Hourigan** Votes	Transfer of **Ryan, T** Votes	Transfer of **Gilligan** Votes	Transfer of **Kennedy** Votes	Transfer of **Wade** Votes	Transfer of **Power** Surplus
(+104) 1,680	*(+240)* 1,920				
(+128) 5,657	*(+185)* 5,842	*(+137)* 5,979	*(+590)* 6,569	*(+417)* 6,986	*(+176)* 7,162
(+83) 2,650	*(+190)* 2,840	*(+539)* 3,379			
(+125) 5,631	*(+151)* 5,782	*(+90)* 5,872	*(+452)* 6,324	*(+629)* 6,953	*(+770)* 7,723
(+359) 5,715	*(+212)* 5,927	*(+396)* 6,323	*(+635)* 6,958	*(+298)* 7,256	*(+211)* 7,467
(+73) 6,080	*(+173)* 6,253	*(+172)* 6,425	*(+426)* 6,851	*(+2,640)* 9,491	
(+73) 1,478					
(+29) 4,134	*(+132)* 4,266	*(+57)* 4,323	*(+206)* 4,529		
103	195	529	1070	545	

Limerick West

Elected

John Cregan (FF)	1st Count
Michael Collins (FF)*	2nd Count
Dan Neville (FG)*	4th Count

Voting by Party

1st Preference	Number	%	% 1997
Fianna Fáil	19,059	53.43	32.44
Fine Gael	14,856	41.65	37.19
Green Party	948	2.66	—
Christian Solidarity	144	0.40	—
Others	662	1.86	21.96

Statistics

Population	62,970	
Electorate	53,879	
Total Poll	36,145	67.09
Spoiled Votes	476	1.32
Valid Poll	35,669	66.20
Seats	3	
Quota	8,918	
Candidates	7	

Seats

FF	2
FG	1
FF gain from FG	

The Limerick West constituency received 2,097 population in the Croom area from Limerick East in the 1998 revision.

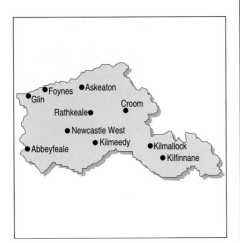

John Cregan (FF)

Home Address
Church Street, Drumcollogher, Co Limerick
Constituency Office
Church Street, Newcastle West, Co Limerick
Telephone
Constituency office (069) 77671;
Fax (069) 77672
Birth Place/Date
Drumcollogher. 21 May 1961
Married
Patsy Breen. 1 son, 2 daughters
Education
St Joseph's National School; St Mary's Secondary School, Drumcollogher
Occupation
Public representative. Fomerly Telecom Éireann employee

John Cregan is a new Dáil deputy. He was a Senator, Labour Panel, 1998–2002. Member, Oireachtas Committee on Justice, Equality and Law Reform in 28th Dáil.

Member, Limerick County Council since 1991. Member, Mid Western Health Board; Association of Health Boards in Ireland.

Michael Collins (FF)

Home Address
White Oaks, Rod House Hill, Patrickswell, Co Limerick
Constituency Office
Convent Terrace, Abbeyfeale, Co Limerick
Telephone
Home (061) 355081; *Constituency office* ((068) 31126; *Fax* (061) 355902;
Mobile 086 245 3773
Birth Place/Date
Abbeyfeale. 29 November 1940
Married
Una Farrell. 1 son, 2 daughters
Education
St Munchin's College, Limerick
Occupation
Full-time public representative

Michael Collins was first elected to the Dáil in 1997. He served on Oireachtas committees dealing with Agriculture, European Affairs and Arts, Heritage and the Gaeltacht.

Member, Limerick County Council 1979–99 (Chairperson 1990/91). He is a brother of Gerry Collins, Dáil deputy for Limerick West 1967–97; Member of the European Parliament since 1994 and a former Minister in the posts of Foreign Affairs, Justice and Post and Telegraphs.

He is a son of James J. Collins, Dáil deputy for Limerick West 1948–67.

Dan Neville (FG)

Home Address
Kiltannan, Croagh, Co Limerick
Telephone
Home/Constituency office (061) 396351;
Fax (061) 396351; *Mobile* 086 243 5536
Birth Place/Date
Croagh. 12 December 1946
Married
Goretti O'Callaghan. 2 sons, 2 daughters
Education
Adare CBS, Co Limerick; University of
Limerick, School of Management Studies;
University College, Cork (Industrial
Engineering, Personnel Management, Social
Science)
Occupation
Full-time public representative. Formerly
personnel manager

Dan Neville is Fine Gael deputy spokesperson
on Health and Children. He was a member of
the Oireachtas Committee on Health and
Children in the 28th Dáil. He was first elected
to the Dáil in 1997 when Fine Gael took two
seats in Limerick West for the first time. In
this election Dan Neville defeated his running
mate Michael Finucane by only one vote as
Fianna Fáil won back a second seat. Dan
Neville was a candidate in the general
elections of 1987 and 1992. He was a
Senator, Labour Panel, 1989–97; Deputy
Leader of Fine Gael in the Seanad and
spokesperson on Justice and Law Reform
1992–97.

Member, Limerick County Council since 1985.

President of the Irish Association of
Suicidology.

Seats 3 Quota 8,918	1st Count	2nd Count Transfer of **Cregan** Surplus	3rd Count Transfer of **Collins** Surplus	4th Count Transfer of **Briody, Mac Domhnaill, O'Riordan** Votes
BRIODY, Marcus (GP)	948	*(+54)* 1,002	*(+136)* 1,138	
COLLINS, Michael* (FF)	8,236	*(+1,290)* 9,526		
CREGAN, John (FF)	10,823			
FINUCANE, Michael* (FG)	7,410	*(+274)* 7,684	*(+183)* 7,867	*(+696)* 8,563
MAC DOMHNAILL, Mike (Ind)	662	*(+48)* 710	*(+79)* 789	
NEVILLE, Dan* (FG)	7,446	*(+232)* 7,678	*(+184)* 7,862	*(+702)* 8,564
O'RIORDAN, Patrick (CSP)	144	*(+7)* 151	*(+26)* 177	
NON-TRANSFERABLE				706

Longford-Roscommon

Elected

Denis Naughten (FG)*	8th Count
Michael Finneran (FF)	10th Count
Peter Kelly (FF)	10th Count
Mae Sexton (PD)	10th Count

Voting by Party

1st Preference	Number	%	% 1997
Fianna Fáil	20,251	40.76	47.02
Fine Gael	15,251	30.69	36.91
Labour	638	1.28	1.48
Prog Democrats	4,679	9.42	4.84
Green Party	426	0.86	—
Sinn Féin	1,673	3.37	—
Christian Solidarity	80	0.16	—
Others	6,691	13.47	9.75

Statistics

Population	82,141	
Electorate	70,650	
Total Poll	50,310	71.21
Spoiled Votes	621	1.23
Valid Poll	49,689	70.33
Seats	4	
Quota	9,938	
Candidates	15	

Seats

FF	2
FG	1
PD	1
PD gain from FG	

The Longford-Roscommon constituency is unchanged since the 1997 General Election.

Denis Naughten (FG)

Home Address
Ardkeenan, Drum, Athlone, Co Roscommon
Constituency Office
Abbey Street, Roscommon
Telephone
Home (0902) 37324; *Constituency Office* (0903) 27557; *Fax* (0903) 27556
Birth Place/Date
Drum, Athlone. June 1973
Education
St Aloysius College, Athlone; University College, Dublin; University College, Cork (BSc)
Occupation
Full-time public representative. Formerly research scientist

Denis Naughten was first elected in 1997 as the youngest TD in the 28th Dáil. Previously Senator, Agricultural Panel, 1997. Party spokesperson on Adult Education, Youth Affairs and School Transport 1997–2000; Enterprise, Trade and Employment 2000–01; deputy spokesperson on Public Enterprise 2001–02. Member of following committees in last Dáil: Education and Science, and Tourism, Sport and Recreation 1997–2000; Enterprise and Small Business 2000–01; Tourism, Sport and Recreation 2001–02.

Member, Roscommon County Council since 1997; Western Health Board since 1997; Association of Health Boards 1997–99.

He is son of the late Liam Naughten, Dáil deputy 1982–89; Senator, Agricultural Panel 1981–82 and 1989–96; Leas-Chathoirleach of the Seanad 1989–95 and Cathaoirleach 1995–96.

Michael Finneran (FF)

Home Address
Riverside Avenue, Roscommon
Telephone
Home (0903) 22245
Birth Place/Date
Roscommon. 10 September 1947
Married
Elizabeth Walsh. 2 sons, 2 daughters
Education
Fevagh National School, Co Roscommon; Summerhill College, Sligo
Occupation
Public Representative. Formerly psychiatric nurse

Michael Finneran is a new Dáil deputy after over a decade in the Seanad. He contested Longford-Roscommon in the general elections of 1992 and 1997. Senator, Administrative Panel, 1989–2002. Government spokesperson on Finance in Seanad 1997–2002.

One of two Irish representatives on the Consultative Council to the European Commission, 1988–92, forerunner to the Committee of the Regions.

Member, Roscommon County Council since 1989; Western Health Board since 1985.

Peter Kelly (FF)

Home Address
Lanherne, Battery Road, Longford
Constituency Office
Church Street, Longford
Telephone
Home (043) 46304; *Constituency Office*
(043) 45070
Birth Place/Date
Longford. 17 August 1944
Married
Maura Hester. 2 sons, 1 daughter
Education
St Michael's Boys' School, Longford; St
Mary's College, Dundalk, Co Louth
Occupation
Full-time public representative. Formerly
funeral director and publican

Peter Kelly is a new Dáil deputy. Member,
Fianna Fáil National Executive.

Member, Longford County Council since 1985
and a former chairperson. Member, County
Longford Tourism; Midland Regional
Authority.

Mae Sexton (PD)

Home Address
46 Demense, Longford
Telephone
Home (043) 41142; *Office* (043) 48300
Birth Place/Date
Dublin. 28 April 1955
Married
Tommy Sexton. 1 son, 1 daughter
Education
Convent of Mercy, Longford
Occupation
Full-time public representative. Formerly
company administrator

Mae Sexton is a new Dáil deputy.

Member, Longford County Council, Longford
Urban District Council, Midland Regional
Authority. Member of Chamber of Commerce
and of Irish delegation to European
Committee of the Regions, Brussels.

Longford-Roscommon

Seats 4 Quota 9,938	1st Count	2nd Count Transfer of **Killalea, Lenihan** Votes	3rd Count Transfer of **Ansbro** Votes	4th Count Transfer of **Baxter, Flanagan** Votes
ANSBRO, Catherine (GP)	426	*(+9)* 435		
BAXTER, Hugh (Lab)	638	*(+2)* 640	*(+84)* 724	
BELTON, Louis* (FG)	4,762	*(+5)* 4,767	*(+21)* 4,788	*(+133)* 4,921
CONNOR, John (FG)	3,829	*(+51)* 3,880	*(+19)* 3,899	*(+143)* 4,042
CROSBY, Tom (Ind)	2,123	*(+10)* 2,133	*(+11)* 2,144	*(+107)* 2,251
FINNERAN, Michael (FF)	6,502	*(+19)* 6,521	*(+16)* 6,537	*(+75)* 6,612
FLANAGAN, Luke 'Ming' (Ind)	779	*(+11)* 790	*(+50)* 840	
KELLY, Greg (FF)	6,430	*(+41)* 6,471	*(+19)* 6,490	*(+180)* 6,670
KELLY, Peter (FF)	7,319	*(+4)* 7,323	*(+11)* 7,334	*(+73)* 7,407
KILLALEA, Vincent (Ind)	191			
LENIHAN, Brian (CSP)	80			
NAUGHTEN, Denis* (FG)	6,660	*(+26)* 6,686	*(+36)* 6,722	*(+199)* 6,921
QUINN, Una (Ind)	3,598	*(+52)* 3,650	*(+88)* 3,738	*(+262)* 4,000
SEXTON, Mae (PD)	4,679	*(+20)* 4,699	*(+52)* 4,751	*(+154)* 4,905
WHELAN, Paul (SF)	1,673	*(+13)* 1,686	*(+16)* 1,702	*(+170)* 1,872
NON-TRANSFERABLE		8	12	68

Longford-Roscommon

5th Count	6th Count	7th Count	8th Count	9th Count	10th Count
Transfer of **Whelan** Votes	Transfer of **Crosby** Votes	Transfer of **Connor** Votes	Transfer of **Quinn** Votes	Transfer of **Naughton** Surplus	Transfer of **Belton** Votes
(+116) 5,037	*(+156)* 5,193	*(+512)* 5,705	*(+127)* 5,832	*(+383)* 6,215	
(+108) 4,150	*(+139)* 4,289				
(+171) 2,422					
(+118) 6,730	*(+428)* 7,158	*(+136)* 7,294	*(+887)* 8,181	*(+544)* 8,725	*(+191)* 8,916
(+227) 6,897	*(+117)* 7,014	*(+726)* 7,740	*(+719)* 8,459	*(+228)* 8,687	*(+175)* 8,862
(+227) 7,634	*(+238)* 7,872	*(+33)* 7,905	*(+75)* 7,980	*(+25)* 8,005	*(+1,313)* 9,318
(+155) 7,076	*(+355)* 7,431	*(+2,075)* 9,506	*(+2,108)* 11,614		
(+331) 4,331	*(+528)* 4,859	*(+506)* 5,365			
(+293) 5,198	*(+299)* 5,497	*(+61)* 5,558	*(+513)* 6,071	*(+230)* 6,301	*(+2,616)* 8,917
126	162	240	936	266	1,920

Louth

Elected

Dermot Ahern (FF)*	1st Count
Fergus O'Dowd (FG)	8th Count
Séamus Kirk (FF)*	8th Count
Arthur Morgan (SF)	8th Count

Voting by Party

1st Preference	Number	%	% 1997
Fianna Fáil	20,751	43.57	40.02
Fine Gael	9,635	20.23	27.90
Labour	3,185	6.69	10.50
Green Party	1,979	4.16	3.12
Sinn Féin	7,121	14.95	8.11
Christian Solidarity	79	0.17	—
Workers' Party	176	0.37	—
Others	4,697	9.86	5.04

Statistics

Population	92,166	
Electorate	81,952	
Total Poll	48,274	58.91
Spoiled Votes	651	1.35
Valid Poll	47,623	58.11
Seats	4	
Quota	9,525	
Candidates	15	

Seats

FF	2
FG	1
SF	1

SF gain from Lab

The Louth constituency is unchanged since the 1997 General Election.

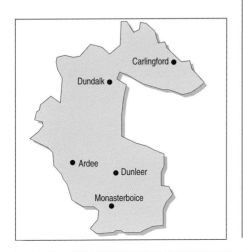

Dermot Ahern (FF)

Home Address
Hill Cottage, The Crescent, Blackrock, Co Louth
Business Address
Department of Communications, the Marine and Natural Resources, Leeson Lane, Dublin 2
Constituency Office
18 Francis Street, Dundalk, Co Louth
Telephone
Office (01) 6789807; *Fax* (01) 6763616; *Constituency Office* (042) 9339609 or (042) 9329016
Birth Place/Date
Drogheda. 2 February 1955
Married
Maeve Coleman. 2 daughters
Education
St Mary's College, Dundalk; University College, Dublin (BCL); Incorporated Law Society of Ireland
Occupation
Government Minister. Formerly solicitor

Dermot Ahern was appointed Minister for Communications, the Marine and Natural Resources in June 2002.

He was Minister for Social, Community and Family Affairs 1997–2002. He was Minister of State at the Department of the Taoiseach with special responsibility as Government Chief Whip, and Minister of State at the Department of Defence November 1991–February 1992. He was Assistant Government Chief Whip 1988–91. He was first elected to the Dáil in 1987.

He was Fianna Fáil Chief Whip, Leader of the House in opposition and in charge of party Parliamentary Strategy and Legislative Proposals in the Dáil 1995–97. Member of the British-Irish Inter-Parliamentary Body 1991–97 (co-chairman 1993–95).

Member of Louth County Council 1979–91.

Fergus O'Dowd (FG)

Home Address
24 St Mary's Villas, Drogheda, Co Louth
Telephone
Home (041) 983 3392
Birth Place/Date
Thurles, Co Tipperary. September 1948
Married
Margaret Thornton. 3 sons
Education
Drogheda CBS; Diploma in General and Rural Science
Occupation
Full-time public representative. Formerly teacher

Fergus O'Dowd is a new Dáil deputy. He was appointed front bench spokesperson for Community, Rural and Gaeltacht Affairs. He was a member of the Seanad (Administrative Panel) 1997–2002.

Member, Louth County Council since 1979. Member, Drogheda Corporation since 1974. Served three terms as Mayor (1977–78, 1981–82, 1994–95). Member, North Eastern Health Board. Founding Chairman of the Droichead Arts Centre, Drogheda. Campaigned for closure of Sellafield nuclear re-processing plant and against a local incinerator.

Séamus Kirk (FF)

Home Address
Rathiddy, Knockbridge, Co Louth
Telephone
Home (042) 93 31032
Birth Place/Date
Drumkeith, Co Louth. 26 April 1945
Married
Mary McGeough. 3 sons, 1 daughter
Education
Dundalk CBS
Occupation
Full-time public representative. Farmer

Séamus Kirk is Chairman of the Fianna Fáil Parliamentary Party. He was first elected to the Dáil in November 1982. Minister of State at the Department of Agriculture and Food with special responsibility for Horticulture, March 1987–February 1992. During the 28th Dáil he was a member of the All-Party Committee on the Constitution and the Oireachtas committees on Local Government and European Affairs.

Member, Forum for Peace and Reconciliation 1994–96. Member of the British-Irish Inter-Parliamentary Body.

Member, Louth County Council 1974–85; Louth County Health Committee 1974–85; Louth County Committee of Agriculture 1974–85; East Border Region Committee 1974–85.

Member, Gaelic Athletic Association since 1958. Member, Tidy Towns Committee.

Arthur Morgan (SF)

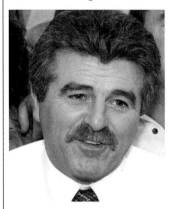

Home Address
Omeath, Co Louth
Constituency Office
7 Williamson's Place, Dundalk, and Rope Walk, Drogheda
Telephone
Constituency Office Telephone/Fax
(042) 9328859
Birth Place/Date
Omeath. 23 July 1954
Married
Marion Traynor
Education
St Brigid's National School, Omeath; St Michael's College, Omeath
Occupation
Full-time public representative. Formerly company director

Arthur Morgan is a new Dáil deputy. He contested the general elections in Louth in 1987 and 1989.

He is a former member of the Sinn Féin Ard Comhairle 1997–2001. He was a member of the party's background team in the negotiation of the Good Friday Agreement 1998. He was convicted for the possession of explosives and weapons and imprisoned in the H-Blocks in the Maze Prison 1977–84. He took part in the H-Block protest in the early 1980s. He made the case in 1986 to the Louth Comhairle Ceanntair that Sinn Féin should abandon its abstentionist policy.

Member, Louth County Council since 1999.

Louth

Seats 4 Quota 9,525	1st Count	2nd Count Transfer of **Maguire, Short, Ó Gógáin, McMahon** Votes	3rd Count Transfer of **Godfrey, Bellew** Votes
AHERN, Dermot* (FF)	9,603		
BELL, Michael* (Lab)	3,185	*(+52)* 3,237	*(+151)* 3,388
BELLEW, Martin (Ind)	1,307	*(+103)* 1,410	
BRENNAN, Terry (FG)	4,130	*(+77)* 4,207	*(+235)* 4,442
GODFREY, Frank (Ind)	473	*(+29)* 502	
GREHAN, Mary (Ind)	2,384	*(+112)* 2,496	*(+525)* 3,021
KIRK, Séamus* (FF)	6,495	*(+66)* 6,561	*(+207)* 6,768
MAGUIRE, Michael F (CSP)	79		
MAHER, Frank (FF)	4,653	*(+15)* 4,668	*(+139)* 4,807
MARTIN, Bernadette (GP)	1,979	*(+130)* 2,109	*(+197)* 2,306
MCMAHON, Aidan Francis (Ind)	294		
MORGAN, Arthur (SF)	7,121	*(+154)* 7,275	*(+213)* 7,488
O'DOWD, Fergus (FG)	5,505	*(+35)* 5,540	*(+146)* 5,686
Ó GÓGÁIN, Liam (Ind)	239		
SHORT, Peter (WP)	176		
NON-TRANSFERABLE		15	99

4th Count	5th Count	6th Count	7th Count	8th Count
Transfer of **Ahern** Surplus	Transfer of **Martin** Votes	Transfer of **Grehan** Votes	Transfer of **Bell** Votes	Transfer of **Maher** Votes
(+3) 3,391	*(+341)* 3,732	*(+385)* 4,117		
(+7) 4,449	*(+221)* 4,670	*(+724)* 5,394	*(+652)* 6,046	*(+87)* 6,133
(+9) 3,030	*(+491)* 3,521			
(+43) 6,811	*(+182)* 6,993	*(+651)* 7,644	*(+316)* 7,960	*(+2,027)* 9,987
(+4) 4,811	*(+135)* 4,946	*(+72)* 5,018	*(+625)* 5,643	
(+3) 2,309				
(+7) 7,495	*(+310)* 7,805	*(+669)* 8,474	*(+518)* 8,992	*(+485)* 9,477
(+2) 5,688	*(+410)* 6,098	*(+248)* 6,346	*(+1,394)* 7,740	*(+2,435)* 10,175
	219	772	612	609

Mayo

Elected

Jerry Cowley (Ind)	5thCount
Michael Ring (FG)*	5th Count
Enda Kenny (FG)*	9th Count
John Carty (FF)	10th Count
Beverly Cooper-Flynn (FF)*	10th Count

Voting by Party

1st Preference	Number	%	% 1997
Fianna Fáil	25,380	39.98	42.95
Fine Gael	23,862	37.59	48.75
Prog Democrats	919	1.45	—
Green Party	669	1.05	1.52
Sinn Féin	2,085	3.28	—
Others	10,565	16.64	5.59

Statistics

Population	111,524	
Electorate	94,854	
Total Poll	64,270	67.76
Spoiled Votes	790	1.23
Valid Poll	63,480	66.92
Seats	5	
Quota	10,581	
Candidates	14	

Seats

FF	2
FG	2
Ind	1
Ind gain from FG	

The Mayo constituency is unchanged since the 1997 General Election.

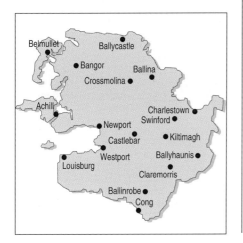

Jerry Cowley (Ind)

Home Address
Mulranny, Co Mayo
Telephone
Office (098) 36287; *Fax* (098) 36287;
Mobile 087 224 9691
Birth Place/Date
Galway. 11 November 1952
Married
Teresa Staunton. 3 sons, 2 daughters
Education
De La Salle School, Castlebar, Co Mayo;
Breaffy National School, Ballina, Co Mayo; St
Muredach's College, Ballina; University
College, Galway (MB, BCH, BAO, DCH,
D.Obst); MRCGP; MICGP; LLB, BL
Occupation
Full-time public representative. Medical
doctor. Barrister

Jerry Cowley is a new Dáil deputy. He
campaigned on a platform of improved
medical facilities for the Western region.
He had the distinction of receiving votes from
every box in the Mayo constituency.

Former chairperson and co-founder of the
National Federation of Group Water Schemes.
Director, Irish Council for Social Housing.
Chairperson, Campaign for North-South
Helicopter Medical Services. Chairperson,
St Brendan's Village, Mulranny (sheltered
housing). Chairperson, Safe Home
Programme.

Michael Ring (FG)

Home Address
The Paddock, Wesport, Co. Mayo
Constituency Office
Quay Street, Wesport
Telephone
Home (098) 25734; *Constituency Office*
(098) 27012; *Fax* (098) 27644
Birth Place/Date
Westport. 24 December 1953
Married
Ann Fitzgerald. 1 son, 2 daughters
Education
Westport Vocational School
Occupation
Full-time public representative

Michael Ring was first elected to the Dáil in a
by-election in June 1994 in the old Mayo
West constituency following the resignation
of Deputy Pádraig Flynn (FF) to become an EU
Commissioner. Was party spokesperson on
Agriculture – Livestock, Breeding and
Horticulture 1997–2000; deputy spokesperson
on Health 2000–02.

Member of Joint Committee on Health and
Children in last Dáil. Member British-Irish
Inter-Parliamentary Body.

Member, Mayo County Council since 1991
and a number of subsidiary committees;
Westport Urban District Council since 1979
(chairman 1982/83 and 1988/89).

Enda Kenny (FG)

Home Address
Tucker Street, Castlebar, Co Mayo
Telephone
Home (094) 25600
Birth Place/Date
Castlebar. April 1951
Married
Fionnuala O'Kelly. 2 sons, 1 daughter
Education
St Gerald's Secondary School, Castlebar; St
Patrick's Training College, Drumcondra,
Dublin; University College, Galway
Occupation
Leader of Fine Gael. Formerly national school
teacher

Enda Kenny was elected Leader of Fine Gael
in June 2002 following the resignation of
Michael Noonan in the wake of what was
seen as a disastrous election for the party. It
lost 23 seats. Enda Kenny had been defeated
by Mr Noonan in the contest for the
leadership in January 2001. He was Minister
for Tourism and Trade 1994–97. He was
Minister of State at the Department of
Education and at the Department of Labour
with special responsibility for Youth Affairs,
February 1986–March 1987. He was first
elected to the Dáil in November 1975.

He served as party spokesperson on Arts,
Heritage, Gaeltacht and the Islands 1997–2002.
Fine Gael Chief Whip 1992–94 and
spokesperson on Regional Development 1994.
Spokesperson on the Gaeltacht 1987–88 and in
1982; on Western Development 1982; on
Youth Affairs and Sport 1977–80. Chairperson,
Fine Gael Economic Affairs Committee
1991–92. Member, New Ireland Forum. British-
Irish Inter-Parliamentary Body 1991–92.

Member, Mayo County Council 1975–95;
former chairperson, Mayo Vocational
Education Committee, Western Health Board.

He is a son of the late Henry Kenny, Dáil
deputy for Mayo South 1954–69 and for Mayo
West 1969–75, and Parliamentary Secretary
to the Minister for Finance 1973–75.

John Carty (FF)

Home Address
Carrowmore, Knock, Co Mayo
Constituency Office
Ballyhaunis Road, Claremorris, Co Mayo
Telephone
Home (094) 88149; *Constituency office*
(094) 72707
Birth Place/Date
Knock. 12 August 1950
Married
Kathleen Regan. 6 sons, 2 daughters
Education
St Patrick's College, Ballyhaunis, Co Mayo;
Warrenstown Agricultural College, Co Meath;
St Patrick's College, Maynooth (Diploma in
Local History)
Occupation
Full-time public representative. Formerly
Agricultural Officer. Farmer

John Carty is a new Dáil deputy. He secured
his seat at the expense of Fianna Fáil running
mate, Tom Moffat.

He is a member of Mayo County Council
since 1999. Chairperson, Strategic Policy
Committee on Housing and Mayo County
Development Board. Member, Western
Railway Committee and Mayo Tourism Board.
Vice-President of Aghamore GAA Club.
Chairperson, South Mayo Family Research
Centre, Ballinrobe.

Beverly Cooper-Flynn (FF)

Home Address
2 The Manor Village, Westport Road,
Castlebar, Co Mayo
Constituency Office
Newtown, Castlebar
Telephone
Home (094) 26800; *Constituency Office*
(094) 27035; *Mobile* (087) 256 0229
Birth Place/Date
Tuam, Co Galway. 9 June 1966
Education
St Joseph's Secondary School, Castlebar;
University College, Dublin (BComm), IPM, ACII
Occupation
Full-time public representative. Formerly
financial services manager

Beverly Cooper-Flynn was first elected to the
Dáil in 1997. She was a candidate in the Mayo
West by-election in June 1994. She was twice
expelled from the Fianna Fáil Parliamentary
Party during the 28th Dáil. Firstly in February
1999 for voting against a Dáil motion asking her
father, Pádraig Flynn, to clarify his position on
allegations he received a financial contribution.
She was re-admitted in November 1999.
Secondly, in April 2001 following her libel case
against RTÉ which she won but had to pay the
costs. She ran as a Fianna Fáil candidate in this
election with the backing of the party.

Former member of Public Accounts
Committee. Member of National Economic
and Social Forum. Member of following
committees in 28th Dáil: Equality, Defence
and Women's Rights; Health and Children.

Member of Mayo County Council since
September 1996. Member, Western Health
Board (Chairperson 1999/2000).

She is a daughter of Pádraig Flynn, Fianna Fáil
TD for Mayo West 1977–93, a former Minister
for Justice, Industry and Commerce,
Environment, Trade, Commerce and Tourism
and the Gaeltacht. EU Commissioner
1993–2000.

Mayo

Seats 5 Quota 10,581	1st Count	2nd Count	3rd Count	4th Count
		Transfer of **King, Crowley, Heffron** Votes	Transfer of **Holmes** Votes	Transfer of **Wood** Votes
CAFFREY, Ernie (FG)	2,290	*(+129)* 2,419	*(+67)* 2,486	*(+72)* 2,558
CARTY, John (FF)	6,457	*(+55)* 6,512	*(+43)* 6,555	*(+201)* 6,756
CHAMBERS, Frank (FF)	5,726	*(+66)* 5,792	*(+253)* 6,045	*(+221)* 6,266
COOPER-FLYNN, Beverly* (FF)	6,661	*(+80)* 6,741	*(+145)* 6,886	*(+237)* 7,123
COWLEY, Jerry (Ind)	8,709	*(+504)* 9,213	*(+595)* 9,808	*(+765)* 10,573
CROWLEY, Ann (GP)	669			
HEFFRON, Billy (PD)	919			
HIGGINS, Jim* (FG)	5,858	*(+113)* 5,971	*(+64)* 6,035	*(+120)* 6,155
HOLMES, Michael (Ind)	1,754	*(+119)* 1,873		
KENNY, Enda* (FG)	5,834	*(+120)* 5,954	*(+91)* 6,045	*(+97)* 6,142
KING, Thomas (Ind)	102			
MOFFAT, Tom* (FF)	6,536	*(+213)* 6,749	*(+143)* 6,892	*(+192)* 7,084
RING, Michael* (FG)	9,880	*(+165)* 10,045	*(+339)* 10,384	*(+192)* 10,576
WOOD, Vincent (SF)	2,085	*(+96)* 2,181	*(+93)* 2,274	
NON-TRANSFERABLE		30	40	177

Mayo

5th Count	6th Count	7th Count	8th Count	9th Count	10th Count
Transfer of **Caffrey** Votes	Transfer of **Cowley** Surplus	Transfer of **Ring** Surplus	Transfer of **Chambers** Votes	Transfer of **Higgins** Votes	Transfer of **Kenny** Surplus
(+61) 6,817	(+5) 6,822	(+2) 6,824	(+1,460) 8,284	(+1,247) 9,531	(+626) 10,157
(+41) 6,307	(+8) 6,315	(+4) 6,319			
(+44) 7,167	(+11) 7,178	(+9) 7,187	(+2,330) 9,517	(+232) 9,749	(+161) 9,910
(+555) 11,128					
(+678) 6,833	(+165) 6,998	(+102) 7,100	(+120) 7,220		
(+336) 6,478	(+98) 6,576	(+131) 6,707	(+600) 7,307	(+4,615) 11,922	
(+437) 7,521	(+140) 7,661	(+36) 7,697	(+928) 8,625	(+253) 8,878	(+309) 9,187
(+331) 10,907					
75	120	42	881	873	245

Meath

Elected

Noel Dempsey (FF)*	1st Count
John Bruton (FG)*	8th Count
Mary Wallace (FF)*	9th Count
Damien English (FG)	9th Count
Johnny Brady (FF)*	9th Count

Voting by Party

1st Preference	Number	%	% 1997
Fianna Fáil	28,786	44.92	41.88
Fine Gael	17,452	27.23	36.92
Labour	2,727	4.26	6.52
Green Party	2,337	3.65	1.95
Sinn Féin	6,042	9.43	3.53
Christian Solidarity	180	0.28	1.82
Others	6,557	10.23	4.56

Statistics

Population	109,732	
Electorate	108,717	
Total Poll	64,081	58.94
Spoiled Votes	—	
Valid Poll	64,081	58.94
Seats	5	
Quota	10,681	
Candidates	14	

Seats

FF	3
FG	2
No change	

The Meath constituency is unchanged since the 1997 General Election. Meath was one of the three constituencies where electronic voting was used for the first time.

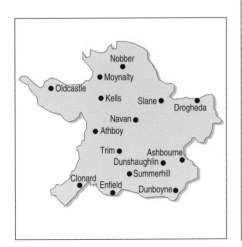

Noel Dempsey (FF)

Home Address
Newtown, Trim. Co Meath
Business Address
Department of Education and Science, Marlborough Street, Dublin 1
Telephone
Home/Constituency Office (046) 31146; *Fax* (046) 36643 *Office* ; (01) 8734700 *Fax* (01) 872 9093
Birth Place/Date
Trim. 6 January 1953
Married
Bernadette Rattigan. 2 sons, 2 daughters
Education
St Michael's CBS, Trim; University College, Dublin; St Patrick's College, Maynooth (BA, HDipEd); Diploma in Career Guidance; Diploma in Youth Leadership
Occupation
Government Minister. Formerly career guidance counsellor

Noel Dempsey was appointed Minister for Education and Science in June 2000.

He was Minister for the Environment and Local Government 1997–2002. He was Minister of State at the Department of the Taoiseach with special responsibility as Government Chief Whip, and at the Department of Finance with special responsibility for the Office of Public Works, and at the Department of Defence 1993–94. He was Minister of State at the Departments of the Taoiseach and Defence (Chief Whip) February 1992–January 1993. He has been a Dáil deputy since 1987.

Party spokesperson on the Environment 1995–97. Party convenor on Forum for Peace and Reconciliation.

Former member, Meath County Council 1977–92 (chairman 1986/87); Trim Urban District Council (chairman 1981/82, 1985/86 and 1991/92).

John Bruton (FG)

Home Address
Cornelstown, Dunboyne, Co Meath
Telephone
Office (01) 6183107
Birth Place/Date
Dublin. 18 May 1947
Married
Finola Gill. 1 son, 3 daughters
Education
Clongowes Wood College, Co Kildare; King's Inns (BA Economics and Politics, BL)
Occupation
Full-time public representative

John Bruton was Taoiseach 1994–97 leading a three-party coalition of Fine Gael, Labour and Democratic Left. Leader of Fine Gael 1990–2001. Deputy Leader 1987–90.

He was Minister for Finance 1986–87; Minister for Public Service January–March 1987; Minister for Industry, Trade, Commerce and Tourism 1983–86; Minister for Industry and Energy 1982–83; Minister for Finance 1981–82; Leader of the House 1982–86 with responsibility for implementing Dáil reform; Parliamentary Secretary to the Minister for Education 1973–77; Parliamentary Secretary to the Minister for Industry and Commerce 1975–77. He was first elected in 1969 as the youngest member of the 19th Dáil.

He is vice-president of the European People's Party since 1999. Member of the Praesidium of the Convention on the Future of Europe since 2002. Author of the report of the Joint Oireachtas Committee on Europe on 'The Future of the European Union' published in February 2002.

Member of the Parliamentary Assembly of the Council of Europe 1989–91. President Irish Council of the European Movement 1990–96.

Brother of Richard Bruton, Dáil deputy for Dublin North-Central since 1992.

Mary Wallace (FF)

Home Address
Fairyhouse Road, Ratoath, Co Meath
Telephone
Home (01) 825 6259
Birth Place/Date
Dublin. June 1959
Married
Declan Gannon. 1 son
Education
Loreto Convent, Balbriggan, Co Dublin; Loreto
Convent, North Great George's Street, Dublin;
Rathmines College of Commerce, Dublin (Dip
Hospital & Health Services Administration)
Occupation
Public representative. Formerly personnel
executive

Mary Wallace was Minister of State at the
Department of Justice, Equality and Law
Reform with special responsibility for Equality
and Disabilities 1997–2002. She was first
elected to the Dáil in 1989. She contested the
1987 general election. Was Senator,
Administrative Panel, 1987–89. Party
spokesperson for people with disabilities and
carers 1995–97. Chairperson, Oireachtas Joint
Committee on Women's Rights 1995–97
vice-chairperson 1989–92).

Chairperson of Fianna Fáil National Women's
Committee 1992–94. Chairperson of the
National Steering Committee on Violence
Against Women 1998–2002.

Member, Meath County Council 1982–97;
North-Eastern Health Board 1985–89; Meath
Vocational Education Committee 1991–95;
Meath County Committee of Agriculture
1982–87 (Chairperson 1986/87);
Blanchardstown Hospital 1977–87.

Damien English (FG)

Home Address
40 Watergate Street, Navan, Co Meath
Constituency Office
16 Bridge Street, Navan
Telephone
Constituency office (046) 71667;
Mobile 086 814 3495
Website homepage.eircom.net\~denglish
Birth Place/Date
Drogheda, Co Louth. 21 February 1978
Education
Kells Community School; Chartered Institute
of Management Accountants
Occupation
Full-time public representative

Damien English is a new Dáil deputy. He is
the youngest TD. He was appointed deputy
spokesperson in Arts, Sport and Tourism.

He has been a member of Meath County
Council since 1999 when he was elected at
21 years of age. He is a member of the Meath
County Development Board and of the Navan
Shamrock Festival Board.

Johnny Brady (FF)

Home Address
Springville, Kilskyre, Kells, Co Meath
Telephone
Office (046) 40852
Birth Place/Date
Meath. January 1948
Married
Kathleen Clarke. 1 son
Education
Kells Vocational School
Occupation
Full-time public representative. Farmer

Johnny Brady was elected to the Dáil in 1997
in his first general election.

Member of the following committees in last
Dáil: Agriculture, Food and the Marine (whip);
Social, Community and Family Affairs.

He has been a member of Meath County
Council since 1974 (chairman 1995/96).
Former member of Meath County Committee
of Agriculture and of the North-Eastern Health
Board.

He served as chairman of Meath Juvenile
GAA Hurling Board for six years and with local
youth organisations.

Meath

Seats 5 Quota 10,681	1st Count	2nd Count	3rd Count	4th Count
		Transfer of **Dempsey** Surplus	Transfer of **Redmond, Colwell** Votes	Transfer of **O'Brien** Votes
BRADY, Johnny* (FF)	8,493	*(+258)* 8,751	*(+36)* 8,787	*(+46)* 8,833
BRUTON, John* (FG)	7,617	*(+76)* 7,693	*(+32)* 7,725	*(+155)* 7,880
COLWELL, Jane (Ind)	263	*(+2)* 265		
DEMPSEY, Noel* (FF)	11,534			
ENGLISH, Damien (FG)	5,958	*(+61)* 6,019	*(+52)* 6,071	*(+68)* 6,139
FARRELLY, John* (FG)	3,877	*(+15)* 3,892	*(+11)* 3,903	*(+34)* 3,937
FITZGERALD, Brian (Ind)	3,722	*(+29)* 3,751	*(+56)* 3,807	*(+113)* 3,920
KELLY, Tom (Ind)	1,373	*(+7)* 1,380	*(+23)* 1,403	*(+163)* 1,566
O'BRIEN, Pat (Ind)	1,199	*(+3)* 1,202	*(+42)* 1,244	
O'BYRNE, Fergal (GP)	2,337	*(+16)* 2,353	*(+53)* 2,406	*(+224)* 2,630
REDMOND, Michael (CSP)	180	*(+1)* 181		
REILLY, Joe (SF)	6,042	*(+51)* 6,093	*(+51)* 6,144	*(+123)* 6,267
WALLACE, Mary* (FF)	8,759	*(+313)* 9,072	*(+32)* 9,104	*(+180)* 9,284
WARD, Peter (Lab)	2,727	*(+21)* 2,748	*(+21)* 2,769	*(+75)* 2,844
NON-TRANSFERABLE			37	63

5th Count	6th Count	7th Count	8th Count	9th Count
Transfer of **Kelly** Votes	Transfer of **O'Byrne** Votes	Transfer of **Ward** Votes	Transfer of **Farrelly** Votes	Transfer of **Fitzgerald** Votes
(+46) 8,879	*(+108)* 8,987	*(+123)* 9,110	*(+467)* 9,577	*(+299)* 9,876
(+241) 8,121	*(+333)* 8,454	*(+694)* 9,148	*(+1,733)* 10,881	
(+126) 6,265	*(+374)* 6,639	*(+737)* 7,376	*(+1,349)* 8,725	*(+1,429)* 10,154
(+41) 3,978	*(+74)* 4,052	*(+221)* 4,273		
(+185) 4,105	*(+359)* 4,464	*(+675)* 5,139	*(+119)* 5,258	
(+200) 2,830				
(+118) 6,385	*(+325)* 6,710	*(+412)* 7,122	*(+226)* 7,348	*(+732)* 8,080
(+361) 9,645	*(+362)* 10,007	*(+254)* 10,261	*(+113)* 10,374	*(+1,261)* 11,635
(+120) 2,964	*(+631)* 3,595			
128	264	479	266	1,537

Sligo-Leitrim

Elected

Marian Harkin (Ind)	4th Count
Jimmy Devins (FF)	6th Count
John Perry (FG)*	6th Count
John Ellis (FF)*	7th Count

Voting by Party

1st Preference	Number	%	% 1997
Fianna Fáil	19,086	38.97	40.41
Fine Gael	13,059	26.67	36.63
Labour	2,429	4.96	10.86
Sinn Féin	5,001	10.21	7.10
Christian Solidarity	166	0.34	3.01
Others	9,230	18.85	0.34

Statistics

Population	80,878	
Electorate	70,460	
Total Poll	49,494	70.24
Spoiled Votes	523	1.06
Valid Poll	48,971	69.50
Seats	4	
Quota	9,795	
Candidates	12	

Seats

FF	2
FG	1
Ind	1
Ind gain from FG	

The Sligo-Leitrim constituency is unchanged since the 1997 General Election.

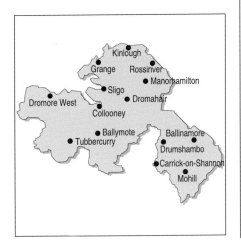

Marian Harkin (Ind)

Home Address
24 The Park, Strandhill Road, Sligo
Constituency Office
1 Dominick Street, Sligo
Telephone
Constituency Office (071) 45888/45689;
Mobile 086 8341758
Birth Place/Date
Sligo. 26 November 1953
Married
Widowed. 2 sons
Education
Marist Convent, Tubbercurry, Co Sligo;
University College, Dublin (BSc, HDipEd)
Occupation
Public representative. Formerly secondary
school teacher

Marian Harkin is a new Dáil deputy.
Campaigned on a platform of regional
development for the West and greater
medical facilities. Contested the 1999
European Parliament election in Connacht-
Ulster when she won 47,500 first preference
votes.

Member, Council of the West. Board member
of Ulster Community Investment Trust, a
cross-border community bank.

Jimmy Devins (FF)

Address
Mail Coach Road, Sligo
Telephone
Constituency Office (071) 52970;
Fax (071) 52971
Birth Place/Date
Sligo. 20 September 1948
Married
Mary Tracey. 4 daughters
Education
St John's National School; Blackrock College,
Co Dublin; University College, Dublin (MB,
BCh, BAO); Trinity College, Dublin (MSc in
Family Medicine); DCH, D.Obst, MICGP
Occupation
Public representative. Medical doctor

Jimmy Devins is a new Dáil deputy.

Member, Sligo County Council since 1991;
Border Regional Authority; Border and Mid-
West Assembly. Former chairperson of the
Institute of Technology, Sligo.

John Perry (FG)

Home Address
Grianán Iuda, Carrownanty, Ballymote,
Co Sligo
Constituency Office
Teeling Street, Ballymote; Westward Town
Centre, Sligo
Telephone
Home (071) 89227; *Constituency Office*
(071) 89333/51011; *Fax* (071) 51119;
Mobile 087 245 9407
Birth Place/Date
Ballymote. 15 August 1956
Married
Marie Mulvey. 1 son
Education
Corran College, Ballymote
Occupation
Full-time public representative.

John Perry was first elected to the Dáil in
1997 at his first attempt.

He was the Fine Gael nominee for Chairman
of the Public Accounts Committee. He is the
Fine Gael Director of Organisation.

He was party spokesperson on Science,
Technology, Small Business and Enterprise,
Border Counties 1997–2002.

Elected to Sligo County Council 1999.
Chairman, Ballymote Community Enterprise.
Director, Co Sligo Enterprise Board; Sligo
Airport; Sligo Tourism and Marketing Forum.
Member of community and development
committees and organisations.

Winner of the *Irish Quality Business* award in
1991 and 1992. Recipient of Sligo *Person of
the Year* award, 1993.

John Ellis (FF)

Home Address
Fenagh, Co Leitrim
Telephone
Home (078) 44252; *Fax* (078) 44017; *Mobile*
087 259 4978
Birth Place/Date
Fenagh. 2 May 1952
Married
Patricia Donnelly. 2 sons, 1 daughter
Education
St Felim's College, Ballinamore, Co Leitrim
Occupation
Full-time public representative. Farmer

John Ellis has been a member of the Dáil
since 1987. He was previously a Dáil deputy
June 1981–November 1982. Senator 1977–81
and 1983–87, Agricultural Panel. He contested
Dáil general elections in Roscommon-Leitrim
in 1977 and Sligo-Leitrim in November 1982.

Member, Oireachtas committees on
Agriculture, Food and the Marine and on
Education and Science in the 28th Dáil.
Member, British-Irish Inter-Parliamentary
Body. Member, Public Accounts Committee
1993–97.

Member, Leitrim County Council since 1974
(chairperson 1986/87); General Council of
County Councils 1979–91; General Council of
Committees of Agriculture 1979–88.

Member, Midland and Western Livestock
Improvement Society. Member, Gaelic
Athletic Association.

Sligo-Leitrim

	1st Count	2nd Count	3rd Count
Seats 4		Transfer of **Lacken, Ford, McCrea, McSharry** Votes	Transfer of **Bree** Votes
Quota 9,795			
BREE, Declan (Lab)	2,429	*(+101)* 2,530	
DEVINS, Jimmy (FF)	6,307	*(+120)* 6,427	*(+397)* 6,824
ELLIS, John* (FF)	6,434	*(+31)* 6,465	*(+41)* 6,506
FORD, Martin (Ind)	203		
HARKIN, Marian (Ind)	8,610	*(+186)* 8,796	*(+828)* 9,624
LACKEN, John (CSP)	166		
MCCREA, John (Ind)	114		
MACMANUS, Seán (SF)	5,001	*(+99)* 5,100	*(+516)* 5,616
MCSHARRY, Andrew Michael (Ind)	303		
PERRY, John* (FG)	6,897	*(+86)* 6,983	*(+308)* 7,291
REYNOLDS, Gerry* (FG)	6,162	*(+74)* 6,236	*(+202)* 6,438
SCANLON, Éamon (FF)	6,345	*(+36)* 6,381	*(+82)* 6,463
NON-TRANSFERABLE		53	156

4th Count	5th Count	6th Count	7th Count
Transfer of **MacManus** Votes	Transfer of **Harkin** Surplus	Transfer of **Scanlon** Votes	Transfer of **Devins** Surplus
(+767) 7,591	*(+303)* 7,894	*(+2,727)* 10,621	
(+776) 7,282	*(+221)* 7,503	*(+996)* 8,499	*(+772)* 9,271
(+1,773) 11,397			
(+408) 7,699	*(+224)* 7,923	*(+2,516)* 10,439	
(+501) 6,939	*(+212)* 7,151	*(+152)* 7,303	*(+54)* 7,357
(+393) 6,856	*(+125)* 6,981		
998	517	590	

Tipperary North

Elected

Voting by Party

1st Preference	Number	%	% 1997
Fianna Fáil	17,475	42.66	42.29
Fine Gael	6,108	14.91	11.32
Labour	5,537	13.52	10.33
Prog Democrats	1,446	3.53	3.48
Others	10,400	25.39	29.35

Statistics

Population	67,417	
Electorate	59,427	
Total Poll	41,412	69.69
Spoiled Votes	446	1.08
Valid Poll	40,966	68.93
Seats	3	
Quota	10,242	
Candidates	6	

Seats

FF	2
Ind	1
No change	

The Tipperary North constituency is unchanged since the 1997 General Election.

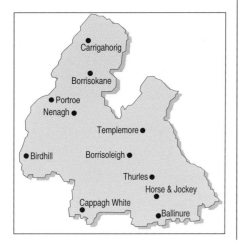

Michael Lowry (Ind)

Home Address
Glenreigh, Holycross, Thurles, Co Tipperary
Business Address
Abbey Road, Thurles
Telephone
Business (0504) 22022; *Fax* (0504) 23349
Birth Place/Date
Holycross. 13 March 1954
Married
Catherine McGrath. 2 sons, 1 daughter
Education
Thurles CBS
Occupation
Public representative. Company director

Michael Lowry was first elected for Fine Gael to the Dáil in 1987. He was Minister for Transport, Energy and Communications 1994–November 1996 when he resigned. He resigned from the Fine Gael Parliamentary Party in 1997. He has topped the poll and been elected on the first count in the two subsequent general elections.

Chairman, Fine Gael Parliamentary Party 1993–94. Member of front bench 1993–94. Fine Gael Leader of the British-Irish Inter-Parliamentary Body 1994.

Member, Tipperary North County Council 1979–95. He was elected again in 1999 with two and a half quotas. He served on the County Development Team, Mid-Western Health Board and Association of Health Boards in Ireland.

Former Chairman, Semple Stadium Management Committee. Former Chairman, County Tipperary Gaelic Athletic Association Board and Mid-Tipperary GAA Board.

Máire Hoctor (FF)

Home Address
Teach Ruadháin, 40 Melrose, Nenagh, Co Tipperary
Constituency Office
Kickham Street, Nenagh
Telephone
Constituency Office (067) 32943;
Fax (067) 50470
Birth Place/Date
Nenagh. 20 January 1963
Education
St Mary's Secondary School, Nenagh; St Patrick's College, Maynooth, Co Kildare (BA Th, HDipEd)
Occupation
Full-time public representative. Formerly secondary school teacher

Máire Hoctor is a new Dáil deputy. She topped the poll in Tipperary North in her first general election and she is the only new female Fianna Fáil deputy.

Member, Tipperary North County Council since 1999 when she also topped the poll. Member, Nenagh Town Council since 1994.

Member, Mid-West Regional Authority; vice-chairperson Tipperary North Vocational Educational Committee. Director, County Enterprise Board; Nenagh Community Network. Chairperson, Nenagh Reparations Project.

Michael Smith (FF)

Home Address
Lismackin, Roscrea, Co Tipperary
Business Address
Department of Defence, Infirmary Road, Dublin 7
Telephone
Home (0505) 43157; *Office* (01) 804 2101
Birth Place/Date
Roscrea. November 1940
Married
Mary Therese Ryan. 1 son, 6 daughters
Education
Templemore CBS, Co Tipperary; University College, Cork (DPA)
Occupation
Full-time public representative. Formerly farmer

Michael Smith was re-appointed Minister for Defence in June 2002, a position which he held October 1997–June 2002. He was Minister of State at the Department of Education and at the Department of Enterprise, Trade and Employment with special responsibility for Science and Technology July–October 1997. He was Minister for the Environment 1992–94. He was also Minister for Education November–December 1994. He was Minister of State at the Department of Industry and Commerce, with special responsibility for Science and Technology, 1989–91. He was Minister for Energy, November 1988–July 1989; Minister of State at the Department of Energy, with special responsibility for Forestry, March 1987–November 1988. Minister of State at the Department of Agriculture December 1980–June 1981. He was first elected to the Dáil in 1969 and represented Tipperary North until 1973 when he lost his seat to the Labour Party. He regained the seat in 1977 at the expense of Fine Gael but lost his seat again in February 1982. He was a candidate in the November 1982 election. Senator, Agricultural Panel, 1982–83; Cultural and Educational Panel 1983–87.

Seats 3 Quota 10,242	1st Count	2nd Count Transfer of **Dwan** Votes	3rd Count Transfer of **O'Meara** Votes	4th Count Transfer of **Hoctor** Surplus
COONAN, Noel J (FG)	6,108	*(+328)* 6,436	*(+2,649)* 9,085	*(+352)* 9,437
DWAN, Bill (PD)	1,446			
HOCTOR, Máire* (FF)	8,949	*(+371)* 9,320	*(+1,720)* 11,040	
LOWRY, Michael* (Ind)	10,400			
O'MEARA, Kathleen (Lab)	5,537	*(+340)* 5,877		
SMITH, Michael* (FF)	8,526	*(+316)* 8,842	*(+800)* 9,642	*(+446)* 10,088
NON-TRANSFERABLE		91	708	

Tipperary South

Elected

Voting by Party

1st Preference	Number	%	% 1997
Fianna Fáil	14,121	38.51	37.28
Fine Gael	8,997	24.54	24.09
Labour	3,353	9.14	16.11
Sinn Féin	1,210	3.30	—
Christian Solidarity	120	0.33	—
Others	8,865	24.18	16.49

Statistics

Population	67,605	
Electorate	56,092	
Total Poll	37,056	66.06
Spoiled Votes	390	1.05
Valid Poll	36,666	65.37
Seats	3	
Quota	9,167	
Candidates	8	

Seats

FF	1
FG	1
Ind	1

No change. Michael Ferris, who won a seat for Labour in 1997, died in March 2000 and Seamus Healy won the subsequent by-election. Theresa Ahearn, who retained her seat for Fine Gael in 1997, died in September 2000 and Tom Hayes of Fine Gael won the subsequent by-election.

Tom Hayes (FG)

Home Address
Cahervillahow, Golden, Co Tipperary
Constituency Office
2 Brighton Place, Clonmel, Co Tipperary
Telephone
Home (062) 62892; *Fax* (062) 62893;
Mobile 087 8105016;
Office (052) 80731; *Fax* (052) 82895
Birth Place/Date
Golden, Co Tipperary. 16 February 1952
Married
Marian Thornton. 3 sons
Education
Thomastown National School; Mount Mellary Secondary School, Vocational School, Tipperary Town; University College, Cork (Diploma in Social Studies)
Occupation
Public representative and farmer

Tom Hayes was elected Chairman of the Fine Gael Parliamentary Party in September 2002. He was appointed deputy spokesperson for Agriculture and Food in June 2002.

He was elected to the Dáil on 1 July 2001 at the by-election caused by the death of Fine Gael colleague, Theresa Ahearn. He had been narrowly beaten in the by-election the previous year caused by the death of the Labour TD, Michael Ferris. He had previously served in the Seanad (Agricultural Panel) from 1997. Party spokesman on agriculture in the Seanad. Served on following committees: Agriculture and Strategic Management.

Member of Tipperary South Riding County Council since 1991. Served on Vocational Education Committee, County Enterprise Board, Cashel Heritage Committee. Member of GAA, Macra na Feirme and IFA.

Noel Davern (FF)

Home Address
Tannersrath, Clonmel, Co Tipperary
Telephone
Home (052) 22991; *Fax* (052) 29800
Birth Place/Date
Cashel, Co Tipperary. December 1945
Married
Ann Marie Carroll. 2 sons, 1 daughter
Education
Cashel CBS; Franciscan College, Gormanstown, Co Meath
Occupation
Full-time public representative

Noel Davern was Minister of State at the Department of Agriculture and Food with special responsibility for Livestock Breeding and Horticulture 1997–2002. In February 2001 at the time of the foot-and-mouth epidemic he also became responsible for the food industry. He was Minister for Education November 1991–February 1992. He was first elected to the Dáil in 1969, winning a seat previously held by his brother, Don Davern, Parliamentary Secretary to the Minister for Agriculture, who died while in office. Noel Davern continued as a Dáil deputy until 1981 but did not contest the general election in that year. He had been elected to the European Parliament in 1979 but failed to be re-elected in 1984. He was re-elected to the Dáil in 1987 and has been a TD since.

Member, Tipperary South Riding County Council 1985–92; Vocational Education Committee; ACOT Committee; National Museum Advisory Committee.

He is a son of Michael Davern, Dáil deputy for Tipperary South 1948–65, and brother of Don Davern, Dáil deputy for the same constituency 1965–68.

Seamus Healy (Ind)

Home Address
Scrouthea, Old Bridge, Clonmel, Co Tipperary
Constituency Office
56 Queen Street, Clonmel
Telephone
Home (052) 23184; *Constituency Office*
(052) 21883; *Fax* (052) 70860
Birth Place/Date
Scrouthea. 9 August 1950
Married
Widower. 4 daughters
Education
High School, Clonmel
Occupation
Full-time public representative. Former
hospital administrator

Seamus Healy was first elected to the Dáil in
the by-election of June 2000 caused by the
death of the Labour deputy, Michael Ferris.
He had contested the general election of 1997
for Tipperary South and also in 1992.

He was elected to Tipperary South County
Council in 1991. Has been a member of
Clonmel Borough Council since 1985. Former
President, Clonmel Trades and Labour
Council. President, St Patrick's Day Society.
Member, Scouting Ireland.

Seats 3 Quota 9,167	1st Count	2nd Count Transfer of **Larkin, Ó Súilleabháin** Votes	3rd Count Transfer of **Wood, Landy** Votes
DAVERN, Noel* (FF)	8,888	*(+197)* 9,085	*(+944)* 10,029
HAYES, Tom* (FG)	8,997	*(+136)* 9,133	*(+1,591)* 10,724
HEALY, Seamus* (Ind)	7,350	*(+415)* 7,765	*(+1,712)* 9,477
LANDY, Denis (Lab)	3,353	*(+202)* 3,555	
LARKIN, Michael (CSP)	120		
MANSERGH, Martin (FF)	5,233	*(+200)* 5,433	*(+455)* 5,888
Ó SÚILLEABHÁIN, Muiris (SF)	1,210		
WOOD, Tom (Ind)	1,515	*(+116)* 1,631	
NON-TRANSFERABLE		64	484

Waterford

Elected

Martin Cullen (FF)*	5th Count
John Deasy (FG)	6th Count
Brian O'Shea (Lab)*	7th Count
Ollie Wilkinson (FF)	7th Count

Voting by Party

1st Preference	Number	%	% 1997
Fianna Fáil	21,576	46.34	35.79
Fine Gael	10,003	21.48	24.55
Labour	6,219	13.36	11.77
Prog Democrats	2,137	4.59	6.46
Green Party	1,361	2.92	1.81
Sinn Féin	2,955	6.35	—
Socialist			
Workers' Party	300	0.64	1.57
Workers' Party	1,270	2.73	9.24
Others	742	1.59	8.48

Statistics

Population	93,193	
Electorate	73,725	
Total Poll	47,120	63.91
Spoiled Votes	557	1.18
Valid Poll	46,563	63.16
Seats	4	
Quota	9,313	
Candidates	14	

Seats

FF	2
FG	1
Lab	1
No change	

The Waterford constituency is unchanged since the 1997 General Election.

Martin Cullen (FF)

Home Address
Abbey House, Abbey Road, Ferrybank, Waterford
Business Address
Department of the Environment and Local Government, Custom House, Dublin 1
Telephone
Home (051) 851112; *Business* (01) 8882000; *Fax* (01) 8882888; *Constituency Office* (051) 851112; *Fax* (051) 851543
Birth Place/Date
Waterford. November 1954
Married
Married. 3 sons, 1 daughter
Education
Waterpark College, Waterford; Waterford Regional Technical College (member, Marketing Institute of Ireland)
Occupation
Government Minister. Formerly Chief Executive of the Federation of Transport Operators

Martin Cullen was appointed Minister for the Environment and Local Government in June 2002. He was the first Waterford deputy to be appointed to a Cabinet post in many years. He served as Minister of State at the Department of Finance, with special responsibility for the Office of Public Works, 1997–2002. He was first elected to the Dáil as a Progressive Democrat deputy in 1987, lost his seat in the 1989 general election and regained it in 1992. During the 27th Dáil he joined Fianna Fáil. Senator, Taoiseach's nominee, 1989–92. Spokesperson on Enterprise and Employment 1993; Industry and Commerce 1988–89; Tourism, Transport and Communications 1987–88.

Member, Waterford City Council 1991–97 (Mayor 1993/94: his father and grandfather were both mayors of Waterford). Former director, Waterford Economic Development Board and South-East Regional Tourism Organisation.

Founder member, Waterford Round Table 1979.

John Deasy (FG)

Home Address
Kilrush, Dungarvan, Co Waterford
Constituency Office
20 Grattan Square, Dungarvan
Telephone
Constituency office (058) 43003; *Fax* (058) 45315
Birth Place/Date
Abbeyside, Dungarvan. 8 October 1967
Education
Coláiste na Rinne, Ring, Dungarvan; St Augustine's College, Dungarvan; Mercyhurst College, Erie, Pennsylvania, USA (BA History/Communications); University College, Cork (BCL)
Occupation
Public representative. Former US Congressional aide

John Deasy is a new Dáil deputy. He was appointed front bench spokesperson for Justice, Equality and Law Reform.

Member of Waterford County Council since 1999 when he topped the poll in the Dungarvan district. Member, Dungarvan Town Council since 1999. Chairman, Waterford County Development Board. Chairman, Strategic Policy Committee on Housing, Social, Cultural, Heritage and Corporate Affairs. Board member, Waterford Regional Airport. Was Manager of Public Affairs for multinational waste management company 1991–92.

He is son of Austin Deasy, Dáil deputy 1977–2002; Senator 1973–77.

Brian O'Shea (Lab)

Home Address
61 Sweetbriar Lane, Tramore, Co Waterford
Telephone
Home (051) 381913; *Fax* (051) 386427;
Mobile 087 2943292
Birth Place/Date
Waterford. 9 December 1944
Married
Eileen Walsh. 2 sons, 4 daughters
Education
Mount Sion CBS, Waterford; St Patrick's
Teachers' Training College, Dublin
Occupation
Full-time public representative. Formerly
national school teacher

Brian O'Shea was first elected to the Dáil in
1989. He contested general elections in 1987
and 1982 in Waterford. Party spokesperson
on Arts, Heritage, Gaeltacht and the Islands,
and Communications and Sport 1998–2002;
on Defence 1997–98. Member of following
committees in last Dáil: Strategic
Management Initiative; Heritage and the Irish
Language.

Minister of State at the Department of Health,
with special responsibility for Mental
Handicap, Health Promotion, Food Safety and
Public Health 1994–97. Minister of State at
the Department of Agriculture, with special
responsibility for Food and Horticulture
1993–94.

Senator, Industrial and Commercial Panel,
1987–89.

Member, Waterford County Council 1985–93;
Waterford City Council 1985–93; Tramore
Town Commissioners 1979–93.

Former chairman, South-Eastern Airport
Company; former president of Waterford
Council of Trade Unions; former president of
Tramore Community Care Organisation;
former chairman of Waterford City Branch of
INTO.

Ollie Wilkinson (FF)

Home Address
Killahala, Cappoquin, Co Waterford
Telephone
Home (058) 54413; *Fax* (058) 42911
Mobile 087 6553999
Birth Place/Date
Dungarvan. 4 October 1944
Married
Bridget Morrissey. 5 sons, 5 daughters
Education
Tourin National School; Lismore CBS
Occupation
Full-time public representative. Retired farmer

Ollie Wilkinson is a new Dáil deputy. He
contested the Waterford constituency in the
1997 general election.

Member of Waterford County Council since
1985. Chairperson and Mayor 2001 to 2002.
Chairperson of Cappoquin Community
Development Company.

Lifetime involvement with the GAA at club
and county level. Played hurling at senior,
intermediate and under-21 levels.

Waterford

	1st Count	2nd Count	3rd Count
Seats 4 Quota 9,313		Transfer of **Walsh, Waters, Kelly, Halpin** Votes	Transfer of **Halligan** Votes
CULLEN, Martin* (FF)	8,529	*(+77)* 8,606	*(+128)* 8,734
CULLINANE, David (SF)	2,955	*(+135)* 3,090	*(+320)* 3,410
CUMMINS, Maurice (FG)	2,799	*(+63)* 2,862	*(+147)* 3,009
DEASY, John (FG)	7,204	*(+99)* 7,303	*(+60)* 7,363
FLYNN, Michael (PD)	2,137	*(+50)* 2,187	*(+64)* 2,251
HALLIGAN, John (WP)	1,270	*(+128)* 1,398	
HALPIN, Conor (Ind)	289		
KELLY, Jimmy (SWP)	300		
KENNEALLY, Brendan* (FF)	5,735	*(+45)* 5,780	*(+140)* 5,920
MCCANN, Brendan (GP)	1,361	*(+172)* 1,533	*(+113)* 1,646
O'SHEA, Brian* (Lab)	6,219	*(+145)* 6,364	*(+285)* 6,649
WALSH, Eddie (Ind)	118		
WATERS, Declan (Ind)	335		
WILKINSON, Ollie (FF)	7,312	*(+55)* 7,367	*(+16)* 7,383
NON-TRANSFERABLE		73	125

4th Count	5th Count	6th Count	7th Count
Transfer of **McCann** Votes	Transfer of **Flynn** Votes	Transfer of **Cummins** Votes	Transfer of **Cullinane** Votes
(+120) 8,854	*(+578)* 9,432		
(+175) 3,585	*(+129)* 3,714	*(+157)* 3,871	
(+112) 3,121	*(+220)* 3,341		
(+218) 7,581	*(+537)* 8,118	*(+1,880)* 9,998	
(+213) 2,464			
(+49) 5,969	*(+196)* 6,165	*(+260)* 6,425	*(+692)* 7,117
(+533) 7,182	*(+467)* 7,649	*(+667)* 8,316	*(+1,208)* 9,524
(+60) 7,443	*(+192)* 7,635	*(+88)* 7,723	*(+481)* 8,204
166	145	289	1,490

Westmeath

Elected

Voting by Party

1st Preference	Number	%	% 1997
Fianna Fáil	14,336	41.65	45.67
Fine Gael	9,363	27.20	25.88
Labour	8,967	26.05	25.51
Sinn Féin	1,185	3.44	—
Christian Solidarity	126	0.37	—
Others	444	1.29	3.94

Statistics

Population	63,314	
Electorate	56,012	
Total Poll	34,978	62.45
Spoiled Votes	557	1.59
Valid Poll	34,421	61.45
Seats	3	
Quota	8,606	
Candidates	8	

Seats

FF	1
FG	1
Lab	1
No change	

The constituency of Westmeath is unchanged since the 1997 General Election.

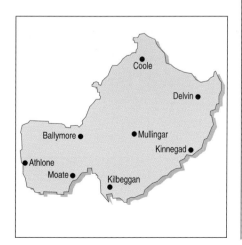

Willie Penrose (Lab)

Home Address
Ballintue, Ballynacargy, Co Westmeath
Constituency Office
Convent Lane, Bishopgate Street, Mullingar, Co Westmeath
Telephone
Home (044) 73264; *Constituency Office* (044) 43966
Birth Place/Date
Mullingar, Co Westmeath. August 1956
Married
Anne Fitzsimons. 3 daughters
Education
St Mary's CBS, Mullingar; Multyfarnham Agricultural College, Co Westmeath; University College, Dublin (BAgrSc, MAgrSc [Economics]); King's Inns, Dublin (Diploma in Legal Studies, Barrister-at-Law)
Occupation
Public representative. Barrister

Willie Penrose was appointed party spokesperson for the Environment and Local Government in June 2002. He was first elected to the Dáil in 1992. He was spokesperson on Agriculture 1997–2002.

Member, Westmeath County Council 1984–2002 and the Council's Planning and Environmental Committee, Agricultural Committee and Coiste Gaeilge.

Member, Ballynacargy GAA Club; Cullion Hurling Club; GAA County Board Committee on Cusack Park, Mullingar Development. Member, Royal Canal Development Group.

Donie Cassidy (FF)

Address
Castlepollard, Co Westmeath
Constituency Office
Mullingar, Co Westmeath
Telephone
Home (044) 61176; *Constituency Office* (044) 43585
Birth Place/Date
Castlepollard. 15 September 1945
Married
Anne Geraghty. 4 sons
Occupation
Full-time public representative. Businessman

Donie Cassidy is a new Dáil deputy. He had been a senator since April 1982. Leader of the House 1997–2002. He is the first senator to have served 20 years in the Seanad before becoming elected to the Dáil.

Member, Westmeath County Council since 1985 (Chairperson 1989/90); Midland Health Board since 1985; Westmeath Vocational Education Committee since 1979. Substitute member of European Parliament since 1984.

President of Castlepollard Development Committee. Vice-President of Castlepollard Hurling Club. He played minor hurling for Westmeath. Life member of Mullingar Golf Club. Former President and Captain of Delvin Golf Club.

Paul McGrath (FG)

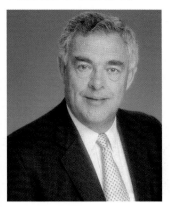

Home Address
Carna, Irishtown, Mullingar, Co Westmeath
Constituency Office
Mary Street, Mullingar
Telephone
Home/Office (044) 40746; *Fax* (044) 40087;
Mobile 087 250 9374
Birth Place/Date
Ballymore, Co Westmeath. February 1948
Married
Josephine Carney. 2 sons, 2 daughters
Education
St Finian's College, Mullingar; Trinity College,
Dublin, and All Saints College, Leeds
Occupation
Full-time public representative. Formerly
national school teacher

Paul McGrath was re-appointed party deputy
spokesperson on Finance in June 2002.

He was party deputy spokesperson on
Finance 1997–2002. He was first elected to
the Dáil in 1989 for the old constituency of
Longford-Westmeath and since 1992 has
represented Westmeath. Member of
Committee on Social, Community and Family
Affairs in last Dáil. Chairperson, Committee on
the Family 1995–97. Spokesperson on Public
Works 1993–94; on Education 1994.

Member, Westmeath County Council since
1991. He has served as a Director, Mullingar
Arts Centre and a Director of the National
Transport Museum. He has also served as
member of Mullingar Youth Club; Midland
Regional Youth Council; National Federation of
Youth Clubs; Royal Canal Employment
Project; Mullingar Show Committee; Mullingar
Squash Club; Leinster Squash Rackets
Association; Mullingar Shamrocks GFC;
Mullingar Golf Club.

Seats 3 Quota 8,606	1st Count	2nd Count Transfer of **Penrose** Surplus	3rd Count Transfer of **Walsh, Lynam** **Hogg, McFadden** Votes
CASSIDY, Donie (FF)	7,892	*(+90)* 7,982	*(+576)* 8,558
HOGG, Niamh (SF)	1,185	*(+31)* 1,216	
LYNAM, Veronica (Ind)	444	*(+16)* 460	
MCFADDEN, Nicky (FG)	3,793	*(+31)* 3,824	
MCGRATH, Paul* (FG)	5,570	*(+145)* 5,715	*(+2,770)* 8,485
O'ROURKE, Mary* (FF)	6,444	*(+47)* 6,491	*(+1,544)* 8,035
PENROSE, Willie* (Lab)	8,967		
WALSH, Patrick (CSP)	126	*(+1)* 127	
NON-TRANSFERABLE			737

Wexford

Elected

Voting by Party

1st Preference	Number	%	% 1997
Fianna Fáil	24,226	40.09	38.95
Fine Gael	15,552	25.74	38.58
Labour	7,995	13.23	17.08
Sinn Féin	4,964	8.22	—
Christian Solidarity	173	0.29	—
Others	7,513	12.43	1.11

Statistics

Population	104,371	
Electorate	94,969	
Total Poll	61,440	64.69
Spoiled Votes	1,017	1.66
Valid Poll	60,423	63.62
Seats	5	
Quota	10,071	
Candidates	12	

Seats

FF	2
FG	1
Lab	1
Ind	1
Ind gain from FG	

The constituency of Wexford is unchanged since the 1998 General Election.

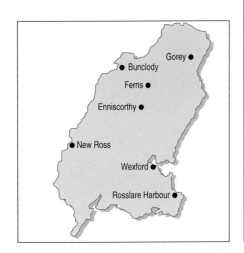

John Browne (FF)

Home Address
Kilcannon, Enniscorthy, Co Wexford
Business Address
Department of Communications, the Marine and Natural Resources, Leeson Lane, Dublin 2
Telephone
Home (054) 35046; *Office* (01) 619 9200
Birth Place/Date
Marshalstown, Enniscorthy, August 1948
Married
Judy Doyle. 1 son, 3 daughters
Education
St Mary's CBS, Enniscorthy
Occupation
Full-time public representative

John Browne was appointed Minister of State at the Department of Communications, the Marine and Natural Resources in June 2002.

He was Chairman of Oireachtas Committee on Agriculture, Food and the Marine 1997–2002. Minister of State at the Department of the Environment, with special responsibility for Environmental Protection, 1993–94. He was Minister of State at the Department of Agriculture and Food, with special responsibility for the Food Industry, 1992–93. He was first elected to the Dáil in November 1982 at his first attempt. Assistant party Chief Whip 1982–87.

Member, Wexford County Council; Enniscorthy Urban District Council; Wexford County Health Committee 1979–92.

Member, Gaelic Athletic Association since 1965.

Brendan Howlin (Lab)

Home Address
Whiterock Hill, Wexford
Telephone
Constituency Office (053) 24036
Website: www.brendanhowlin.ie
Birth Place/Date
Wexford. May 1956
Education
Wexford CBS; St Patrick's College, Drumcondra, Dublin
Occupation
Full-time public representative. Formerly national school teacher

Brendan Howlin was appointed spokesperson for Finance in June 2002.

He was elected Deputy Leader of the Labour Party in 1997. Party spokesman on Justice 1997–2002. Member of Committee on Justice, Equality, Defence and Women's Rights and of Committee on Members' Interests in last Dáil. He was Minister for the Environment 1994–97; Minister for Health 1993–94. He was first elected to the Dáil in 1987. He contested the November 1982 general election. Was a Senator, Taoiseach's nominee, 1982–87. Party spokesperson on Health and Youth Affairs 1989–93; on Health and Women's Rights 1987–89. Spokesman on Education in Seanad 1983–87.

Member, Wexford County Council 1985–93; Wexford Borough Council 1981–93 (Alderman, 1985/93. Mayor 1986/87). Former member of Town of Wexford Vocational Education Committee.

Former Chairman, Wexford Branch of INTO. Former Vice-Chairman of Wexford Council of Trade Unions.

Paul Kehoe (FG)

Home Address
Coolteigue, Bree, Enniscorthy, Co Wexford
Telephone
Home (054) 47852; *Mobile* 087 995 4949
Birth Place/Date
Wexford. 11 January 1973
Education
St Mary's CBS, Enniscorthy; Kildalton
Agricultural College
Occupation
Full-time public representative. Farmer

Paul Kehoe is a new Dáil deputy. He was
appointed deputy spokesperson for
Communications, Marine and Natural
Resources.

He has been a member of Fine Gael for 12
years and has been the County Youth Officer.
Former Youth Officer with Co Wexford GAA.
Former Chairman Macra na Feirme. Winner of
Macra National Leadership Award 2001.

Member, Fleadh Cheoil na hÉireann; Irish
Handicapped Children's Pilgrimage Trust.

Liam Twomey (Ind)

Address
Rosslare Medical Centre, Rosslare Strand,
Co Wexford
Telephone
Office (053) 32800; *Mobile* 086 8267940
Birth Place/Date
Cork. 3 April 1967
Married
Elizabeth O'Sullivan. 2 sons
Education
St Finnbarr's, Farenferris, Cork; Trinity
College, Dublin (MB, BCH, BAO, BA) MICGP;
Diploma Geriatric Medicine
Occupation
Full-time public representative. Medical doctor

Liam Twomey is a new Dáil deputy. He
campaigned on a platform of improved
medical services.

Member, Irish Medical Organisation
(Chairperson of Wexford Branch). Public
Relations Officer for Co Wexford of MICGP.

Tony Dempsey (FF)

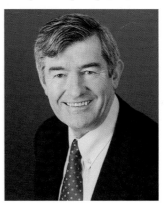

Home Address
Ardbracan House, Barntown, Co Wexford
Constituency Office
45 Commercial Quay, Wexford
Telephone
Home (053) 20011; *Constituency office*
(053) 46878
Birth Place/Date
Davidstown, Co Wexford. 11 May 1944
Married
Gemma Dunne. 4 sons, 1 daughter
Education
Davidstown National School; Enniscorthy
CBS; University College, Dublin, St Patrick's
College, Maynooth (BA, HDipEd)
Occupation
Public representative. Formerly vocational
school principal

Tony Dempsey is a new Dáil deputy. He took
the last seat by beating his Fianna Fáil running
mate, Hugh Byrne, by less than 100 votes.

He has a strong involvement with the Gaelic
Athletic Association. Is a member of the
Central Council for more than 20 years. Is the
manager of the Wexford senior hurling team
and has trained and managed numerous
Wexford hurling and football teams at various
levels.

Wexford

Seats 5 Quota 10,071	1st Count	2nd Count Transfer of **O'Connor, Ó Bolguidhir** Votes		3rd Count Transfer of **Doyle, S** Votes	
BROWNE, John* (FF)	9,150	*(+31)* 9,181		*(+337)* 9,518	
BYRNE, Hugh* (FF)	7,556	*(+18)* 7,574		*(+46)* 7,620	
D'ARCY, Michael J* (FG)	4,564	*(+33)* 4,597		*(+28)* 4,625	
DEMPSEY, Tony (FF)	7,520	*(+40)* 7,560		*(+75)* 7,635	
DWYER, John (SF)	4,964	*(+56)* 5,020		*(+128)* 5,148	
DOYLE, Avril (FG)	3,940	*(+29)* 3,969		*(+42)* 4,011	
DOYLE, Seán (Ind)	1,274	*(+41)* 1,315			
HOWLIN, Brendan* (Lab)	7,995	*(+78)* 8,073		*(+128)* 8,201	
KEHOE, Paul (FG)	7,048	*(+51)* 7,099		*(+288)* 7,387	
Ó BOLGUIDHIR, Miranda (Ind)	424				
O'CONNOR, Michael (CSP)	173				
TWOMEY, Liam (Ind)	5,815	*(+195)* 6,010		*(+203)* 6,213	
NON-TRANSFERABLE		25		40	

Wexford

4th Count Transfer of **Doyle, A** Votes	5th Count Transfer of **Dwyer** Votes	6th Count Transfer of **D'Arcy** Votes	7th Count Transfer of **Kehoe** Surplus	8th Count Transfer of **Browne** Surplus
(+91) 9,609	*(+569)* 10,178			
(+135) 7,755	*(+481)* 8,236	*(+466)* 8,702	*(+311)* 9,013	*(+59)* 9,072
(+1,020) 5,645	*(+190)* 5,835			
(+158) 7,793	*(+403)* 8,196	*(+627)* 8,823	*(+279)* 9,102	*(+48)* 9,150
(+69) 5,217				
(+723) 8,924	*(+1,211)* 10,135			
(+1,404) 8,791	*(+404)* 9,195	*(+3,436)* 12,631		
(+361) 6,574	*(+1,488)* 8,062	*(+678)* 8,740	*(+1,342)* 10,082	
50	471	628	628	

Wicklow

Voting by Party

1st Preference	Number	%	% 1997
Fianna Fáil	17,083	31.27	29.87
Fine Gael	8,722	15.97	19.71
Labour	16,144	29.55	13.80
Green Party	3,213	5.88	2.48
Sinn Féin	1,529	2.80	—
Socialist Workers' Party	400	0.73	—
Others	7,535	13.79	20.84

Statistics

Population	106,092	
Electorate	86,763	
Total Poll	55,296	63.72
Spoiled Votes	736	1.33
Valid Poll	54,560	62.88
Seats	5	
Quota	9,094	
Candidates	15	

Seats

FF	2
FG	1
Lab	1
Ind	1
No change	

The Wicklow constituency is unchanged since the 1997 General Election.

Dick Roche (FF)

Home Address/Constituency Office
2 Herbert Terrace, Herbert Road, Bray, Co Wicklow
Business Address
Department of the Taoiseach, Merrion Street, Dublin 2
Telephone
Home (01) 286 3211; *Office* (01) 619 4399; *Fax* (01) 286 7666
Website www.dickroche.com
Birth Place/Date
Wexford. March 1947
Married
Eleanor Griffin. 3 sons, 1 daughter
Education
Wexford CBS; University College, Dublin (BComm, DPA, MPA)
Occupation
Public representative. University lecturer

Dick Roche was a Dáil deputy 1987–92 and was re-elected in 1997. Having lost his seat in the 1992 general election, he was elected to the Seanad, Administrative Panel, during 1993–97. He was Taoiseach's nominee November 1992–February 1993.

Chairman Oireachtas Joint Committee on the Strategic Management Initiative 1997–2002. Party spokesperson on Public Finance in Seanad 1992–97 and on Public Service Reform 1994–97. Chairman, Oireachtas Joint Committee on State-Sponsored Bodies 1989–92.

Member, Wicklow County Council 1985–2002.

Member, Institute of Public Administration; International Ombudsman Institute; Associate of Graduates in Public Administration; Irish Council of the European Movement; Irish Commission for Justice and Peace (chairman 1985/86).

Liz McManus (Lab)

Home Address
1 Martello Terrace, Bray, Co Wicklow
Constituency Office
2 Belton House, Castle Street, Bray
Telephone
Constituency Office (01) 2760583; *Fax* (01) 2760584
Birth Place/Date
Montreal, Canada. March 1947
Married
John McManus. 3 sons, 1 daughter
Education
Holy Child Convent, Killiney, Co Dublin; University College, Dublin (BArch)
Occupation
Public representative. Writer. Formerly architect

Liz McManus was appointed spokesperson for Health and Children in June 2002.

She was first elected to the Dáil in 1992. She was the first woman to be elected to the Dáil for Democratic Left. She was Labour spokesperson for Health in the last Dáil. Before the parties merged, she was Democratic Left spokesperson on Health and Children, Justice, Equality and Law Reform, Arts, Heritage, Gaeltacht and the Islands.

She was Minister of State at the Department of the Environment, with special responsibility for Housing and Urban Renewal, 1994–97. Democratic Left spokesperson on Agriculture and Food, Equality and Law Reform and Health 1993–94. Chairperson, Task Force on the Needs of the Travelling Community 1993.

She has served on Wicklow County Council; County Wicklow Library Committee; County Wicklow National Monuments Advisory Committee; Bray Urban District Council (chairperson 1984–85). Director, Wicklow Tourism. Founder of Bray Women's Refuge. Established Bray Economic Action Committee.

Liz McManus won the Hennessy/New Irish Writing Award, the Listowel Award and the Irish PEN Award for her fiction. In 1990 she published her first novel, *Acts of Subversion*, which was nominated for the Aer Lingus/*Irish Times* Award for new writing.

Billy Timmins (FG)

Home Address
Sruhaun, Baltinglass, Co Wicklow
Constituency Office
Weaver Square, Baltinglass
Telephone
Home (0508) 81655; *Constituency Office*
(0508) 81016; *Mobile* 087 8159090
Birth Place/Date
Baltinglass. October 1959
Married
Madeleine Hyland. 2 sons, 3 daughters
Education
Patrician College, Ballyfin, Co Laois; University
College, Galway (BA, Diploma in Public
Relations, Marketing and Advertising)
Occupation
Full-time public representative. Formerly army
officer who served with the United Nations in
Lebanon and Cyprus

Billy Timmins was appointed spokesperson on
Agriculture and Food in June 2002. He was
elected to the Dáil on his first attempt in
1997. He won the seat previously held by his
father, Godfrey Timmins. Party spokesperson
on Defence – Peacekeeping and Humanitarian
Relief 1997–2000; Housing 2000–01; Deputy
spokesperson, Justice and Defence 2001–02.

Member, National Economic and Social
Forum. Member, Wicklow County Council
since 1999. Won Leinster and All-Ireland club
championship medals in 1990. Hobbies are
sports, reading, hill-walking and history.

Is a son of Godfrey Timmins who was a TD
for Wicklow 1968–87 and 1989–97.

Joe Jacob (FF)

Home Address
Main Street, Rathdrum, Co Wicklow
Telephone
Home (0404) 46528; *Constituency Office*
(0404) 46528; *Fax* (0404) 43026
Birth Place/Date
Kilrush, Co Clare. April 1939
Married
Patty Grant. 3 sons, 3 daughters
Education
De La Salle College, Wicklow; Terenure
College, Dublin
Occupation
Public representative. Formerly distribution
manager with Nítrigin Éireann Teoranta

Joe Jacob was first elected to the Dáil for
Wicklow in 1987. He was Minister of State at
the Department of Public Enterprise with
special responsibility for Energy 1997–2002.
He was Leas-Cheann Comhairle of the Dáil
1993–97.

Chairman of the Fianna Fáil Parliamentary
Party 1992–95.

Member, British-Irish Inter-Parliamentary Body
1991–92. Member of Fianna Fáil delegation to
Forum for Peace and Reconciliation.

Member, Wicklow County Council 1985–97;
Wicklow County Vocational Education
Committee 1985–97 (chairman 1991–93);
Eastern Health Board; Midlands and Eastern
Tourism Organisation; Wicklow Tourism.

Member, Gaelic Athletic Association – player
and administrator.

Mildred Fox (Ind)

Home Address
Lower Calary, Kilmacanogue, Co Wicklow
Telephone
Home (01) 2876386; *Office* (01) 6183548
Birth Place/Date
Dublin. 17 June 1971
Married
Daryl Tighe. 1 daughter
Education
St Kilian's Community School, Bray, Co
Wicklow; University College, Dublin (BA)
Occupation
Full-time public representative. Formerly hotel
front-office manager

Mildred Fox was first elected to the Dáil in
June 1995 in a by-election caused by the
death of her father, Johnny Fox. She was the
youngest member of the 27th Dáil and the
only independent woman deputy in the 27th
Dáil and the 28th Dáil.

In the vote for Taoiseach in June 1997, she
supported Bertie Ahern after outlining to the
Dáil various projects that she had secured for
her constituency.

Member of Wicklow County Council since
1995. Secretary, Wicklow County Board of
Ladies' GAA and playing member of local
football and camogie clubs. Member, Macra
na Feirme.

She is a daughter of Johnny Fox who was an
independent deputy for Wicklow elected in
1992. He had previously been a Fianna Fáil
councillor.

Wicklow

Seats 5 Quota 9,094	1st Count	2nd Count Transfer of **Roche** Surplus	3rd Count Transfer of **Hyland** Votes	4th Count Transfer of **Kenny** Votes
DE BURCA, Deirdre (GP)	3,208	*(+4)* 3,212	*(+28)* 3,240	*(+37)* 3,277
HYLAND, Barbara Mary (Ind)	171	*(+0)* 171		
FOX, Mildred* (Ind)	6,324	*(+18)* 6,342	*(+22)* 6,364	*(+46)* 6,410
JACOB, Joe* (FF)	7,836	*(+63)* 7,899	*(+14)* 7,913	*(+13)* 7,926
KEANE, Mairéad (SF)	1,527	*(+3)* 1,530	*(+6)* 1,536	*(+10)* 1,546
KEARNS, Robert (Ind)	406	*(+0)* 406	*(+6)* 412	*(+6)* 418
KEDDY, Charlie (Ind)	383	*(+1)* 384	*(+8)* 392	*(+12)* 404
KELLY, Nicky (Lab)	6,529	*(+3)* 6,532	*(+4)* 6,536	*(+19)* 6,555
KENNEDY, Catherine (SWP)	399	*(+1)* 400	*(+12)* 412	*(+13)* 425
KENNY, Brian (Ind)	236	*(+1)* 237	*(+10)* 247	
MCMANUS, Liz* (Lab)	7,595	*(+17)* 7,612	*(+24)* 7,636	*(+57)* 7,693
O'ROURKE, Raymond (FG)	1,332	*(+1)* 1,333	*(+20)* 1,353	*(+19)* 1,372
O'SHAUGHNESSY, Jimmy (Lab)	2,029	*(+2)* 2,031	*(+1)* 2,032	*(+0)* 2,032
ROCHE, Dick* (FF)	9,213			
TIMMINS, Billy* (FG)	7,372	*(+5)* 7,377	*(+11)* 7,388	*(+10)* 7,398
NON-TRANSFERABLE			5	5

5th Count	6th Count	7th Count	8th Count	9th Count	10th Count
Transfer of **Kearns, Keddy, Kennedy** Votes	Transfer of **O'Rourke** Votes	Transfer of **Keane** Votes	Transfer of **de Burca, O'Shaughnessy** Votes	Transfer of **McManus** Surplus	Transfer of **Jacob** Surplus
(+223) 3,500	*(+61)* 3,561	*(+465)* 4,026			
(+232) 6,642	*(+84)* 6,726	*(+249)* 6,975	*(+1,272)* 8,247	*(+422)* 8,669	*(+19)* 8,688
(+119) 8,045	*(+28)* 8,073	*(+233)* 8,306	*(+663)* 8,969	*(+156)* 9,125	
(+103) 1,649	*(+10)* 1,659				
(+107) 6,662	*(+29)* 6,691	*(+219)* 6,910	*(+899)* 7,809	*(+848)* 8,657	*(+12)* 8,669
(+208) 7,901	*(+219)* 8,120	*(+190)* 8,310	*(+2,210)* 10,520		
(+25) 1,397					
(+96) 2,128	*(+20)* 2,148	*(+40)* 2,188			
(+68) 7,466	*(+930)* 8,396	*(+80)* 8,476	*(+634)* 9,110		
66	16	183	536		

Summary of Returns (Dáil General Election 2002)

	Fianna Fáil			Fine Gael			Labour		
	No. of 1st preferences	% of 1st preferences	% of increase/ decrease	No. of 1st preferences	% of 1st preferences	% of increase/ decrease	No. of 1st preferences	% of 1st preferences	% of increase/ decrease
Carlow-Kilkenny	30,543	50.20	8.01	13,309	21.87	-7.31	8,004	13.15	-2.03
Cavan-Monaghan	21,614	34.95	-3.49	15,571	25.18	-9.49	550	0.89	-3.07
Clare	22,602	45.38	-4.98	12,680	25.46	-4.62	1,720	3.45	-0.14
Cork East	18,914	41.31	4.87	13,322	29.09	-1.03	9,605	20.98	2.12
Cork North-Central	18,725	41.48	5.95	9,202	20.38	-9.78	5,313	11.77	-0.65
Cork North-West	19,433	50.06	3.56	16,335	42.08	0.96	2,668	6.87	-0.53
Cork South-Central	26,831	48.57	5.96	10,718	19.40	-11.17	3,282	5.94	-2.98
Cork South-West	14,882	39.48	0.42	12,189	32.33	-11.85	3,442	9.13	2.38
Donegal North-East	17,954	49.40	7.59	7,637	21.01	2.14	1,021	2.81	-2.67
Donegal South-West	14,997	42.09	4.05	9,058	25.42	2.44	1,079	3.03	-1.17
Dublin Central	13,488	39.58	-3.25	3,768	11.06	-3.45	4,149	12.17	3.68
Dublin Mid-West	9,122	32.06	32.06	3,276	11.51	11.51	2,563	9.01	9.01
Dublin North	16,803	38.24	-0.41	5,189	11.81	-7.17	6,359	14.47	0.83
Dublin North-Central	20,043	50.05	3.61	6,809	17.00	-9.03	4,203	10.49	1.13
Dublin North-East	11,761	40.12	-0.49	4,504	15.36	-3.54	4,758	16.23	-4.72
Dublin North-West	12,435	47.54	0.50	2,082	7.96	-7.64	4,391	16.79	-4.43
Dublin South	20,250	36.64	-1.98	10,931	19.78	-9.31	5,247	9.49	-1.11
Dublin South-Central	15,106	34.32	-0.11	7,456	16.94	-8.01	8,679	19.72	-1.99
Dublin South-East	8,767	27.03	1.25	5,210	16.06	-11.32	4,032	12.43	-4.24
Dublin South-West	14,235	38.68	8.74	4,654	12.65	-2.85	7,285	19.80	-2.10
Dublin West	10,386	34.63	1.45	3,694	12.32	-4.62	3,810	12.71	0.59
Dún Laoghaire	16,243	30.29	4.46	8,069	15.04	-15.92	12,164	22.68	0.13
Galway East	23,117	46.77	-1.83	15,576	31.52	0.35	0	0.00	-7.92
Galway West	20,442	41.33	-4.62	8,359	16.90	-5.32	5,213	10.54	0.47
Kerry North	11,811	30.15	3.84	8,652	22.09	-2.20	8,773	22.40	-7.51
Kerry South	16,357	44.64	12.85	6,473	17.66	3.89	5,307	14.48	0.43
Kildare North	14,250	43.21	8.35	5,786	17.54	-8.64	7,051	21.38	-6.41
Kildare South	15,152	46.43	8.84	5,795	17.76	-8.73	6,043	18.52	-1.73
Laois-Offaly	32,432	51.30	1.46	14,553	23.02	-5.36	1,600	2.53	-9.08
Limerick East	19,973	39.95	0.23	13,919	27.84	1.33	4,629	9.26	-6.78
Limerick West	19,059	53.43	20.99	14,856	41.65	4.46	0	0.00	-4.22
Longford-Roscommon	20,251	40.76	-6.27	15,251	30.69	-6.22	638	1.28	-0.19
Louth	20,751	43.57	3.56	9,635	20.23	-7.66	3,185	6.69	-3.81
Mayo	25,380	39.98	-2.97	23,862	37.59	-11.16	0	0.00	0.00
Meath	28,786	44.92	3.04	17,452	27.23	-9.69	2,727	4.26	-3.67
Sligo-Leitrim	19,086	38.97	-1.43	13,059	26.67	-9.96	2,429	4.96	-5.90
Tipperary North	17,475	42.66	0.37	6,108	14.91	3.59	5,537	13.52	3.19
Tipperary South	14,121	38.51	1.23	8,997	24.54	0.45	3,353	9.14	-6.97
Waterford	21,576	46.34	10.55	10,003	21.48	-3.07	6,219	13.36	1.59
Westmeath	14,336	41.65	-4.02	9,363	27.20	1.33	8,967	26.05	1.54
Wexford	24,226	40.09	1.15	15,552	25.74	-12.84	7,995	13.23	-6.46
Wicklow	17,049	31.25	1.38	8,704	15.95	-3.76	16,153	29.61	5.81

Progressive Democrats			Green Party			Sinn Féin			Others		
No. of 1st prefer- ences	% of 1st prefer- ences	% of increase/ decrease	No. of 1st prefer- ences	% of 1st prefer- ences	% of increase/ decrease	No. of 1st prefer- ences	% of 1st prefer- ences	% of increase/ decrease	No. of 1st prefer- ences	% of 1st prefer- ences	% of increase/ decrease
0	0.00	-5.64	4,961	8.15	2.63	2,078	3.42	3.42	1,949	3.20	0.93
1,131	1.83	1.83	1,100	1.78	1.78	10,832	17.51	-1.85	11,049	17.87	14.30
0	0.00	-6.93	2,903	5.83	2.24	0	0.00	0.00	9,897	19.87	14.43
0	0.00	-4.25	1,136	2.48	2.48	2,624	5.73	2.17	187	0.41	-6.37
3,126	6.92	-0.58	1,155	2.56	-0.49	2,860	6.34	2.58	4,763	10.55	2.97
0	0.00	0.00	0	0.00	0.00	0	0.00	0.00	383	0.99	-3.99
0	0.00	-4.19	4,952	8.96	2.38	2,063	3.73	3.73	7,394	13.39	6.26
0	0.00	0.00	0	0.00	-3.49	2,207	5.85	5.85	4,978	13.20	6.68
0	0.00	0.00	0	0.00	0.00	3,611	9.93	1.83	6,124	16.85	-8.88
0	0.00	0.00	0	0.00	-4.21	3,829	10.75	10.75	6,672	18.72	-11.86
0	0.00	0.00	1,470	4.31	0.81	4,979	14.61	7.96	6,227	18.27	-5.75
5,706	20.05	20.05	3,508	12.33	12.33	1,855	6.52	6.52	2,426	8.53	8.53
0	0.00	-3.48	7,294	16.60	2.96	1,350	3.07	3.07	6,947	15.81	4.21
0	0.00	-3.30	2,275	5.68	1.86	2,299	5.74	5.74	4,419	11.03	-0.02
1,219	4.16	-3.65	1,656	5.65	2.08	3,003	10.24	4.31	2,417	8.24	6.01
0	0.00	0.00	607	2.32	-1.83	4,781	18.28	18.28	1,862	7.12	-4.87
8,288	15.00	5.61	5,222	9.45	3.35	2,172	3.93	3.93	3,153	5.71	-0.49
1,377	3.13	-1.88	2,299	5.22	1.27	5,591	12.70	7.93	3,508	7.97	2.79
6,093	18.79	7.82	5,264	16.23	4.52	2,398	7.39	7.39	669	2.06	-5.41
0	0.00	-13.64	1,157	3.14	0.00	7,466	20.29	11.39	2,005	5.45	-1.54
2,370	7.90	0.29	748	2.49	-1.83	2,404	8.02	3.02	6,576	21.93	1.10
7,166	13.36	4.82	5,002	9.33	4.24	2,159	4.03	4.03	2,830	5.28	-1.75
0	0.00	-7.41	1,022	2.07	2.07	1,828	3.70	3.70	7,879	15.94	11.05
6,192	12.52	0.25	2,193	4.43	0.99	2,779	5.62	3.11	4,288	8.67	5.12
0	0.00	0.00	0	0.00	0.00	9,496	24.24	8.34	441	1.13	-2.47
0	0.00	0.00	0	0.00	0.00	0	0.00	0.00	8,509	23.22	-17.17
3,919	11.88	5.19	1,974	5.99	1.52	0	0.00	0.00	0	0.00	0.00
3,887	11.91	-1.61	1,208	3.70	3.70	0	0.00	0.00	546	1.67	-0.47
9,088	14.38	7.87	520	0.82	0.82	2,600	4.11	4.11	2,424	3.83	0.17
4,885	9.77	-2.65	917	1.83	0.22	0	0.00	0.00	5,677	11.35	7.66
0	0.00	-4.18	948	2.66	2.66	0	0.00	0.00	806	2.26	-19.70
4,679	9.42	4.58	426	0.86	0.86	1,673	3.37	3.37	6,771	13.63	3.88
0	0.00	-5.32	1,979	4.16	1.04	7,121	14.95	6.84	4,952	10.40	5.36
919	1.45	1.45	669	1.05	-0.46	2,085	3.28	3.28	10,565	16.64	9.87
0	0.00	-2.37	2,337	3.65	1.70	6,042	9.43	5.90	6,737	10.51	5.09
0	0.00	-1.65	0	0.00	0.00	5,001	10.21	3.11	9,396	19.19	15.84
1,446	3.53	0.05	0	0.00	0.00	0	0.00	0.00	10,400	25.39	-7.20
0	0.00	0.00	0	0.00	0.00	1,210	3.30	3.30	8,985	24.50	1.99
2,137	4.59	-1.88	1,361	2.92	1.12	2,955	6.35	6.35	2,312	4.97	-14.66
0	0.00	0.00	0	0.00	0.00	1,185	3.44	3.44	570	1.66	-2.29
0	0.00	0.00	0	0.00	-1.68	4,964	8.22	8.22	7,686	12.72	11.61
0	0.00	-3.30	3,208	5.88	3.40	1,527	2.80	2.80	7,919	14.51	-6.33

General Statistics (Dáil General Election 2002)

Constituency	Population	Seats	Electors on Register	Total Votes Cast	%	Invalid Votes	%	Valid Poll	%	Quota	Candi-dates
Carlow-Kilkenny	113,543	5	97,071	61,688	63.55	844	1.37	60,844	62.68	12,169	11
Cavan-Monaghan	104,257	5	87,087	62,710	72.01	863	1.34	61,847	71.02	10,308	14
Clare	90,530	4	80,412	50,341	62.60	539	1.07	49,802	61.93	9,961	10
Cork East	83,001	4	72,702	46,334	63.73	546	1.18	45,788	62.98	9,158	9
Cork North-Central	104,787	5	79,063	45,692	57.79	548	1.20	45,144	57.01	7,525	13
Cork North-West	62,453	3	53,699	39,393	73.36	574	1.46	38,819	72.29	9,705	6
Cork South-Central	107,591	5	90,237	55,785	61.82	545	0.80	55,240	61.22	9,207	12
Cork South-West	62,678	3	54,274	38,132	70.26	434	1.14	37,698	69.46	9,425	10
Donegal North-East	67,691	3	58,208	36,896	63.39	549	1.49	36,347	62.44	9,087	7
Donegal South-West	62,303	3	54,789	36,135	65.95	500	1.38	35,635	65.04	8,909	10
Dublin Central	88,900	4	62,180	34,517	55.51	483	1.26	34,034	54.73	6,807	10
Dublin Mid-West	67,192	3	55,184	28,693	52.00	237	0.82	28,456	51.57	7,115	13
Dublin North	88,392	4	72,908	43,942	60.27	0	0	43,942	60.27	8,789	12
Dublin North-Central	86,954	4	65,583	40,475	61.72	427	1.05	40,048	61.06	8,010	10
Dublin North-East	68,637	3	52,105	29,634	56.87	316	1.07	29,318	56.27	7,330	10
Dublin North-West	67,129	3	47,641	26,543	55.71	385	1.45	26,158	54.91	6,540	9
Dublin South	114,491	5	92,645	55,690	60.11	427	0.77	55,263	59.65	9,211	11
Dublin South-Central	114,383	5	86,161	44,768	51.96	752	1.68	44,016	51.09	7,337	15
Dublin South-East	89,621	4	59,896	32,720	54.63	287	0.88	32,433	54.15	6,487	11
Dublin South-West	90,594	4	64,947	37,216	57.30	414	1.11	36,802	56.66	7,361	10
Dublin West	67,297	3	52,676	29,988	56.93	–	–	29,988	56.93	7,498	9
Dún Laoghaire	114,674	5	91,522	54,071	59.08	438	0.81	53,633	58.60	8,939	17
Galway East	84,945	4	73,659	49,874	67.71	452	0.91	49,422	67.01	9,885	9
Galway West	103,909	5	80,109	49,944	62.35	478	0.96	49,466	61.75	8,245	17
Kerry North	63,024	3	55,476	39,524	71.25	351	0.89	39,173	70.61	9,794	7
Kerry South	63,106	3	51,761	37,022	71.52	376	1.02	36,646	70.80	9,162	8
Kildare North	68,259	3	60,094	33,271	55.36	291	0.87	32,980	54.88	8,246	6
Kildare South	66,733	3	58,354	33,132	56.78	501	1.51	32,631	55.92	8,158	8
Laois-Offaly	112,062	5	95,373	63,888	66.99	671	1.05	63,217	66.28	10,537	14
Limerick East	105,548	5	80,593	50,513	62.68	513	1.02	50,000	62.04	8,334	15
Limerick West	62,970	3	53,879	36,145	67.09	476	1.32	35,669	66.20	8,918	7
Longford-Roscommon	82,141	4	70,650	50,310	71.21	621	1.23	49,689	70.33	9,938	15
Louth	92,166	4	81,952	48,274	58.91	651	1.35	47,623	58.11	9,525	15
Mayo	111,524	5	94,854	64,270	67.76	790	1.23	63,480	66.92	10,581	14
Meath	109,732	5	108,717	64,081	58.94	0	0	64,081	58.94	10,681	14
Sligo-Leitrim	80,878	4	70,460	49,494	70.24	523	1.06	48,971	69.50	9,795	12
Tipperary North	67,417	3	59,427	41,412	69.69	446	1.08	40,966	68.93	10,242	6
Tipperary South	67,605	3	56,092	37,056	66.06	390	1.05	36,666	65.37	9,167	8
Waterford	93,193	4	73,725	47,120	63.91	557	1.18	46,563	63.16	9,313	14
Westmeath	63,314	3	56,012	34,978	62.45	557	1.59	34,421	61.45	8,606	8
Wexford	104,371	5	94,969	61,440	64.69	1,017	1.66	60,423	63.62	10,071	12
Wicklow	106,092	5	86,763	55,296	63.72	736	1.38	54,560	62.88	9,094	15

The 29th Dáil has 166 deputies, the same as the previous Dáil. Of these 111 (66.87%) were outgoing members of the 28th Dáil, 8 (4.82%) were previous members of the House but not of the 28th Dáil, and 47 (28.31%) are new deputies.

New Deputies

Andrews, Barry (FF) – Dún Laoghaire
Blaney, Niall (Ind) – Donegal North-East
Boyle, Dan (GP) – Cork South-Central
Breen, James (Ind) – Clare
Breen, Pat (FG) – Clare
Callanan, Joe (FF) – Galway East
Carty, John (FF) – Mayo
Cassidy, Donie (FF) – Westmeath
Connolly, Paudge (Ind) – Cavan-Monaghan
Cowley, Jerry (Ind) – Mayo
Cregan, John (FF) – Limerick West
Crowe, Seán (SF) – Dublin South-West
Cuffe, Ciaran (GP) – Dún Laoghaire
Curran, John (FF) – Dublin Mid-West
Deasy, John (FG) – Waterford
Dempsey, Tony (FF) - Wexford
Devins, Jimmy (FF) – Sligo-Leitrim
English, Damien (FG) – Meath
Enright, Olwyn (FG) – Laois-Offaly
Ferris, Martin (SF) – Kerry North
Finneran, Michael (FF) – Longford-Roscommon
Glennon, Jim (FF) – Dublin North
Gogarty, Paul (GP) – Dublin Mid-West
Grealish, Noel (PD) – Galway West
Harkin, Marian (Ind) – Sligo-Leitrim
Hoctor, Máire (FF) – Tipperary North
Kehoe, Paul (FG) – Wexford
Kelly, Peter (FF) – Longford-Roscommon
McEllistrim, Tom (FF) – Kerry North
McGrath, Finian (Ind) – Dublin North-Central
McHugh, Paddy (Ind) – Galway East
Morgan, Arthur (SF) – Louth
Mulcahy, Michael (FF) – Dublin South-Central
Murphy, Gerard (FG) – Cork North-West
O'Connor, Charlie (FF) – Dublin South-West
O'Donovan, Denis (FF) – Cork South-West
O'Dowd, Fergus (FG) – Louth
O'Fearghail, Seán (FF) – Kildare South
O'Malley, Fiona (PD) – Dún Laoghaire
O'Malley, Tim (PD) – Limerick East
Ó Snodaigh, Aengus (SF) – Dublin South-Central
Parlon, Tom (PD) – Laois-Offaly
Power, Peter (FF) – Limerick East
Ryan, Eamonn (GP) – Dublin South
Sexton, Mae (PD) – Longford-Roscommon
Twomey, Liam (Ind) – Wexford
Wilkinson, Ollie (FF) – Waterford

Ex-TDs Re-elected

Costello, Joe (Lab) – Dublin Central
Burton, Joan (Lab) – Dublin West
Fitzpatrick, Dermot (FF) – Dublin Central
Gallagher, Pat the Cope (FF) – Donegal South-West
Lynch, Kathleen (Lab) – Cork North-Central
McDowell, Michael (PD) – Dublin South-East
Nolan, M.J. (FF) – Carlow-Kilkenny
Sherlock, Joe (Lab) – Cork East

Women Deputies

22 women (13.25 %) won seats in the 2002 general election, two more than in 1997 and the highest number so far.

Election	No. of Women Elected
2002	22
1997	20
1992	20
1989	13
1987	14
Nov 1982	14
Feb 1982	8
1981	11
1977	5
1973	4
1969	3

Women Elected 2002

Burton, Joan (Lab) – Dublin West
Cooper-Flynn, Beverly (FF) – Mayo
Coughlan, Mary (FF) – Donegal South-West
Enright, Olwyn (FG) – Laois-Offaly
De Valera, Síle (FF) – Clare
Fox Mildred (Ind) – Wicklow
Hanafin, Mary (FF) – Dún Laoghaire
Harkin, Marian (Ind) – Sligo-Leitrim
Harney, Mary (PD) – Dublin Mid-West
Hoctor, Máire (FF) – Tipperary North
Keaveney, Cecilia (FF) – Donegal North-East
Lynch, Kathleen (Lab) – Cork North-Central
McManus, Liz (Lab) – Wicklow
Mitchell, Olivia (FG) – Dublin South
Moynihan-Cronin, Breeda (Lab) – Kerry South
O'Donnell, Liz (PD) – Dublin South
O'Malley, Fiona (PD) – Dún Laoghaire
O'Sullivan, Jan (Lab) – Limerick East
Sexton, Mae (PD) – Longford-Roscommon
Shortall, Róisín (Lab) – Dublin North-West
Upton, Mary (Lab) – Dublin South-Central
Wallace, Mary (FF) – Meath

Deceased Deputies

Five deputies died during the period of the 28th Dáil:
Ahearn, Theresa (FG) – Tipperary South
Coveney, Hugh (FG) – Cork South-Central
Ferris, Michael (Lab) – Tipperary South
Kemmy, Jim (Lab) – Limerick East
Upton, Pat (Lab) – Dublin South-Central

Resignations

One deputy resigned during the 28th Dáil:
Burke, Ray (FF) – Dublin North

Retiring Deputies

Twenty-two outgoing deputies did not seek re-election in the 2002 election
Andrews, David (FF) – Dún Laoghaire
Barnes, Monica (FG) – Dún Laoghaire
Barrett, Seán (FG) – Dún Laoghaire
Blaney, Harry (Ind) – Donegal North-East
Brennan, Matt (FF) – Sligo-Leitrim
Briscoe, Ben (FF) – Dublin South-Central
Browne, John (FG) – Carlow-Kilkenny
Burke, Liam (FG) – Cork North-Central
Deasy, Austin (FG) – Waterford
De Rossa, Proinsias (Lab) – Dublin North-West
Doherty, Seán (FF) – Longford-Roscommon
Enright, Tom (FG) – Laois-Offaly
Flood, Chris (FF) – Dublin South-West
Foley, Denis (FF) – Kerry North
Gildea, Tom (Ind) – Donegal South-West
Lawlor, Liam (Ind) – Dublin West
McGahon, Brendan (FG) – Louth
Molloy, Robert (PD) – Galway West
O'Kennedy, Michael (FF) – Tipperary North
O'Malley, Desmond (PD) – Limerick East
Reynolds, Albert (FF) – Longford-Roscommon
Yates, Ivan (FG) – Wexford

Lost Seats

Bell, Michael (Lab) - Louth
Belton, Louis (FG) – Westmeath
Boylan, Andrew (FG) – Cavan-Monaghan
Bradford, Paul (FG) – Cork East
Burke, Ulick (FG) – Galway East
Byrne, Hugh (FF) – Wexford
Carey, Donal (FG) – Clare
Clune, Deirdre (FG) – Cork South-Central
Cosgrave, Michael J. (FG) – Dublin North-East
Creed, Michael (FG) – Cork North-West
Currie, Austin (FG) – Dublin Mid-West
Daly, Brendan (FF) – Clare
D'Arcy, Michael (FG) – Wexford
Dukes, Alan (FG) – Kildare South
Farrelly, John V. (FG) – Meath
Finucane, Michael (FG) – Limerick West

Statistics

Fitzgerald, Frances (FG) – Dublin South-East
Flanagan, Charles (FG) – Laois-Offaly
Hayes, Brian (FG) – Dublin South-West
Higgins, Jim (FG) – Mayo
Kenneally, Brendan (FF) – Waterford
Kitt, Michael (FF) – Galway East
McDowell, Derek (Lab)– Dublin North-Central
McGennis, Marian (FF) – Dublin Central
Mitchell, Jim (FG) – Dublin Central
Moffatt, Tom (FF) – Mayo
O'Rourke, Mary (FF) – Westmeath
Owen, Nora (FG) – Dublin North
Reynolds, Gerry (FG) – Sligo-Leitrim
Shatter, Alan (FG) – Dublin South
Sheehan, P.J. (FG) – Cork South-West
Spring, Dick (Lab) – Kerry North
Wade, Eddie (FF) – Limerick East

Defeated Deputies

Thirty-three deputies were defeated in the 2002 election: 8 Fianna Fáil, 22 Fine Gael and 3 Labour. They included former Tánaiste, and Labour Party leader, Dick Spring; former Fianna Fáil Minister, Mary O'Rourke and former Fine Gael Ministers, Jim Mitchell and Nora Owen.

Narrow Margins

The last seat in 18 constituencies was won by less than 500 votes compared with the same for 9 constituencies in 1997. The narrowest margin was just 1 vote which separated Fine Gael colleagues, Dan Neville and Michael Finucane in Limerick West. Seven of the narrow margins involved deputies from the same party.

Seat	Margin
Limerick West	1
Dan Neville (FG) from	
Michael Finucane (FG)	
Cork South-Central	6
John Dennehy (FF) from	
Kathy Sinnott (Ind)	
Cork South-West	35
Jim O'Keefe (FG) from	
P.J. Sheehan (FG)	
Cork North-West	47
Gerard Murphy (FG) from	
Michael Creed (FG)	
Longford-Roscommon	54
Michael Finneran (FF) from	
Greg Kelly (FF)	
Dublin Central	74
Dermot Fitzpatrick (FF) from	
Nicky Kehoe (SF)	
Wexford	78
Tony Dempsey (FF) from	
Hugh Byrne (FF)	

Wicklow	100
Mildred Fox (Ind) from	
Nicky Kelly (Lab)	
Cavan-Monaghan	121
Seymour Crawford (FG) from	
Andrew Boylan (FG)	
Kildare North	135
Bernard Durkan (FG) from	
Paul Kelly (FF)	
Kerry South	153
Jackie Healy-Rae (Ind) from	
Tom Fleming (FF)	
Kildare South	187
Jack Wall (Lab) from	
Alan Dukes (FG)	
Cork East	207
David Stanton (FG) from	
Paul Bradford (FG)	
Limerick East	305
Jan O'Sullivan (Lab) from	
Mary Jackman (FG)	
Galway West	309
Noel Grealish (PD) from	
Margaret Cox (FF)	
Carlow-Kilkenny	394
M.J. Nolan (FF) from	
Jim Townsend (Lab)	
Westmeath	450
Paul McGrath (FG) from	
Mary O'Rourke (FF)	
Kerry North	489
Jimmy Deenihan (FG) from	
Dick Spring (Lab)	

Family Seats

Of the 166 deputies in the 29th Dáil, 18 are sons of former deputies and 7 are daughters. In the 28th Dáil there were 23 sons and 7 daughters.

Síle de Valera and Éamon Ó Cuív are niece/nephew and grandchildren of former deputies. Their grandfather was Éamon de Valera, former Taoiseach and deputy and President of Ireland, and their uncle was Vivion de Valera a former deputy.

Brian and Conor Lenihan are sons and grandsons of former deputies. Seán Haughey is a son of a former Taoiseach, Charles Haughey, and a grandson of a former Taoiseach, Seán Lemass.

Relationships Among Deputies

There are three sets of brothers in the 29th Dáil:
Bertie Ahern (FF, Dublin Central)
Noel Ahern (FF, Dublin North-West)

John Bruton (FG, Meath)
Richard Bruton (FG, Dublin North-Central)
Brian Lenihan (FF, Dublin West)
Conor Lenihan (FF, Dublin South-West)

Leading Vote-getters

Eleven candidates in the 2002 election got a first-preference vote of more than 10,000. The highest was that of Micheál Martin who got 14,764 votes in Cork South-Central. Willie O'Dea got the second highest, a repeat of his performance in 1997 by polling 13,174 votes in Limerick East. The third was Brian Cowen who won 12, 529 votes in Laois-Offaly. Two candidates in Cavan-Monaghan polled over 10,000 votes: Caoimhghín Ó Caoláin who also topped the poll in 1997, and Brendan Smith who polled 10,679.

Top Ten	Votes
Micheál Martin (FF)	14,764
Cork South-Central	
Willie O'Dea (FF)	13,174
Limerick East	
Brian Cowen (FF)	12,529
Laois-Offaly	
Liam Aylward (FF)	12,169
Carlow-Kilkenny	
Noel Dempsey (FF)	11,534
Meath	
Bertie Ahern (FF)	10,896
Dublin Central	
Caoimhghín Ó Caoláin (SF)	10,832
Cavan-Monaghan	
Brendan Smith (FF)	10,679
Cavan-Monaghan	
Ned O'Keefe (FF)	10,574
Cork East	
Michael Moynihan (FF)	10,540
Cork North-West	
Michael Lowry (Ind)	10,400
Tipperary North	

Another way of assessing individual performances at the polls which allows for varying constituency factors such as the size of electorates and number of candidates is the multiple of the quota received by a candidate.

Candidate	Multiple of Quota
Micheál Martin (FF)	1.601
Cork South-Central	
Bertie Ahern (FF)	1.598
Dublin Central	
Willie O'Dea (FF)	1.581
Limerick East	
John Cregan (FF)	1.214
Limerick West	
Éamon Ó Cuív (FF)	1.206
Galway West	

Brian Cowen (FF) 1.189
Laois-Offaly
Ned O'Keefe (FF) 1.155
Cork East
Michael Noonan (FG) 1.144
Limerick East
Charlie McCreevy (FF) 1.101
Kildare North
Michael Moynihan (FF) 1.086
Cork North-West

24 candidates exceeded the quota on the first count: 19 Fianna Fáil, 2 Sinn Féin, 1 Fine Gael, 1 Labour and 1 Independent

Deputies: When First Elected

Date of Entry	General Election	By-elections
2002	47	—
1997	25	5
1992	16	5
1989	12	—
1987	18	—
1982 (Nov)	6	1
1982 (Feb)	6	1
1981	10	—
1977	9	—
1973	—	1
1969	3	—
1965	—	—
1961	1	—
Total	153	13

Dáil Service

Of the 166 deputies in the 29th Dáil, 47 (28.31%) entered the house for the first time in the 2002 general election. In the 1997 general election, 25 (15.06%) of them were elected for the first time and 5 later in by-elections. In the 1992 election, 16 (9.64%) entered the house for the first time and 5 later in by-elections. A total of 98 deputies have, therefore, entered the Dáil in the three elections and by-elections over the past 10 years.

Long-serving Deputies

The longest-serving deputy in the Dáil is Séamus Pattison (Lab, Carlow-Kilkenny), the present Leas-Cheann Comhairle, who was first elected in the 1961 general election. He has served continuously in the house since then and was Ceann Comhairle 1997–2002. He was also an MEP in 1981–83.

After Deputy Pattison the longest serving are: John Bruton (FG, Meath) and Noel Davern (FF,

Tipperary South) elected in 1969 (Michael Smith was first elected in 1969 but lost his seat in 1973 and again in 1982).

Enda Kenny (FG, Mayo) was elected in a 1975 by-election.

Bertie Ahern (FF, Dublin Central), Liam Aylward (FF, Carlow-Kilkenny), Charlie McCreevy (FF, Kildare North), Jim O'Keefe (FG, Cork South-West), Rory O' Hanlon (FF, Cavan-Monaghan), Ruairí Quinn (Lab, Dublin South-East), Joe Walsh (FF, Cork South-West) and Michael Woods (Dublin North-East) were first elected in 1977.

Síle de Valera (FF) was first elected in 1977 for Dublin Mid-County but lost her seat in 1981. She has represented Clare since 1987.

Marital Status and Families of Deputies

Of the 166 deputies returned to the 29th Dáil, 28 (16.87%) had not been married and 7 (4.22%) had been married and were separated. Two of these had re-married.

The married and separated deputies had a total of 441 children. The 116 with families had an average of 3.5 children.

Occupation of Deputies

Virtually all Dáil deputies now describe themselves as 'Full-Time Public Representatives.' In some cases they will also devote a certain amount of time to their previous occupations. In the following list, the occupations listed are those in which they were engaged before being elected.

Education	38
National Teachers	*14*
Secondary Teachers	*14*
Vocational Teachers	*1*
University Lecturers	*6*
Career Guidance/Youth Work	*2*
Pre-School	*1*
Farmers	18
Clerical and Technical	20
Company Directors/Managers	15
Lawyers	16
Solicitors	*9*
Barristers	*7*
Accountants	8
Science/Engineering/Architecture	7
Health Care (doctors, nurses etc)	13
Business interests	18
Trade Union officials	4
Auctioneers	4
Economists	1
Journalists	2
Public Relations	1
Army Officers	1

Changed Seats

In the 2002 general election party strengths changed in 23 constituencies and remained unchanged in 13. There was one new constituency, Dublin Mid-West, and 5 constituencies where the number of seats was reduced or increased by one.

Changed

Carlow-Kilkenny	FF gain from FG
Cavan-Monaghan	Ind gain from FG
Clare	Ind gain from FG
Cork East	Lab gain from FG
Cork North-Central	Lab gain from FG
Cork South-Central	GP gain from FG
Cork South-West	FF gain from FG
Dublin Central	Lab gain from FG
Dublin North	FF gain from FG
Dublin North-Central	Ind gain from Lab
Dublin South	GP gain from FG
Dublin South-East	PD gain from FG
Dún Laoghaire	PD and GP wins from FG
Galway East	Ind gain from FG
Kerry North	SF gain from Lab
Kildare South	FF gain from FG
Laois-Offaly	PD gain from FG
Limerick West	FF gain from FG
Longford-Roscommon	PD gain from FG
Louth	SF gain from Lab
Mayo	Ind gain from FG
Sligo-Leitrim	Ind gain from FG
Wexford	Ind from FG

Non-Qualification for Refund

The system whereby candidates would lose their deposit of £300 if they failed to exceed 25% of the quota was abolished after the 1997 general election as a result of a High Court challenge. Deposits are no longer needed but non-party candidates must have 30 signatures of persons on the electoral register in the constituency to secure a nomination.

Candidates may now obtain reimbursement of certain election expenses up to a maximum of 6,348 on condition that their votes, including transfers, exceed one quarter of the quota.

Of the 463 candidates contesting the 2002 general election, 161 (34.77%) did not qualify for a refund of expenses because their votes, after all transfers had been completed, did not exceed one quarter of the quota.

Statistics

In Dún Laoghaire and Wicklow, this applied to eight candidates in each constituency. In Limerick East, Longford-Roscommon and Louth, this applied to seven candidates in each constituency.

Among the main parties, the candidates who failed to qualify for refunds comprised 9 Fine Gael (10.6% of the party's candidates); 7 Labour (15.2%); 5 Progressive Democrats (25%); 13 Green Party (41.9%); 14 Sinn Féin (37.8%).

All 23 Christian Solidarity Party candidates failed to qualify, as did all 8 Workers' Party candidates and all 7 candidates of the Socialist Workers' Party. In the Socialist Party, 3 (60%) of the 5 candidates did not qualify.

Variations in Party Support by Constituency

Comparisons between the results of the 1997 and 2002 general elections are not possible in every constituency. Dublin Mid-West is a new constituency. Five constituencies have had seat changes and a number of others have had their boundaries adjusted.

Fianna Fáil

Fianna Fáil increased its share of the vote in 29 constituencies and showed a decrease in 12. The changes given below are in percentage points. The overall Fianna Fáil share of the vote was 41.49%, an increase of 2.16 percentage points over 1997.

Major Increases

Limerick West	20.99%
Kerry South	12.85%
Waterford	10.55%
Kildare South	8.84%
Dublin South-West	8.75%
Kildare North	8.35%
Carlow-Kilkenny	8.01%

Major Decreases

Longford-Roscommon	6.26%
Clare	4.98%

Fine Gael

Fine Gael increased its share of the vote in 10 constituencies and showed a decrease in 31. The overall share of the party's vote was 22.48%, a decrease of 5.47 percentage points compared with 1997.

Major Increases

Limerick West	4.46%
Tipperary North	3.59%
Kerry South	3.89%

Major Decreases

Dún Laoghaire	15.92%
Wexford	12.84%
Cork South-West	11.85%
Dublin South-East	11.32%
Cork South-Central	11.17%
Mayo	11.16%

Labour

Labour increased its vote in 19 constituencies and showed a decrease in 18. The overall share of the party's vote was 10.77%, a decrease of 2.14 percentage points compared with 1997 when the Labour and Democratic Left votes in that election are combined. The size of the increases below is partially explained by the merger of the two parties.

Major Increases

Wicklow	15.75%
Dún Laoghaire	14.02%
Cork East	12.85%
Dublin South-West	10.08%
Dublin South-Central	9.31%

Major Decreases

Laois-Offaly	9.08%
Kerry North	7.50%
Tipperary South	6.97%
Cork North-Central	6.50%

Progressive Democrats

The Progressive Democrats increased their share of the vote in 8 constituencies and showed a decrease in 5. The overall share of the party's vote was 3.96%, a decrease of 0.72 percentage points compared with 1997 although the party doubled its number of seats from 4 to 8.

Increases

Dublin South-East	7.82%
Dublin South	5.61%
Kildare North	5.19%
Dún Laoghaire	4.81%
Longford-Roscommon	4.58%

Decreases

Dublin North-East	3.64%
Limerick East	2.65%

Green Party

The Green Party increased its share of the vote in 16 constituencies and showed a decrease in 2. The party's overall share of the vote was 3.85%, an increase of 1.09 percentage points over 1997.

Increases

Dublin South-East	4.52%
Dún Laoghaire	4.24%
Wicklow	3.40%
Dublin South	3.35%

Decrease

Dublin West	1.83%

Sinn Féin

Sinn Féin increased its share of the vote in 14 constituencies where a comparison can be made. The party's overall share of the vote was 6.51%, an increase of 3.96 percentage points over 1997.

Major Increases

Dublin South-West	11.39%
Kerry North	8.33%
Dublin Central	7.96%
Dublin South-Central	7.93%
Louth	6.84%
Meath	5.90%

Educational Background of Deputies

Third level education is taken to include university, technical institute and specialised colleges, e.g. agricultural colleges

Level	Party							Total	%
	FF	FG	Lab	PD	GP	SF	Others		
First Level	—	—	—	—	—	—	2	2	1.2
Second Level	24	5	4	2	—	4	2	41	24.7
Third Level	57	26	17	6	6	1	10	123	74.01

Age Groupings of Deputies

Age	Number of Deputies							Total	%
	FF	FG	Lab	PD	GP	SF	Others		
Over 65	2	—	2	—	—	—	1	5	3.01
61-65	6	1	1	—	—	—	—	8	4.82
56-60	12	7	7	1	—	—	1	28	16.87
51-55	19	7	5	1	—	—	3	35	21.08
46-50	18	5	5	3	—	3	6	40	24.01
41-45	13	5	1	1	2	1	1	24	14.46
36-40	5	—	—	1	3	1	—	10	6.02
31-35	6	1	—	1	1	—	—	9	5.42
26-30	—	4	—	—	—	—	2	6	3.01
21-25	—	1	—	—	—	—	—	1	0.60

Parties' Performance

Party	Candidates	No. Elected	% Elected	% of 1st Prefs	% of Total Seats
FF	106	81	76.41	41.49	48.80
FG	85	31	36.47	22.48	18.67
Lab	46	21	45.65	10.77	12.65
PD	20	8	40.00	3.96	4.82
GP	31	6	19.35	3.85	3.61
SF	37	5	13.51	6.51	3.01
SP	5	1	20.00	0.80	0.60
WP	8	—	—	0.22	—
CSP	23	—	—	0.25	—
SWP	7	—	—	0.18	—
IHA	8	1	12.50	0.66	0.60
Others	87	12	13.79	8.83	7.23
Total	**463**	**166**		**100**	**99.99**

Interparty Transfers

The transfer of votes in second and succeeding counts is one of the most critical factors in the working of Proportional Representation voting. In the following tables, the transfers are analysed, taking into account all counts in all constituencies for which meaningful data are available.

Leakage

One of the most critical aspects of transfers is the ability of a party to ensure that transfers of surpluses of its candidates, or of the votes of eliminated candidates, go to other candidates of that party to the maximum extent possible.

Table 1 shows the percentage of transfers from each party to other candidates of the same party, where at least one other candidate of that party remains in the contest, and the percentage of non-transferable votes.

Coalition Parties

Table 2, page 180 shows the transfers within the two groups of parties that fought the election. These were the outgoing and declared Fianna Fáil-Progressive Democrats Coalition, and the Rainbow Coalition proposed by Fine Gael (Fine Gael-Labour-Green Party), when no other candidate of the party remained in the contest. The Rainbow Coalition was not overtly supported by either Labour or the Green Party.

Table 1

From	% To own party	% Non-transferable
FF	62.70	6.42
FG	63.02	6.48
Lab	49.43	11.29
PD*	45.14	5.02
SF*	57.25	2.51

* 2 counts only each
The Green Party did not field more than one candidate in any constituency.

Statistics

Table 2 Inter-Party Alliances

FIANNA FÁIL – PROGRESSIVE DEMOCRATS

From	% to FF	% to FG	% to Lab	% to PD	% to GP	% to Coalition Partner	% to Others	% Non-transferable
FF*	—	15.21	18.24	66.55	—	66.55	33.45	0.00
PD	34.56	28.25	22.79	—	1.93	34.56	57.96	7.48

* 1 count only

RAINBOW COALITION: FINE GAEL – LABOUR – GREEN PARTY

From	% to FF	% to FG	% to Lab	% to PD	% to GP	% to Coalition Partner	% to Others	% Non-transferable
FG	13.64	—	38.93	4.23	23.66	62.58	29.14	8.28
Lab	21.78	35.58	—	3.84	7.22	42.80	44.41	12.79
GP	18.31	14.89	32.64	3.26	—	47.53	37.96	14.51

Table 3 Destination of Transfers Given

FROM	FF	FG	Lab	PD	GP	SF	SP	WP	SWP	CSP	IHA	Ind	N/T	Total
FF	52.81	16.55	7.57	3.46	2.83	1.95	0.81	0.01	0.01	0.06	0.21	3.95	9.78	100.00
FG	14.24	46.72	12.34	4.10	5.33	0.85	0.30	0.00	0.00	0.00	0.19	6.62	9.31	100.00
Lab	18.43	32.95	10.72	3.01	6.90	4.06	0.06	0.00	0.00	0.00	4.04	7.36	12.46	100.00
PD	30.30	25.24	21.08	9.07	2.43	1.38	0.00	0.00	0.00	0.00	0.00	3.51	6.99	100.00
GP	18.31	14.89	32.64	3.26	0.00	4.66	0.46	0.00	0.00	0.00	4.12	7.15	14.51	100.00
SF	24.09	12.68	13.71	1.70	9.83	2.16	2.35	0.00	0.00	0.01	1.00	13.36	19.13	100.00
SP	8.36	13.37	26.21	2.41	21.05	13.50	0.00	0.00	0.00	0.00	3.66	3.04	8.39	100.00
WP	10.23	6.70	24.40	0.84	10.29	18.90	0.00	8.31	0.96	0.00	0.00	12.80	6.58	100.00
SWP	16.82	10.38	19.03	2.92	12.36	22.71	0.00	3.37	0.00	0.00	4.20	2.81	5.40	100.00
CSP	35.20	13.54	13.85	2.30	13.62	2.83	4.67	0.46	0.15	0.00	1.15	6.50	5.74	100.00
IHA	19.95	16.16	21.26	5.93	13.20	6.53	2.25	0.00	0.13	0.00	0.00	6.14	8.46	100.00
Ind	25.55	25.65	8.67	3.19	4.04	6.96	0.05	0.02	0.09	0.03	0.06	10.01	15.66	100.00
Sub-Total	26.38	27.26	13.09	3.54	5.18	3.14	0.65	0.05	0.02	0.02	1.04	7.43	12.21	100.00
Mixed*	23.64	26.96	16.16	2.70	3.87	4.70	0.52	0.19	0.00	0.00	0.81	10.33	10.12	100.00
All	**26.06**	**27.23**	**13.45**	**3.44**	**5.02**	**3.32**	**0.63**	**0.07**	**0.02**	**0.02**	**1.01**	**7.77**	**11.96**	**100.00**

* Votes or surplus of candidates from more than one party distributed in one count

Table 4 Composition of Transfers Received

Taking all counts into account, whether another candidate of the same party remained in the contest or not, the transfers received by each party from its own candidates and from candidates of other parties are as follows:

FROM	FF	FG	Lab	PD	GP	SF	SP	WP	SWP	CSP	IHA	Ind	N/T	All
FF	35.46	10.63	9.84	17.59	9.86	10.28	22.38	1.57	10.19	67.03	3.59	8.89	14.31	17.50
FG	12.73	39.95	21.37	27.69	24.71	5.94	11.22	0.00	0.00	1.10	4.32	19.82	18.13	23.29
Lab	6.84	11.71	7.71	8.45	13.29	11.83	0.95	0.00	0.00	1.10	38.66	9.16	10.08	9.67
PD	4.28	3.42	5.78	9.70	1.78	1.53	0.00	0.00	0.00	0.00	0.00	1.66	2.15	3.68
GP	4.74	3.69	16.38	6.39	0.00	9.47	4.96	0.00	0.00	0.00	27.50	6.21	8.19	6.75
SF	10.73	5.40	11.83	5.72	22.73	7.54	43.13	0.00	0.00	7.69	11.52	19.95	18.56	11.61
SP	0.18	0.27	1.07	0.38	2.30	2.23	0.00	0.00	0.00	0.00	1.99	0.21	0.39	0.55
WP	0.11	0.07	0.52	0.07	0.59	1.63	0.00	36.29	14.81	0.00	0.00	0.47	0.16	0.29
SWP	0.30	0.17	0.65	0.39	1.13	3.14	0.00	23.50	0.00	0.00	1.91	0.17	0.21	0.46
CSP	0.30	0.11	0.23	0.15	0.61	0.19	1.66	1.57	1.85	0.00	0.26	0.19	0.11	0.22
IHA	1.05	0.81	2.16	2.35	3.59	2.68	4.87	0.00	9.26	0.00	0.00	1.08	0.97	1.37
Ind	12.56	12.07	8.26	11.86	10.31	26.83	1.09	3.66	63.89	23.08	0.82	16.50	16.77	12.81
Sub-Total	89.29	88.31	85.82	90.75	90.90	83.30	90.25	66.58	100.00	100.00	90.56	84.31	90.01	88.20
Mixed*	10.71	11.69	14.18	9.25	9.10	16.70	9.75	33.42	0.00	0.00	9.44	15.69	9.99	11.80
Total	**100**	**100**	**100**	**100**	**100**	**100**	**100**	**100**	**100**	**100**	**100**	**100**	**100**	**100**

* Votes or surplus of candidates from more than one party distributed in one count

Transfer Analysis
By Richard Sinnott

The evidence

As the name of the Irish electoral system (PR-STV) suggests, each voter has a single vote and his or her ballot paper can be thought of as a set of instructions to the returning officer as to what to do with that vote. As it proceeds, the counting of votes leaves a trail of evidence regarding the political preferences and political behaviour of the voters. The two principal features of voting behaviour revealed in this way are the degree of party loyalty and the strength or weakness of inter-party alliances.

However, the trail of evidence is incomplete, complex and, at times, imperfect. It is incomplete principally because the further preferences in the votes of candidates who are elected or are runners-up on the final count are not revealed since, at that stage, the contest is over. The evidence is complex because the distribution of preferences depends on which candidates and which parties are still in contention at any given count. The evidence is imperfect because the process of transferring surplus votes ignores and thus underreports non-transferable votes and because, when such surpluses arise on counts later than the first count, only the votes acquired at the count on which the candidate was elected (the so-called 'last parcel of votes received') are examined in order to determine the destination of the surplus. The evidence is also imperfect because, when a candidate is elected or eliminated at a late stage, the vote being distributed may include votes received from candidates of other parties or of none.

Notwithstanding these qualifications, PR-STV throws up more evidence about the views and the behaviour of the voters than any other voting system, evidence that relates, in particular, to the ability of parties to elicit loyal support from their voters and to the response of the voters to any explicit, implicit or putative alliances between the parties.

Party loyalty

Election 2002 saw a further dip in party loyalty among Irish voters. Party loyalty is revealed by our trail of evidence when a party has more than one candidate in a constituency and one of those candidates has been elected or eliminated while at least one other candidate of the party remains in contention. Loyal votes are those that are passed on to the party colleague(s) of the elected/eliminated candidate instead of 'leaking' to other parties or becoming non-transferable (see Table 1 on page 179). Fianna Fáil loyalty declined to 62.7 per cent in 2002, a drop of almost five percentage points since 1997. But it had also dropped in 1998 relative to 1992 (by 3 points) and in 1992 relative to 1989 (by 9 points). Cumulatively, Fianna Fáil loyalty is down 16.6 percentage points over the last five elections (figures relating to past elections are from previous editions of this Guide). The level of loyalty among Fine Gael voters also declined over the same period (by 12 points), the main fall occurring at a single election – that of 1992. In 2002 the two main parties showed almost identical levels of loyalty, or, if you like, identical levels of leakage. Given other evidence that we have of declining levels of party attachment or party identification among the voters, reversing the trend towards increased vote leakage is likely to be difficult.

Table 1 also shows the level of party loyalty in 2002 for Labour, the PDs and Sinn Féin. These figures should be treated with caution as they are based on very few counts –

three in the case of Labour in 2002 and two each in the case of the PDs and Sinn Féin.

Inter-party alliances

The 2002 election was remarkable for, among other things, the failure of the two putative coalitions to harden into explicit inter-party transfer pacts and into corresponding mutual appeals to party voters to pass their preferences on to the other party or parties in the would-be alliance (see the account of the election on pages 6–8 for details). It might seem at first sight that Fianna Fáil voters responded rather well to such alliance signals as did emanate from the party leadership since it appears that fully two-thirds of them transferred their votes to the Progressive Democrats when no Fianna Fáil candidate remained in contention. However, the figure of 66.55 per cent in Table 2, page 180 should be treated with great caution as it is based on only a single count in a single constituency and, moreover, is based on the transfer of surplus votes with a consequent underestimation of the proportion of non-transferable votes. In short, the published results of the election do not provide any reliable evidence of the rate of transfer from Fianna Fáil to the Progressive Democrats in 2002.

We are on firmer ground in the case of Progressive Democrat to Fianna Fáil transfers. Here we have seven instances and the evidence from them shows that only a minority of PD voters extended a helping hand to Fianna Fáil candidates. This does not necessarily mean that they were opposed to a FF-PD coalition; it may simply have reflected the belief that transferring votes to Fianna Fáil candidates could have contributed to a Fianna Fáil majority and to the redundancy, as for as government formation is concerned, of their own party.

Statistics

On the other side of the political fence, coalition overtures also received a mixed response that reflected the mixed signals coming from the parties. Fine Gael voters showed fairly consistent support for the coalition in their voting preferences – when Fine Gael votes were being transferred with no continuing Fine Gael candidate available to receive them but with either a Labour or a Green Party candidate (or both) available, 62.58 per cent of Fine Gael voters transferred to one or other of the presumed coalition partners. The favour was not returned, at least not in the same measure. In the parallel situations, the rate of Green Party transfers to the other Rainbow Coalition partners was 47.53 per cent and the rate of Labour transfers was 42.8 per cent.

Other transfers

Table 3, page 180, provides a global view of all transfers in all counts, irrespective of which party or parties were available to receive transfers. Because of this, the estimates in Table 3 are very approximate but are somewhat more reliable in the case of the smaller parties. Looking for example at Sinn Féin and taking account of the approximate nature of the estimates, it seems that there was a somewhat lower rate of transfer from Sinn Féin to Fianna Fáil and to Labour in 2002 compared with 1997 and a lower rate of non-transferring or plumping by Sinn Féin (down to about one-fifth). Beneficiaries of these changes were mainly the Greens and candidates of the Independent Health Alliance.

The transfer behaviour of those who voted for independent candidates in 2002 followed a very similar pattern to 1997. Half of such voters transferred (in more or less equal proportions) to Fianna Fáil and Fine Gael. The only slight difference in 2002 is a somewhat higher rate of transfer from independent candidates to Sinn Féin. The transfer behaviour of voters who supported independent candidates attached to the Independent Health Alliance was quite different from that of supporters of independent candidates as such. The main difference was a lower rate of transfer to Fianna Fáil and Fine Gael, a lower rate of plumping and a higher rate of transfer to Labour and the Greens (but not to Sinn Féin).

Transfer patterns can also be looked at from the point of view of the receiving party. Rather than showing the behaviour of the voters, this shows the composition of the total transfer vote received by each party and the particular dependencies involved (see Table 4, page 180).

The future

Allowing for the qualifications noted at the outset, the 2002 election shows a pattern of vote transfers that is more variegated and less in the control of the parties than has tended to be the case in the past. This is reflected in indications of lower party loyalty, lower levels of inter-party transfer and, in general, a greater degree of dispersion of votes in the transfer process. This corresponds to other signs of fragmentation in the party system and poses a considerable challenge to all parties and candidates as they contemplate their options for the next election.

Constituency Profiles

	Highest	Lowest
% Turnout	Cork North-West (73.36%)	Dublin South-Central (51.96%)
% Spoiled Votes	Dublin South-Central (1.68)	Dublin South (0.77)
Quota	Carlow-Kilkenny (12,169)	Dublin South-East (6,487)
Candidates	Dún Laoghaire Galway West } 17 each	Cork North-West Kildare North Tipperary North } 6 each
Candidates/Seat	Longford-Roscommon Louth } 3.75 each	Cork North-West Kildare North Tipperary North } 2 each
Population (1996 Census)	Dún Laoghaire (114,674)	Cork North-West (62,453)
Population/Seat	Waterford (23,298)	Sligo-Leitrim (20,220)
Electorate	Meath (108,717)	Kerry South (51,761)
Electorate/Seat	Meath (21,743)	Dublin South-East (14,974)
FF share of 1st Prefs	Limerick West (53.43%)	Dublin South-East (27.03%)
FG share of 1st Prefs	Cork North-West (42.08%)	Dublin North-West (7.96%)
Lab share of 1st Prefs	Westmeath (26.05%)	Cavan-Monaghan (0.89%) (3 constituencies not contested by Lab)
PD share of 1st Prefs	Dublin Mid-West (20.05%)	Mayo (1.45%) (24 constituencies not contested by PDs)
GP share of 1st Prefs	Dublin North (16.60%)	Mayo (1.05%) (11 constituencies not contested by GP)
SF share of 1st Prefs	Kerry North (24.24%)	Wicklow (2.8%) (8 constituencies not contested by SF)
SP share of 1st Prefs	Dublin West (21.48%)	Dublin South (1.92%) (37 constituencies not contested by SP)
WP share of 1st Prefs	Waterford (2.72%)	Louth (0.37%) (35 constituencies not contested by WP)
SWP share of 1st Prefs	Dún Laoghaire (1.63)	Cork South-Central (0.40%) 35 constituencies not contested by SWP
CSP share of 1st Prefs	Dublin Central (1.07%)	Dublin South-West Longford-Roscommon (0.16% each) (19 constituencies not contested)
HA share of 1st Prefs	Dublin North-Central (9.45%)	Dún Laoghaire Kerry North (0.59% each) (34 constituencies not contested by IHA)

Pre-Election Poll Findings

It is fair to say that the 2002 General Election campaign was characterised by an unprecedented level of media attention afforded to opinion polls. Coverage of the polls reached saturation level on the morning of Friday 3 May, not as a result of that day's opinion poll findings *per se*, but rather as a reaction to the decision taken by MRBI and *The Irish Times* to amend the method of questioning from which party voting intentions are derived.

The new questioning technique was introduced with a view to counteracting the historical propensity of opinion polls in Ireland to overestimate levels of support for Fianna Fáil. Prior to the 2002 Election, MRBI had invested significant resources in attempting to identify the key factor or factors driving this overstatement. During February 2002, for example, MRBI had conducted a bespoke research study, one of the key findings from which was that a significant proportion of all potential voters either could not identify the party to which a TD they could name belonged, or identified their named TD with an incorrect party. Among the latter group, stated support for Fianna Fáil was well above average.

The implications were clear: once the various candidates had been declared, respondents should be asked which candidate, rather than which party, they were likely to vote for. For the last two MRBI pre-election polls of the campaign, therefore, the historical party support question was dropped altogether, with interviewees instead presented with a simulated ballot paper. The ballot paper listed the candidates standing in the respondent's constituency by name, along with the party to which they belonged, where relevant. Respondents then allocated their first, second, third preferences etc, as they would when actually casting their votes. At analysis stage, consolidated party support figures were then calculated by simply adding together the results for all Fianna Fáil candidates, all Fine Gael candidates, and so on.

The table illustrates first preference voting intentions as measured on Monday 13 May, four days before polling day, alongside the actual first preference vote achieved. The third column notes the variation between voting intentions and actual vote achieved. In interpreting these poll findings and the degree to which they provided solid indicators of the performance of the various parties at the actual election, two key factors need to be taken into consideration. Firstly, a statistical

PRE-ELECTION POLL FINDINGS VS. ELECTION OUTCOME

	13 May Opinion Poll	17 May Election Outcome	Variation
Fianna Fáil	45.2	41.5	+3.7
Fine Gael	20.6	22.5	−1.9
Labour	11.6	10.8	+0.8
Sinn Féin	6.7	6.5	+0.2
Progressive Democrats	2.0	4.0	−2.0
Green Party	3.4	3.8	−0.4
Independents	10.6	10.9	−0.3

margin of error of ±3% applies to any such survey of 1,000 respondents. Secondly, and most importantly, the opinion poll was carried out a full four days before people actually cast their votes.

In terms of margins of error, it can be seen that the variation between voting intentions and actual behaviour for Labour, Sinn Féin, the Green Party and Independents is negligible. Indeed, the only party support figures which fractionally exceed the margin of error when compared with the actual vote achieved is Fianna Fáil and, less so, the PDs. It has by now been well documented that when it became apparent from the opinion polls that Fianna Fáil could potentially achieve an overall majority the PDs, most visibly in the person of party president Michael McDowell, launched a vigorous anti-Fianna Fáil majority campaign.

The more recent *Irish Times*/MRBI polls had shown quite clearly that the electorate wanted the return of a Fianna Fáil/PD Government, not a single party administration. In warning against a Fianna Fáil majority, the PDs were thus deliberately tapping into the underlying fears and concerns of the Irish electorate. The campaign was of course a resounding success, with a marginal fall-off in support for Fianna Fáil during the last days of the campaign, and a corresponding uplift in support for the Progressive Democrats.

From a purely numerical perspective therefore, the unique manner in which MRBI employed the ballot paper technique produced a set of figures widely acknowledged to have accurately reflected the electorate's first preference voting intentions four days prior to election day.

In terms of accurately predicting the most likely material outcome of the election with regard to Government make-up and opposition strengths and weaknesses, however, reference should be made to my commentary on the same poll which appeared

in *The Irish Times* on 15 May, and written on the evening of Monday 13 May.

By way of interpreting the poll findings, it was stated that Bertie Ahern seemed almost certain to emerge as the next Taoiseach, and that if Fianna Fáil required support from outside the party, the most likely arrangement appeared to be Fianna Fáil along with the PDs and/or a number of like-minded Independents.

It was also stated that Fine Gael appeared set to lose seats, with the precise extent of its losses impossible to quantify as it would be fighting for a range of seats on the final count. Labour it was said could make but modest gains on its then existing standing of 21 seats, while from Sinn Féin's perspective, it was pointed out that the party's target of three seats seemed probable, with four or more a distinct possibility.

As an overview, it was concluded that as the Green Party and Independents also appeared likely to increase their number of seats, the long-term outcome of the election could well represent a realignment of Irish politics, with the right-of-centre ground belonging to the Fianna Fáil-PD bloc, left-of-centre defaulting to Labour, and Sinn Féin, the Green Party and Socialist Independents representing the more radical left, with Fine Gael facing some difficult decisions.

At a time when some commentators are still questioning the value and veracity of pre-election opinion polls, reasoned consideration should be given to the accuracy of the 2002 *Irish Times*/MRBI series, and the degree to which they kept the electorate informed of the mood of the nation as election day loomed.

Ian McShane,
Managing Director,
MRBI Limited

Dublin North (11 March 1998)

The election was caused by the resignation of Ray Burke (FF). The seat was won by Seán Ryan (Lab) on the 14th count.

Voting		%
Electorate	65,891	
Valid Poll	33,046	50.15
Quota	16,524	

1st Count		%
Condrot-Ruigrok, Rena	780	2.36
Cooney, Benny (Ind)	18	0.05
Daly, Clare (SP)	2,692	8.14
Donnelly, Paul (SF)	1,088	3.29
Fallon, Finian (PD)	533	1.61
Farrelly, Peter	34	0.10
Goulding, Ciaran (Ind)	682	2.06
Holohan, Joe (DL)	225	0.68
Jenkinson, Philip (FG)	3,185	9.63
Keaveney, Angela (CSP)	565	1.70
Kennedy, Michael (FF)	10,334	31.27
Martin, Paul (GP)	1,092	3.30
McDonald, John	107	0.32
Nagle, Alan (Ind)	44	0.13
O'Neill, Noel (NLP)	15	0.05
Rooney, Elaine (Ind)	176	0.53
Ryan, Seán (Lab)	**11,012**	**33.32**
Shields, Gertie (Ind)	452	1.37
Fallon, Jim (Ind)	12	0.04

Limerick East (11 March 1998)

The election was caused by the death of Jim Kemmy (Lab). The seat was won by Jan O'Sullivan (Lab) on the fifth count.

Voting		%
Electorate	78,062	
Valid Poll	42,703	54.70
Quota	21,352	

1st Count		%
Bennis, Nora (NP)	700	1.64
Gilligan, John	850	1.99
Hannan, Noel	108	0.25
Jackman, Mary (FG)	10,445	24.46
Marsh, Sandra (FF)	10,173	23.82
O'Malley, Tim (PD)	4,287	10.04
O'Sullivan, Jan (Lab)	**10,619**	**24.87**
Ryan, John (DL)	3,868	9.01
Shapland, Jenny (SF)	909	2.13
Sheehan, Bernard (Ind)	198	0.46
Sheppard, Eric (GP)	546	1.28

Cork South-Central (23 October 1998)

The election was caused by the death of Hugh Coveney (FG). The seat was won by Simon Coveney (FG) on the third count.

Voting		%
Electorate	86,195	
Valid Poll	43,007	49.90
Quota	21,504	

1st Count		%
Behan, Sinéad (FF)	12,658	29.43
Boyle, Dan (GP)	3,461	8.05
Cooney, Benny (Ind)	197	0.46
Coveney, Simon (FG)	**16,212**	**37.70**
Cremin, Harry (SF)	1,158	2.69
Kelly, Peter (PD)	971	2.26
McEnery, Brian (NLP)	150	0.35
O'Sullivan, Toddy (Lab)	8,171	18.00
Tallon, Jim	29	0.07

Dublin South-Central (27 October 1999)

The election was caused by the death of Pat Upton (Labour). The seat was won by Mary Upton (Lab) on the eighth count.

Voting		%
Electorate	69,771	
Valid Poll	20,116	28.83
Quota	10,059	

1st Count		%
Burns, John (NLP)	106	0.53
Byrne, Catherine (FG)	4,037	20.07
Goodwillie, John (GP)	1,263	6.28
Kelly, Shay (WP)	555	2.76
MacMeanmain, Manus (CSP)	399	1.98
Mulcahy, Michael (FF)	6,050	30.08
Murphy, Eamonn	383	1.90
Ó Snodaigh, Aengus (SF)	1,686	8.38
Upton, Mary (Lab)	**5,637**	**28.02**

Tipperary South (22 June 2000)

The by-election was caused by the death of Michael Ferris (Lab). The seat was won by Seamus Healy (Ind) on the third count.

Voting		%
Electorate	53,984	
Valid Poll	30,576	56.64
Quota	15,289	

1st Count		%
Ferris, Ellen (Lab)	5,133	16.79
Hayes, Tom (FG)	8,184	26.77
Healy, Seamus (Ind)	**9,419**	**30.81**
Heney, Mary (CSP)	784	2.56
McInerney, Raymond (NLP)	97	0.32
O'Brien, Barry (FF)	6,959	22.76

Tipperary South (30 June 2001)

The by-election was caused by the death of Theresa Ahearn (FG). The seat was won by Tom Hayes (FG) on the third count.

Voting		%
Electorate	54,903	
Valid Poll	31,907	58.12
Quota	15,954	

1st Count		%
Hayes, Tom (FG)	**11,446**	**35.87**
Landy, Denis (Lab)	4,103	12.86
Maguire, Michael (FF)	8,461	26.52
Prendergast, Phil (Ind)	7,897	24.75

Seanad Éireann (elected July 2002)

Fianna Fáil	30	Progressive Democrats	4
Fine Gael	15		
Labour	5	Others	6

	Senator	Whip	Panel/Constituency
	Bannon, James	FG	Industrial and Commercial
*	Bohan, Eddie	FF	Industrial and Commercial
	Bradford, Paul	FG	Agricultural
	Brady, Cyprian	FF	Taoiseach's Nominee
	Brennan, Michael	FF	Taoiseach's Nominee
	Browne, Fergal	FG	Labour
	Burke, Paddy	FG	Agricultural
	Burke, Ulick	FG	Agricultural
*	Callanan, Peter	FF	Agricultural
*	Coghlan, Paul	FG	Industrial and Commercial
	Coonan, Noel	FG	Cultural and Educational
*	Cox, Margaret	FF	Industrial and Commercial
	Cummins, Maurice	FG	Labour
	Daly, Brendan	FF	Labour
*	Dardis, John	PD	Taoiseach's Nominee
	Dooley, Timmy	FF	Administrative
	Feeney, Geraldine	FF	Labour
	Feighan, Frank	FG	Administrative
	Finucane, Michael	FG	Labour
*	Fitzgerald, Liam	FF	Labour
*	Glynn, Camillus	FF	Administrative
	Hanafin, John	FF	Labour
	Hayes, Brian	FG	Cultural and Educational
*	Hayes, Maurice	Ind	Taoiseach's Nominee
*	Henry, Mary	Ind	University of Dublin
	Higgins, Jim	FG	Labour
	Kenneally, Brendan	FF	Taoiseach's Nominee
*	Kett, Tony	FF	Administrative
*	Kiely, Rory	FF	Agricultural
	Kitt, Michael	FF	Taoiseach's Nominee
	Leyden, Terry	FF	Labour
*	Lydon, Don	FF	Labour
	MacSharry, Marc	FF	Industrial and Commercial
	Mansergh, Martin	FF	Agricultural
	McCarthy, Michael	Lab	Labour
	McDowell, Derek	Lab	Industrial and Commercial
	McHugh, Joe	FG	Administrative
	Minihan, John	PD	Taoiseach's Nominee
*	Mooney, Paschal	FF	Cultural and Educational
	Morrissey, Tom	PD	Taoiseach's Nominee
*	Moylan, Pat	FF	Taoiseach's Nominee

	Senator	Whip	Panel/Constituency
*	Norris, David	Ind	University of Dublin
*	O'Brien, Francis	FF	Agricultural
*	O'Meara, Kathleen	Lab	Agricultural
*	Ó Murchú, Labhrás	FF	Cultural and Educational
*	Ormonde, Ann	FF	Cultural and Educational
	O'Rourke, Mary	FF	Taoiseach's Nominee
*	O'Toole, Joe	Ind	National University of Ireland
	Phelan, John Paul	FG	Agricultural
	Phelan, Kieran	FF	Industrial and Commercial
*	Quinn, Feargal	Ind	National University of Ireland
*	Ross, Shane	Ind	University of Dublin
*	Ryan, Brendan	Lab	National University of Ireland
	Scanlon, Eamon	FF	Agricultural
	Terry, Sheila	FG	Industrial and Commercial
	Tuffy, Joanna	Lab	Administrative
*	Walsh, Jim	FF	Agricultural
	Walsh, Kate	PD	Taoiseach's Nominee
	White, Mary M.	FF	Industrial and Commercial
	Wilson, Diarmuid	FF	Administrative

Voting in the Seanad Elections held as a consequence of the dissolution of the 28th Dáil was for 49 of the 60 seats, the remaining 11 members being nominated later by the Taoiseach. Of the 49 elected members, 43 were returned from the Vocational Panels and 6 from the University Constituencies. Voting was completed on 17 July for the University Constituencies and for the Vocational Panels.

Of the seats on the Vocational Panels, Fianna Fáil won 24, Fine Gael 15 and Labour 4. Of the University members, 5 are Independent and 1 is Labour. Of the Taoiseach's nominees, 6 accept the Fianna Fáil whip, 4 accept the Progressive Democrats whip and 1 has not accepted any whip.

In the list, an asterisk denotes an outgoing senator. There were 24 re-elected or re-nominated; 11 had lost their Dáil seats in the 2002 general election.

Elected (5 Seats)

Paschal Mooney (FF)*
12th Count
Labhrás Ó Murchú (FF)*
14th Count
Brian Hayes (FG)
16th Count
Noel Coonan (FG)
16th Count
Ann Ormonde (FF)*
17th Count

Paschal Mooney (FF)

Address Carrick Road,
Drumshanbo, Co Leitrim
Tel. (078) 41236/41013;
Fax (078) 41237
b. Dublin. October 1947
m. Sheila Baldrey. 3s, 2d
Educ. Presentation Bros, Carrick-on-Shannon; Camden Inst, London
Occ. Journalist, broadcaster, public representative
Senator since 1987. Member, National Economic and Social Forum and National Forum on Europe. Member Leitrim CC since 1991, Chairman 1994/95. Vice-Chairman Leitrim VEC, Chairman Leitrim Sports Advisory Body.

Labhrás Ó Murchú (FF)

Address An Boithrín Glas, Caiseal, Co Thiobraid Árann
Tel. (062) 61552; **Fax** (062) 61552
b. Cashel, Co Tipperary. 14 August 1939
m. Una Ronan
Educ. Cashel CBS
Occ. Director-General, Comhaltas Ceoltóirí Éireann
Senator since 1997. Chairman of Irish Family History Foundation and of Fondúireacht An Phiarsaigh.

Noel Coonan (FG)

Address Gortnagoona, Roscrea, Co Tipperary
Tel. H (0505) 43382; Office (0504) 32544; Mobile 086 242 7733
b. Roscrea. 6 January 1951
Educ. CBS Templemore, Co Tipperary
Occ. Full-time public representative.
New senator. Contested Tipperary North in the 2002 general election. Member of Tipperary North CC since 1991 and Templemore UDC since 1994. Member, Mid-Western Health Board.

Brian Hayes (FG)

Address 48 Dunmore Park, Kingswood Heights, Tallaght, Dublin 24
Tel. H (01) 462 6545
b. Dublin. 23 August 1969
Educ. St Joseph's College, Garbally, Ballinasloe, Co Galway; Maynooth College (BA); TCD (HDipEd)
Occ. Public representative. Formerly National Youth and Education Officer, Fine Gael; secondary school teacher
Dáil deputy 1997–2002. Senator, 1995–97. Member South Dublin CC since 1995.

Ann Ormonde (FF)

Address 2 Auburn Road, Dublin 4
Tel. H (01) 260 1577;
b. Kilmacthomas, Co Waterford
Educ. Our Lady's College, Presentation Convent, Clonmel; UCD (MA,BComm, HDipEd, Dip Career Guidance)
Occ. Full-time public representative. Formerly career guidance counsellor
Senator since 1993. Member Dublin CC since 1985, now South Dublin CC. Contested general elections of 1987, 1989, 1992 and 1997.

Candidates

Name	(County, Party)	Vote (1st Pref)
Nominating Bodies Sub-Panel		
Brassil, John Joseph	(Kerry, FF)	72
Crowley, Aidan	(Mayo, FF)	10
Dillon, Ellen	(Kildare, Ind)	1
Hammond, Richard	(Dublin, FG)	8
Harty, Mary	(Limerick, FG)	64
Herity, Michael	(Dublin, Ind)	12
McKenna, Tony	(Tipperary, FF)	59
Mooney, Paschal	(Leitrim, FF)	114
Ó Baoill, Seán	(Donegal, Ind)	47
Ó Murchú, Helen	(Dublin, Ind)	22
Ó Murchú, Labhrás	(Tipperary, FF)	106
Ormonde, Ann	(Dublin, FF)	101
Spearman, Thomas	(Dublin, Ind)	4
Taylor-Quinn, Madeleine	(Clare, FG)	68
Oireachtas Sub-Panel		
Coonan, Noel	(Tipperary, FG)	101
Hayes, Brian	(Dublin, FG)	109
Hoy, Kevin	(Dublin, Ind)	0
Kelly, Paul	(Kildare, FF)	44
Maher, Frank	(Louth, FF)	14

Agricultural Panel

Elected (11 Seats)

Francis O'Brien (FF)*	1st Count
Kathleen O'Meara (Lab)*	1st Count
Paddy Burke (FG)*	14th Count
Peter Callanan (FF)*	17th Count
Jim Walsh (FF)*	17th Count
Rory Kiely (FF)*	18th Count
Paul Bradford (FG)	22nd Count
Martin Mansergh (FF)	23rd Count
Ulick Burke (FG)	25th Count
John Paul Phelan (FG)	25th Count
Eamon Scanlon (FF)	26th Count

Candidates

Name	(County, Party)	Vote (1st Pref)

Nominating Bodies Sub-Panel

Name	(County, Party)	Vote
Boylan, Andrew	(Cavan, FG)	25
Bradford, Paul	(Cork, FG)	50
Burke, Paddy	(Mayo, FG)	69
Callanan, Peter	(Cork, FF)	61
Connor, John	(Roscommon, FG)	37
Fitzgerald, Michael	(Tipperary, FG)	26
Fleming, Thomas	(Kerry, FF)	28
Higgins, Albert	(Sligo, FF)	10
Hoade, Mary	(Galway, FF)	26
Kelly, Gerry	(Cork, FG)	8
Kiely, Rory	(Limerick, FF)	63
Killilea, Donagh	(Galway, FF)	13
Mansergh, Martin	(Tipperary, FF)	52
McGowan, Patrick	(Donegal, FF)	23
Moylan, Pat	(Offaly, FF)	45
Murphy, Kevin	(Cork, FG)	19
Moynihan, Bernard	(Cork, Ind)	1
O'Brien, Francis	(Monaghan, FF)	91
Phelan, John Paul	(Kilkenny, FG)	36

Oireachtas Sub-Panel

Name	(County, Party)	Vote
Bailey, John	(Dublin, FG)	37
Burke, Ulick	(Galway, FG)	39
Chambers, Frank	(Mayo, FF)	17
Farrell, Mary	(Carlow, Ind)	0
Hunt, Bridget	(Mayo, Ind)	0
O'Meara, Kathleen	(Tipperary, Lab)	87
Scanlon, Eamon	(Sligo, FF)	27
Sharkey, Paddy	(Louth, Ind)	0
Walsh, Jim	(Wexford, FF)	65

Francis O'Brien (FF)

Address Corwillan, Latton, Castleblaney, Co Monaghan
Tel. *H* (042) 9741152
b. Ballybay, Co Monaghan. April 1943
m. Gertrude Smith. 3s, 1d
Educ. Drumfreehan National School, Latton, Co Monaghan
Occ. Public representative. Farmer
Francis O'Brien has been a senator since 1989.
Member, Monaghan CC since 1979 (chair 1986/87); East Border Region Committee since 1987 (chair 1991/92).

Kathleen O'Meara (Lab)

Address 15 Knights Crescent, Nenagh, Co Tipperary
Business Address 76 Silver Street, Nenagh.
Tel. (067) 34190
b. Roscrea, Co Tipperary. January 1960
m. Kevin Dolan. 1s, 1d
Educ. Sacred Heart College, Roscrea; University College, Galway; National Institute of Higher Education, Dublin
Occ. Public representative. Formerly journalist
Kathleen O'Meara has been a senator since 1997.

Paddy Burke (FG)

Address 161 Knockaphunta, Westport Road, Castlebar, Co Mayo
Tel. *H* (094) 22568;
Mobile 087 244 1802
b. Castlebar. January 1955
m. Dolores Barrett
Educ. Ballinafad College, Castlebar; Rockwell Agricultural College, Co Tipperary; Franciscan Brothers Agricultural College, Mount Bellew, Co Galway
Occ. Public representative. Self-employed
Paddy Burke has been a senator since 1993. Member, Mayo CC since 1979.

Peter Callanan (FF)

Address Ballymountain, Inishshannon, Co Cork
Tel. *H* (021) 4775192
b. Clonakilty, Co Cork
m. Sheila Harrington. 4s, 2d
Educ. Mount Melleray College, Co Waterford
Occ. Farmer
Peter Callanan has been a senator since 1997.
Member, Cork CC since 1979 (vice-chair 1989/90); local farming and sporting organisations.

Jim Walsh (FF)

Address Mountgarrett Castle , New Ross, Co Wexford
Tel. *H* (051) 421771
m. Marie Furlong. 1s, 2d
Educ. New Ross CBS
Occ. Formerly company director. Farmer
Jim Walsh has been a senator since 1997.
Member, Wexford CC since 1979 (chair 1992/93); New Ross UDC since 1974 (chair 8 times).

Paul Bradford (FG)

Address Mourne Abbey, Mallow, Co Cork
Tel. *H* (022) 29375
b. Mallow. December 1963
Educ. Patrician Academy, Mallow
Occ. Public representative. Farmer
Paul Bradford was a member of the Dáil from 1989–2002. Senator 1987–89 (spokesperson on Communications and Energy). He contested the Dáil general elections in 1987 and 2002. Member Cork CC since 1985.

Ulick Burke (FG)

Address Eagle Hill, Abbey, Loughrea, Co Galway
Tel. *H* (0509) 45218; *Mobile* 087 2855863; *Constituency Office* (091) 847 437
b. Loughrea, Co Galway. November 1943
m. Maeve Haughton. 5s, 2d
Educ. St Molaisse's College, Portumna, Co Galway; University College, Galway (BA, HDipEd)
Occ. Full-time public representative. Formerly teacher
Ulick Burke was a member of the Dáil 1997–2002. He was a senator 1981–82 and 1983–87.

Eamon Scanlon (FF)

Address Keenaghan, Ballymote, Co Sligo
Tel. *H* (071) 83113
b. Ballymote. 20 September 1954
m. Ann Killoran. 4s, 2d
Educ. Ballymote Corran College
Occ. Butcher, Auctioneer
Eamon Scanlon is a new senator. He contested the Sligo-Leitrim constituency in the 2002 general election.
Member, Sligo CC since 1991.

Rory Kiely (FF)

Address Cloncrippa, Feenagh, Kilmallock, Co Limerick
Tel. *H* (063) 85033; *Mobile* 087 2855 836
b. Feenagh. May 1934
m. Eileen O'Connor. 2s, 2d
Educ. Rath Luirc CBS, Co Cork
Occ. Elected Cathoirleach Sept. 2002
Rory Kiely has been a senator 1977–82 and since 1983. He contested the Dáil election of 1969.
Chairman Limerick County GAA Board 1969–81.

Martin Mansergh (FF)

Address Friarsfield House, Tipperary
Tel. *H* (062) 51226
b. England. 1946
m. Elizabeth Young. 1s, 4d
Educ. King's School, Canterbury; Christ Church, Oxford (MA, PhD)
Occ. Former Special Advisor to taoisigh, Charles Haughey, Albert Reynolds and Bertie Ahern on Northern Ireland and Economic and Social Affairs. Former Department of Foreign Affairs official
Martin Mansreagh is a new senator. He contested in Tipperary South in the 2002 general election.

John Paul Phelan (FG)

Address Smithstown, Tullogher, Co Kilkenny
Tel. *H* (051) 427 326; *Mobile* 087 805 2088
b. Waterford. 27 September 1978
Educ. Good Counsel College, New Ross, Co Wexford; Waterford Institute of Technology
Occ. Full-time public representative
John Paul Phelan is a new senator. He is the youngest member of the Seanad.
Member, Kilkenny CC since 1999.

Labour Panel

Elected (11 Seats)

Liam Fitzgerald (FF)*	1st Count
Jim Higgins (FG)	7th Count
Don Lydon (FF	9th Count
Michael McCarthy (Lab)	12th Count
Brendan Daly (FF)	14th Count
Geraldine Feeney (FF)	14th Count
Terry Leyden (FF)	14th Count
John Gerard Hanafin (FF)	15th Count
Maurice Cummins (FG)	19th Count
Michael Finucane (FG)	20th Count
Fergal Browne (FG)	21st Count

Candidates

Name	(County, Party)	Vote (1st Pref)

Nominating Bodies Sub-Panel

Name	(County, Party)	Vote
Collins, Seán	(Louth, FF)	25
Cregan, Denis (Dino)	(Cork, FG)	50
Cummins, Maurice	(Waterford, FG)	54
Feeney, Geraldine	(Sligo, FF)	45
Geraghty, Des	(Dublin, Lab)	39
Hanafin, John	(Tipperary, FF)	44
Keegan, Garry	(Dublin, FF)	18
Kelly, Rody	(Carlow, FF)	23
Kiely, Dan	(Kerry, FF)	32
Leyden, Terry	(Roscommon, FF)	50
Lyons, Seán	(Dublin, Ind)	13
Ridge, Therese	(Dublin, FG)	30

Oireachtas Sub-Panel

Name	(County, Party)	Vote
Andrews, Chris	(Dublin, FF)	25
Browne, Fergal	(Carlow, FG)	48
Daly, Brendan	(Clare, FF)	45
Finucane, Michael	(Limerick, FG)	51
Fitzgerald, Liam	(Dublin, FF)	85
Higgins, Jim	(Mayo, FG)	68
Lydon, Don	(Dublin, FF)	66
McCarthy, Michael	(Cork, Lab)	64
Sinnott, Kathryn (Kathy)	(Cork, Ind)	44
Wade, Eddie	(Limerick, FF)	36

Liam Fitzgerald (FF)

Address 117 Tonlegee Road, Raheny, Dublin 5
Tel. *H* (01) 847 0632; *Mobile* 087 231 9200
b. Limerick, September 1949
m. Brid Lynch. 3s, 2d
Educ. Doon CBS, Co Limerick; St Patrick's Teacher Training College, UCD (BA, HDipEd)
Occ. Full-time public representative. Formerly teacher Senator since 1997. TD 1981–Feb 1982 and Nov 1982–97. Member Dublin City Council since 1985.

Don Lydon (FF)

Address Santo Antonio, Stillorgan Park Avenue, Stillorgan, Co Dublin
Tel. *H* (01)288 8741
b. August 1938
m. Maeve Ryan
Educ. St Eunan's College, Letterkenny, Co Donegal; UCG;UCD
Occ. Psychologist Senator since 1987. Dublin CC since 1985, now Dún Laoghaire-Rathdown CC. Member, Psychological Associations of Ireland, Britain and America.

Jim Higgins (FG)

Address Devlis, Ballyhaunis, Co Mayo
Tel. (0907) 30052
b. Ballyhaunis. May 1945
m. Marian Hannan. 4 d
Educ. St Jarlath's College, Tuam, Co Galway; UCG (BA, HDipEd)
Occ. Public representative. Formerly teacher
TD 1987–2002. Senator 1981–82 (Taoiseach's nominee); 1983–87 (Labour Panel). Minister of State and Government Whip 1995–97. Member Mayo CC 1979–95.

Michael McCarthy (Lab)

Address 47 Castle Street, Dunmanway, Co Cork
Tel. *H* (023) 45011
b. Bantry, Co Cork. 15 November 1976
Educ. Coláiste Chairbre, Dunmanway
Occ. Pharmaceutical company employee
New senator. Contested Cork South-West constituency in the 2002 general election. Member Cork CC since 1999.

Brendan Daly (FF)

Address Cooraclare, Kilrush, Co Clare
Tel. *H* (065) 9059040
b. Cooraclare. February 1940
m. Patricia Carmody. 2s, 1d
Educ. CBS Kilrush
Occ. Full-time public representative
TD 1973–92 and 1997–2002. Senator (Agricultural Panel) 1993–97. Minister and Minister of State in various portfolios including the Marine, Defence, Social Welfare, Fisheries and Forestry.

Terry Leyden (FF)

Address Castlecoote, Roscommon, Co Roscommon
Tel. *H* (0903) 26422; *Mobile* 087 7978922
Website: www.terryleyden.com
b. Roscommon. 1 October 1945
m. Mary Margaret O'Connor. 3d, 1s
Educ. Roscommon CBS and Vocational School, UCG
Occ. Full-time public representative. Former architectural designer
New senator. TD 1977–92.

Maurice Cummins (FG)

Address 34 Ursuline Court, Waterford
Tel. *H* (051) 855486
b. Waterford. 25 February 1953
m. Anne O'Shea. 1s,1d
Educ. De La Salle, Newtown, Waterford
Occ. Full-time public representative. Formerly claims manager.
New senator. Contested Waterford constituency in 2002 general election.

Fergal Browne (FG)

Address 61 Old Burrin, Carlow
Tel. *H* (0503) 35356
b. Carlow. September 1973
Educ. St Mary's Academy, Carlow; St Patrick's College, Drumcondra, Dublin; Maynooth NUI
Occ. Teacher
New Senator. Member, Carlow UDC since 1999. Son of John Browne, Fine Gael TD 1989–2002.

Geraldine Feeney (FF)

Address Ard Caoin, Sligo, Co Sligo
Tel. *H* (071) 45690; *Mobile* 087 2306 944
b. Tullamore, Co Offaly. 9th September 1957
m. Widowed. 2s, 2d
Educ. Sacred Heart School, Tullamore; UCG
Occ. Public relations consultant
New senator

John Gerard Hanafin (FF)

Address The Retreat, Richmond, Templemore, Co Tipperary
Tel. *H* (0504) 31560
b. Thurles. 27 September 1960
m. Linda Cummins. 2s, 1d
Educ. CBS Thurles; Cistercian College, Roscrea; UCD; UCC; College of Marketing and Design, Dublin; Institute of Public Administration, Dublin
Occ. Valuer and auctioneer
New Senator. Son of former senator Des Hanafin and brother of Mary Hanafin, Minister of State. Member, North Tipperary CC. Co-opted 1998. Elected 1999.

Michael Finucane (FG)

Address Ardnacrohy, Newcastle West, Co Limerick
Tel. *H* (069) 62742; *Mobile* 087 821 8972
b. Limerick. February 1943
m. Hannah Hartnett. 1s, 2d
Educ. St Senan's Secondary School, Foynes, Co Limerick
Occ. Full-time public representative. Formerly shipping agency manager
New senator. TD 1989–2002. Member, Limerick CC since 1985; Mid-Western Health Board since 1995.

Industrial and Commercial Panel

Elected (9 Seats)

Derek McDowell (Lab)	22nd Count
Kieran Phelan (FF)	28th Count
James Bannon (FG)	30th Count
Eddie Bohan (FF)*	32nd Count
Paul Coghlan (FG)	32nd Count
Margaret Cox (FF)*	32nd Count
MacSharry, Marc (FF)	32nd Count
Mary M. White (FF)	32nd Count
Sheila Terry (FG)	33rd Count

Candidates

Name	(County, Party)	Vote (1st Pref)

Nominating Bodies Sub-Panel

Name	(County, Party)	Vote (1st Pref)
Bannon, James	(Longford, FG)	46
Bohan, Eddie	(Dublin, FF)	60
Bridgett, Andrew	(Kildare, FF)	3
Butler, Larry	(Dublin, FF)	38
Caffrey, Ernie	(Mayo, FG)	33
Cahill, Michael	(Kerry, FF)	23
Clune, Deirdre	(Cork, FG)	35
Coghlan, Paul	(Kerry, FG)	47
Colleary, Aidan	(Sligo, FF)	24
Dowling, Patrick	(Kilkenny, FG)	12
Egan, John	(Tipperary, FF)	23
Fitzgerald, Ted	(Kerry, FF)	13
Hanley, Val	(Galway, FF)	20
Hennessy, Séamus	(Cork, Ind)	0
Hughes, Brendan	(Monaghan, FF)	32
Hunter-McGowan, Thomas	(Cork, Ind)	3
Jackman, Mary	(Limerick, FG)	22
Keogh, Helen	(Dublin, FG)	14
Killally, Gerard	(Offaly, FF)	13
Lucey, Cormac	(Dublin, FG)	10
MacSharry, Marc	(Sligo, FF)	42
McDonagh, Michael	(Galway, FG)	17
McGrath, Michael	(Cork, FF)	25
McPadden, James	(Leitrim, FG)	33
O'Keefe, Kevin	(Cork, FF)	18
O'Meara, Pat	(Tipperary, FF)	18
Ó Muire, Toal	(Dublin, Ind)	0
Phelan, Kieran	(Laois, FF)	55
Regan, Michael	(Galway, FF)	9
White, Mary M.	(Dublin, FF)	39

Oireachtas Sub-Panel

Name	(County, Party)	Vote (1st Pref)
Cox, Margaret	(Galway, FF)	29
Kenneally, Brendan	(Waterford, FF)	26
McDowell, Derek	(Dublin, Lab)	84
Moffat, Tom	(Mayo, FF)	14
Mullins, John	(Dublin, FG)	7
Reilly, Jim	(Kildare, FG)	13
Terry, Sheila	(Dublin, FG)	23
White, Mary A.	(Carlow, GP)	32

Derek McDowell (Lab)

Address 3 Dunluce Road, Clontarf, Dublin
Tel. *H* (01) 833 6138
b. Dublin. September 1958
m. Vicki Barrett
Educ. Ardscoil Rís, Marino, Dublin, TCD (BA)
Occ. Public representative. Solicitor
New Senator. TD for Dublin North-Central 1992–2002. Contested 1989 general election. Labour Party spokesperson on Finance in 28th Dáil. Member, Dublin City Council since 1991.

Kieran Phelan (FF)

Address Raheen Upper, Donaghmore, Portlaoise, Co Laois
Tel. *H* (0505) 46562; *Mobile* 087 287 6088
b. Rathdowney, Co Laois. 19 November 1949
m. Mary Clancy. 4d, 1s
Educ. CBS Roscrea
Occ. Farmer, Auctioneer
New Senator. Member, Laois County Council since 1991.

James Bannon (FG)

Address Newtown, Legan, Co Longford
Tel. *H* (044) 57575
b. 6 March 1958
Educ. Our Lady's Secondary School, Ballymahon, Co Longford
Occ. Auctioneer/Farmer. Public representative
New senator. Member Longford CC since 1985.

Eddie Bohan (FF)

Address 18 Orwell Park, Dublin 6
Tel. B (01) 4912396
b. Longford. November 1932
m. Betty Lambert. 1s, 3d
Educ. Longford Secondary School
Occ. Auctioneer, Publican
Senator since 1987. Deputy spokesperson on Justice and Law Reform and Finance 1997–2002. Former President of Vintners' Federation of Ireland. Former Chairman of Dublin Licensed Vintners.

Newly elected Irish President of the European Parliament Pat Cox addresses the European Deputies in the European Parliament in Strasbourg, 15 January 2002.

The European Parliament

The European Parliament which meets in Strasbourg and Brussels consists of 626 representatives from the 15 EU member states. Ireland has 15 MEPs. (Northern Ireland has 3.)

The EP is directly elected every five years under a proportional representation system. Since the Maastricht Treaty of 1993, any citizen of a member state of the EU who lives in another member state may vote or stand for election in his or her country of residence.

In the chamber, the MEPs sit in political groups and not in national delegations. Currently there are eight political groups plus some 'non-attached' members. Fine Gael MEPs sit with the European People's Party/ European Democrats; Labour with the Party of European Socialists; Fianna Fáil with the Union for Europe of the Nations; the Greens with the Greens/ European Free Alliance.

These groups include members from over 100 national political parties. Women now represent almost 30 per cent of the total MEPs compared with 16 per cent at the time of the first direct election in 1979.

The powers of the EP have been steadily increasing since that time. They fall into three groups:

• Law-making
• EU Budget
• Supervising the Executive.

The EP's power of co-decision in law-making puts it on an equal status with the EU Council of Ministers in a growing number of areas. These are: the free movement of workers, internal market, research and development, environment, consumer protection, education, culture and health.

The EP adopts the EU Budget for the following year each December. If it fails to agree the amount of expenditure with the Council after two readings, it can reject the draft Budget as a whole and the process has to begin again. The EP has the last word on spending on the regions, the fight against unemployment – especially among young people and women – and cultural and educational programmes. It can increase expenditure within a ceiling agreed with the Council and the Commission.

The EP originally supervised the actions of the Commission only but now this extends to the activities of the Council of Ministers, the European Council of Heads of State and Government and the political co-operation bodies.

The EP has a crucial role in the appointment of the Commission whose members are nominated by national governments. After approving the nomination of the President of the Commission, the Parliament holds hearings with the nominee Commissioners and then approves the Commission by a vote of confidence.

The EP also has the power to dismiss the whole Commission by a vote of censure. This has not happened so far but in March 1999, following a report by a committee of experts mandated by the Parliament to examine abuses, the Commission headed by President Santer chose to resign rather than face formal censure.

Pat Cox (Munster)

Pat Cox, an Independent MEP from Munster, had the honour of being the first Irish member to be elected President of the European Parliament in January 2002. He will serve in that post until June 2004. He is also President of the Liberal Democratic and Reform Group in the EP. As President of the EP, Mr Cox's duties include: directing the activities of the Parliament; presiding over and closing the sittings; chairing the meetings of the EP's Conference of Presidents, of groups and of the Bureau; representing the Parliament in external relations, on ceremonial occasions and in administrative, legal or financial matters. He signs into law the EU Budget and co-signs with the President-in-Office of the Council all legislation adopted under the co-decision procedure. One of his most prestigious roles is to address the Heads of State and Government at the opening of European Council meetings.

Mr Cox was born in Limerick on 28 November 1952. He was educated at St Munchin's CBS, Ard Scoil Rís, Limerick and Trinity College, Dublin. He lectured in economics at the University of Limerick and later became a television current affairs broadcaster with RTÉ. He was a founder member and general secretary of the Progressive Democrats. He was first elected to the EP in July 1989. He was also a member of the Dáil for Cork South Central in 1992–94.

Gerard Collins (Munster)

Fianna Fáil member. Born in Abbeyfeale, County Limerick, 16 October 1938. BA from UCD. Fianna Fáil general secretary 1964–67. Member of Dáil (1967–97). Served at various times as Minister for Post and Telegraphs, Justice and Foreign Affairs. Elected to EP 1994. Leader of Fianna Fáil group which is affiliated to the 30-member Union for Europe of the Nations Group. EP Committees: Regional Policy, Transport and Tourism; Foreign Affairs, Human Rights, Common Security and Defence Policy.

Brian Crowley (Munster)

Fianna Fáil member. Born 4 March 1964. Diploma in law from UCC. Senator (1993). Member of Council of State (1997). Elected to EP 1994. Committees: Legal Affairs and Internal Market; Employment and Social Affairs; Fisheries.

John Cushnahan (Munster)

Fine Gael member. Born in Belfast, 23 July 1948. BEd Queen's University, Belfast. Former general secretary and leader of Alliance Party. Northern Ireland Assembly (1982–86). Elected to EP 1989. Committees: Foreign Affairs, Human Rights, Common Security and Defence Policy.

Nuala Ahern (Leinster)

Green Party member. Born in Northern Ireland, 5 February 1949. Psychologist. Former Wicklow county councillor. Founder member of Irish Women's Environmental Network. Elected to EP 1994. Committees: Industry, External Trade, Research and Energy; Culture, Youth, Education, Media and Sport.

The European Parliament

Avril Doyle (Leinster)

Fine Gael member. Born in Dublin, 18 April 1949. BSc from UCD. Former Mayor of Wexford. Former Minister of State. Member of Dáil and Seanad at various times since 1982. Elected to EP 1999. Committees: Environment, Public Health and Consumer Policy; Agriculture and Rural Development.

Liam Hyland (Leinster)

Fianna Fáil member. Born in Portlaoise, 23 April 1933. Diploma in economic and political science. Former Minister of State for Agriculture and Rural Development. Former member of Dáil and Seanad. Elected to EP 1994. Committees: Agriculture and Rural Development; Development and Cooperation.

Joe McCartin (Connacht/Ulster)

Fine Gael member. Born in Ballinamore, County Leitrim, 24 April 1939. Farmer and company director. Former member of Dáil and Seanad. Elected to EP 1979. Committees: Budgets; Budgetary Control.

Jim Fitzsimons (Leinster)

Fianna Fáil member. Born in Navan, 16 December 1936. Former Minister for Energy (1982). Member of Dáil (1977–87). Elected to EP 1984. Committees: Petitions; Environment, Public Health and Consumer Policy; Citizens' Freedoms and Rights, Justice and Home Affairs.

Seán Ó Neachtáin (Connacht/Ulster)

Fianna Fáil member. Replaced Pat the Cope Gallagher in June 2002 when the latter was elected to Dáil Éireann and appointed a Minister of State.
Born in Spiddal, Co. Galway, 22 May 1947. BA, HDipEd from University College, Galway. Former teacher.
Member EU Committee of the Regions 1994–2002. Chairman, European Alliance Group 1998-2002. Vice-Chair Commission for Education and Culture.

Dana Rosemary Scallon (Connacht/Ulster)

Independent member. Born in London, 30 August 1950. Formerly TV presenter, actress, singer, musician. Winner of 1970 Eurovision Song Contest. Independent Presidential candidate 1997. Elected to EP 1999. Committees: Regional Policy, Transport and Tourism; Culture, Youth, Education, Media and Sport; Citizens' Freedoms and Rights, Justice and Home Affairs.

Niall Andrews (Dublin)

Fianna Fáil member. Born in Dublin, 19 August 1937. Former RTÉ programme executive. Former Minister of State at Department for the Environment. Former member of the Dáil. Elected to EP 1984. Committees: Citizens' Freedoms and Rights, Justice and Home Affairs; Foreign Affairs, Human Rights, Common Security and Defence Policy.

Proinsias De Rossa (Dublin)

Labour member. Born in Dublin, 15 May 1940. Member of Dáil (1982–2000). Former leader of the Workers' Party and Democratic Left. President of the Labour Party. Minister for Social Welfare (1994–97). Member of the EP in 1989–92 and elected again 1999. Committees: Petitions; Employment and Social Affairs; Environment, Public Health and Consumer Policy.

Mary Banotti (Dublin)

Fine Gael member. Born in Dublin, 29 May 1939. Nurse/ industrial welfare officer for Irish Distillers (1972–84). Fine Gael Presidential candidate 1997. Elected to EP 1984. Committees: Citizens' Freedoms and Rights, Justice and Home Affairs; Employment and Social Affairs; Women's Rights and Equal Opportunities; Petitions.

Patricia McKenna (Dublin)

Green Party member. Born in Castleshane, County Monaghan, 13 March 1957. Diplomas in Visual Education, Fine Art and Art Education. Elected to EP 1994. Committees: Fisheries; Environment, Public Health, and Consumer Policy; Citizens' Freedoms and Rights, Justice and Home Affairs.

The European Parliament

The sixth election to the European Parliament was held on 11 June 1999.
The results are summarised on this page and details of the counts in each of the four constituencies are given in the following pages.

Connacht-Ulster

Elected

Pat the Cope Gallagher (FF)*
Joe McCartin (FG)*
Dana Rosemary Scallon (Ind)

	Number	%
Electorate	541,552	
Total Poll	332,236	61.35
Spoiled Votes	12,085	3.64
Valid Poll	320,151	59.12
Seats	3	
Quota	80,038	
Candidates	11	

Voting by Party

1st Pref	Number	%	% 1994
Fianna Fáil	113,988	35.6	42.47
Fine Gael	63,632	19.9	29.65
Labour	10,522	3.3	8.52
Sinn Féin	20,457	6.4	5.99
Others	111,552	34.8	0.53

Seats

FF	1
FG	1
Ind	1

FF loss to Ind

Dublin

Elected

Mary Banotti (FG)*
Niall Andrews (FF)*
Patricia McKenna (GP)*
Proinsias De Rossa (Lab)

	Number	%
Electorate	793,200	
Total Poll	286,684	36.14
Spoiled Votes	6,013	2.10
Valid Poll	280,671	35.38
Seats	4	
Quota	56,135	
Candidates	13	

Voting by Party

1st Pref	Number	%	% 1994
Fianna Fáil	69,241	24.67	20.85
Fine Gael	84,466	30.09	23.82
Labour	44,638	15.90	14.07
Green Party	35,659	12.70	14.54
Sinn Féin	18,633	6.64	2.95
Socialist Party	10,619	3.78	—
Christian Solidarity Party	9,425	3.36	—
Natural Law Party	1,006	0.36	—
Others	6,984	2.49	6.44

Seats

FF	1
FG	1
Lab	1
GP	1

No change

Leinster

Elected

Avril Doyle (FG)
Jim Fitzsimons (FF)*
Liam Hyland (FF)*
Nuala Ahern (GP)*

	Number	%
Electorate	706,601	
Total Poll	357,064	50.53
Spoiled Votes	14,725	4.12
Valid Poll	342,339	48.45
Seats	4	
Quota	68,468	
Candidates	8	

Voting by Party

1st Pref	Number	%	% 1994
Fianna Fáil	117,227	34.24	33.46
Fine Gael	116,610	34.06	27.73
Labour	38,112	11.13	15.46
Green Party	47,184	13.78	11.81
Sinn Féin	20,015	5.85	2.49
Natural Law Party	3,191	0.93	0.45

Seats

FF	2
FG	1
GP	1

No change

Munster

Elected

Brian Crowley (FF)*
Gerard Collins (FF)*
Pat Cox (Ind)*
John Cushnahan (FG)*

	Number	%
Electorate	823,008	
Total Poll	462,303	56.17
Spoiled Votes	13,724	2.97
Valid Poll	448,579	54.50
Seats	4	
Quota	89,716	
Candidates	10	

Voting by Party

1st Pref	Number	%	% 1994
Fianna Fáil	237,301	52.90	42.11
Fine Gael	77,463	17.27	18.69
Labour	28,270	6.30	6.99
Green Party	10,257	2.29	2.75
Sinn Féin	29,060	6.48	1.42
Others	66,228	14.76	13.36

Seats

FF	2
FG	1
Ind	1

No change

Seats 3 Quota 80,038	1st Count Number of Votes	2nd Count Transfer of **Raymond and Campbell** Votes	3rd Count Transfer of **Sharkey** Votes	4th Count Transfer of **McManus, Gibbon and Flanagan** Votes	5th Count Transfer of **Treacy** Votes	6th Count Transfer of **Gallagher** Surplus
CAMPBELL, Paul (NLP)	1,920	−1,920	—	—	—	—
FLANAGAN, Ming Luke (NON-P)	5,000	+539 5,539	+111 5,650	−5,650	—	—
GALLAGHER, Pat the Cope (FF)	66,055	+326 66,381	+521 66,902	+5,771 72,673	+25,585 98,258	−18,220 80,038
GIBBONS, Gerard (LAB)	10,522	+305 10,827	+145 10,972	−10,972	—	—
HARKIN, Marian (NON-P)	47,372	+340 47,712	+920 48,632	+7,509 56,141	+4,175 60,316	+3,836 64,152
MCMANUS, Seán (SF)	20,457	+114 20,571	+230 20,801	−20,801	—	—
MCCARTIN, John Joseph (FG)	63,632	+179 63,811	+695 64,506	+3,882 68,388	+4,376 72,764	+2,511 75,275
RAYMOND, Paul (NON-P)	840	−840	—	—	—	—
SCALLON, Dana Rosemary (NON-P)	51,086	+280 51,366	+1,436 52,802	+6,642 59,444	+8,443 67,887	+4,968 72,855
SHARKEY, Liam (NON-P)	5,334	+70 5,404	−5,404	—	—	—
TREACY, Noel (FF)	47,933	+127 48,060	+410 48,470	+2,984 51,454	−51,454	—
Non-transferable papers not effective	—	+480 480	+936 1,416	+10,635 12,051	+8,875 20,926	+6,905 27,831
TOTAL	320,151	320,151	320,151	320,151	320,151	320,151

Dublin

Seats 4 Quota 56,135	1st Count — Number of Votes	2nd Count — Transfer of Burns, Godwin & Goulding Votes	3rd Count — Transfer of Casey Votes	4th Count — Transfer of Higgins Votes	5th Count — Transfer of Malone Votes	6th Count — Transfer of Crowe Votes	7th Count — Transfer of Briscoe Votes	8th Count — Transfer of Andrews Surplus
ANDREWS, Niall (FF)	44,176	+555 / 44,731	+1,236 / 45,967	+514 / 46,481	+1,450 / 47,931	+2,508 / 50,439	+20,984 / 71,423	−15,288 / 56,135
BANOTTI, Mary (FG)	56,593	— / 56,593	— / 56,593	— / 56,593	— / 56,593	— / 56,593	— / 56,593	— / 56,593
BRISCOE, Ben (FF)	25,065	+392 / 25,457	+1,460 / 26,917	+405 / 27,322	+1,157 / 28,479	+1,889 / 30,368	—	
BURNS, John (NLP)	1,006	−1,006	—	—	—	—	—	—
CASEY, Gerard (CSP)	9,425	+442 / 9,867	−9,867	—	—	—	—	—
CROWE, Seán (SF)	18,633	+437 / 19,070	+665 / 19,735	+1,412 / 21,147	+556 / 21,703	−21,703	—	—
DE ROSSA, Proinsías (LAB)	28,748	+774 / 29,522	+360 / 29,882	+1,967 / 31,849	+5,971 / 37,820	+3,785 / 41,605	+1,931 / 43,536	+3,482 / 47,018
GODWIN, Adam (NON-P)	1,438	−1,438	—	—	—	—	—	—
GOULDING, Ciaran (NON-P)	5,546	−5,546	—	—	—	—	—	—
HIGGINS, Joe (SP)	10,619	+741 / 11,360	+337 / 11,697	−11,697	—	—	—	—
MCKENNA, Patricia (GP)	35,659	+2,329 / 37,988	+1,830 / 39,818	+3,844 / 43,662	+4,637 / 48,299	+6,584 / 54,883	+2,109 / 56,992	— / 56,992
MALONE, Bernie (LAB)	15,890	+680 / 16,570	+412 / 16,982	+1,290 / 18,272	−18,272	—	—	—
MITCHELL, Jim (FG)	27,873	+610 / 28,483	+1,919 / 30,402	+894 / 31,296	+2,549 / 33,845	+1,097 / 34,942	+2,109 / 37,051	+4,438 / 41,489
Non-transferable papers not effective	—	+1,030 / 1,030	+1,648 / 2,678	+1,371 / 4,049	+1,952 / 6,001	+5,840 / 11,841	+3,235 / 15,076	+7,368 / 22,444
TOTAL	280,671	280,671	280,671	280,671	280,671	280,671	280,671	280,671

Seats 4 Quota 68,468	1st Count Number of Votes	2nd Count Transfer of **Garrett and Morgan** Votes	3rd Count Transfer of **Butler** Votes
AHERN, Nuala (GP)	47,184	+5,434 52,618	+14,190 66,808
BUTLER, Seán (LAB)	38,112	+2,737 40,849	−40,849
DOYLE, Avril (FG)	67,881	+1,614 69,495	69,495
FITZSIMONS, Jim (FF)	58,750	+2,689 61,439	+4,678 66,117
GARRETT, Desmond (NLP)	3,191	-3,191	—
GILLIS, Alan (FG)	48,729	+1,311 50,040	+6,841 56,881
HYLAND, Liam (FF)	58,477	+3,454 61,931	+3,565 65,496
MORGAN, Arthur (SF)	20,015	−20,015 _	
Non-transferable papers not effective	—	5,967	+11,575 17,542
TOTAL	342,339	342,339	342,339

Munster

	1st Count	2nd Count	3rd Count	4th Count	5th Count	6th Count
Seats 4 **Quota 89,716**	Number of Votes	Transfer of **Crowley** Surplus	Transfer of **Collins** Surplus	Transfer of **Luck, Nutty** and **Riordan** Votes	Transfer of **Ferris** Votes	Transfer of **Corr** Votes
COLLINS, Gerard (FF)	83,106	+34,677 117,783	−28,067 89,716	89,716	89,716	89,716
CORR, Jim (FG)	31,363	+3,663 35,026	+2,530 37,556	+1,137 38,693	+1,976 40,669	−40,669
COX, Pat (IND)	63,954	+12,249 76,203	+9,054 85,257	+3,100 88,357	+6,647 95,004	95,004
CROWLEY, Brian (FF)	154,195	−64,479 89,716	89,716	89,716	89,716	89,716
CUSHNAHAN, John (FG)	46,100	+2,909 49,009	+1,487 50,496	+987 51,483	+2,014 53,497	+24,735 78,232
DESMOND, Paula (LAB)	28,270	+5,732 34,002	+2,882 36,884	+3,862 40,746	+6,141 46,887	+5,944 52,831
FERRIS, Martin (SF)	29,060	+2,723 31,783	+2,652 34,435	+2,099 36,534	−36,534	
LUCK, Stewart (NLP)	1,267	+335 1,602	+295 1,897	−1,897	—	—
NUTTY, Ben (GP)	10,257	+2,073 12,330	+1,313 13,643	−13,643	—	—
RIORDAN, Denis (Non-P)	1,007	+118 1,125	+143 1,268	−1,268	—	—
Non-transferable papers not effective	—	—	7,711 +7,711	+5,623 13,334	+19,756 33,090	+9,990 43,080

212

The Commission was created as an independent body to represent European interests common to all Member States of the Union. It is the driving force in the legislative process, proposing the legislation on which the European Parliament and the Council of Ministers have to take a decision.

It is responsible for implementing common policies such as agriculture (CAP), administers the Budget and manages the Community programmes. In day-to-day running of common policies, the Commission relies heavily on national administrations. In external affairs, the Commission represents the Community and conducts international negotiations, for example in the World Trade Organisation.

The Commission monitors compliance with the treaties and the decisions taken by the Community institutions, for example in the field of competition where it has the power to fine companies for breaches of the rules.

The Commission is composed of 20 independent members (two each from France, Germany, Italy, Spain and the United Kingdom and one each from all the other countries). It is appointed for a five-year term, by agreement among the Member States, and is subject to a vote of appointment by the European Parliament, to which it is answerable, before it can be sworn in.

The Treaty of Nice when ratified would limit the Commission to one member per Member State from 2005. A ceiling on the number of Commissioners would be imposed once the Union has 27 members. The Council would then have to take a unanimous decision on the exact number of Commissioners which must be less than 27. The nationality of Commissioners would be determined by a system of rotation which would be fair to all countries.

Romano Prodi. President. Responsible for the Secretariat-General, Legal Service, Media and Communications. Italian member. Law degree. Former Prime Minister of Italy and a Minister for Industry. Was chairman of the Institute for Industrial Reconstruction (IRI) and of the Ulivo centre-left coalition. Taught political economics and industrial organisation at University of Bologna and Free University of Trento. Studied at Stanford Research Institute and was a visiting professor at Harvard University. Born 1939.

Loyola de Palacio del Valle-Lersundi. Vice-President responsible for Relations with the European Parliament and transport and energy. Spanish member. Law degree. Minister for Agriculture, Fisheries and Food and member of Spanish parliament 1996–99. Senator and vice-president of the Popular Group 1986–89. Former secretary-general of Federation of Press Associations. Born 1950.

Neil Kinnock. Vice-President. Responsible for Administrative Reform. British member. Degree in industrial relations and history. Labour MP 1970–95 for Bedwelty and Islwyn in Wales. Leader of Labour Party 1983–92. Former vice-president of the Socialist International. Member of the Commission 1995–99 responsible for transport. Born 1942.

Mario Monti. Competition. Italian member. Was responsible in Commission in 1995–99 for internal market, financial services and financial integration, customs and taxation. Degree in economics and management. Post-graduate studies at Yale University. Was professor at the University of Turin and professor, rector and president of Bocconi University. Member of Treasury Committee on debt management and Treasury Committee on banking law reform. Born 1943.

The European Commission

Franz Fischler. Agriculture and fisheries. Austrian member. Was responsible for agriculture and rural development in the Commission 1995–99. Federal Minister of Agriculture and Forestry 1989–94. Taught in the Department of Regional Agricultural Planning at the Institute for Farm Management in Vienna. Later worked in the Tyrol Chamber of Agriculture. Born 1946.

Frederik Bolkestein. Internal market. Dutch member. Degrees in mathematics and physics, philosophy, Greek, economics and law. Former Minister of Defence and State Secretary for Foreign Trade. Was Liberal member of parliament and is President of Liberal International. Worked for Shell Group in 1960–76 in foreign postings. Director of Shell Chimie, Paris, in 1973–76. Born 1933.

Pedro Solbes Mira. Economic and monetary affairs. Spanish member. Degrees in political science and law, Madrid University. Former Minister of Agriculture, Fisheries and Food and of Economic Affairs and Finance. Commercial attaché to Spanish Mission to the EC in 1973–1978. Director-General for Commercial Policy 1979-82. Member of task force negotiating Spain's entry to EC. Co-ordinator of first Spanish Presidency of EC. Secretary of State for relations with EC at Ministry of Foreign Affairs 1985–91. Born 1942.

Gunter Verheugen. Enlargement. German member. Studied history, sociology and politics in Cologne and Bonn. Was also trainee journalist. Worked as head of public relations at Federal Ministry of the Interior and in the Foreign Office. General Secretary of the Free Democratic Party 1978–82. Joined the Social Democratic Party 1982. Editor of party newspaper, *Vorwarts*. Member of the Bundestag 1983–99. Member of Foreign Affairs Committee. Minister of State at Foreign Office 1998–99. Born 1944.

Erkki Liikanen. Enterprise and information society. Finnish member. Responsible in the Commission in 1995–99 for the budget, personnel and administration, translation and in-house computer services. Master's degree in political science. Has served as a member of parliament and of the Nordic Council. Former secretary-general of Social Democratic Party. Served as Minister of Finance and Minister in Ministry of the Interior. Was Head of the Finnish Mission to the European Union. Born 1950.

Philippe Busquin. Research. Belgian member. Degree in physics and post-graduate studies in the environment. Former Minister for National Education and for Social Affairs. In Wallonia was Minister for Economic Affairs and for the Budget and Energy. Since 1992 was President of the Socialist Party and Vice-President of the Socialist International. Member of the House of Representatives 1978–95. Elected to the Senate in 1995. Lectured in physics in Free University of Brussels 1962–77. Born 1941.

Poul Nielson. Development and humanitarian aid. Danish member. Degree in political science, University of Arhus. Minister of Energy 1979–82. Minister for Development Cooperation 1994–99. Social Democratic Foreign Affairs and Defence Committee 1965–79. Chairman of Danish European Movement. Member of Parliament. Head of Section, Ministry of Foreign Affairs. Taught in Danish School of Public Administration. Born 1943.

Christopher Patten. External relations. British member. History degree from Oxford University. Member of Parliament for Bath 1979–92. Held junior ministerial posts at Northern Ireland Office and Department of Education and Science. Minister for Overseas Development. Secretary of State for the Environment. Chancellor of the Duchy of Lancaster and Chairman of the Conservative Party 1990–92. Governor of Hong Kong 1992–1997. Chairman of Independent Commission on Policing for Northern Ireland 1998–99. Born 1944.

Pascal Lamy. Trade. French member. Degrees in political science, business studies and law. Worked in Inspectorate-General of Finances and the Treasury. Adviser to Minister for Economic Affairs and Finance, Jacques Delors. Deputy Head of Prime Minister Pierre Mauroy's Private Office. Head of the Private Office of the President of the EC Commission, Jacques Delors, 1985–94. Member of the Socialist Party Steering Committee 1985–94. Director-General of Credit Lyonnais 1999. Born 1947.

Michel Barnier. Regional policy, inter-governmental conference. French member. Diploma from Paris Business College. Served in Private Office of the Ministers for the Environment, Youth and Sport, and for Trade and Craft Industries 1973–78. RPR member of the National Assembly for Savoie 1978–93. Minister of the Environment. Minister of State for European Affairs 1995–97. Senator for Savoie 1997–1999. Chairman of the French Association of the Council of European Municipalities and Regions. Born 1951.

Michaele Schreyer. Budget. German member. Studied economics and sociology at University of Cologne and awarded doctorate 1983. Research assistant and adviser to the Greens in the Federal Parliament. Minister for urban development and environmental protection in the State Government of Berlin. Spokeswoman on public finance for the Greens. Chairwoman of the Bundnis 90/Greens group in the Berlin State Parliament. Lecturer in political science at the Free University of Berlin. Born 1951.

Antonio Vitorino. Justice and Home Affairs. Portugese member. Degrees in law and political science. Deputy Prime Minister and Minister of Defence 1995–97. Former professor of law and judge in the Portugese Constitutional Court. Member of Parliament from 1980. Member of European Parliament. Secretary of State for Administration and Justice of Macao Government 1986–87. Born 1957.

David Byrne. Health and consumer protection. Irish member. Arts degree from UCD. Qualified as barrister from Kings Inns. Called to the Bar 1970. Called to Inner Bar 1985. Attorney-General 1997–99. Member of the Constitution Review Group and of Government Review Body on Social Welfare Law. Member of Executive Committee, Irish Maritime Law Association 1974–92. Member of Cabinet sub-committees on social inclusion, European Affairs and on child abuse. Born 1947.

Viviane Reding. Education and culture. Luxembourg member. Doctor of Human Sciences, Sorbonne, Paris. Journalist and editorialist at *Luxemburger Wort*. President, Luxembourg Union of Journalists 1986–1998. Member of Luxembourg Parliament 1979–89. Member of North Atlantic Assembly and leader of Christian Democrat/Conservative group. National President of Christian-Social Women. Member of European Parliament 1989–99. Vice-President of Social Christian Party. Born 1951.

Margot Wallstrom. Environment. Swedish member. Served at various times as Minister of Social Affairs, Minister of Culture and Minister of Civil Affairs dealing with consumer affairs, women and youth. Member of Parliament 1979-1985. Accountant, Alfa Savings Bank, Karlstad. Member of Executive Committee of the Social Democratic Party. Executive Vice-President, Worldview Global Media, Colombo, Sri Lanka 1998–99. Born 1954.

Anna Diamantopoulou. Employment and Social Affairs. Greek member. Degrees in civil engineering and regional development. Deputy Minister for Development. Served as Secretary-General at various times for Youth, Industry and Adult Education. Member of Central Committee of PASOK 1991–99. Member of Parliament. Member of Forum for the cooperation of Balkan peoples. Member of International Women's Network. Born 1959.

Index

Index

Advertisers